To Willie
Re dozen of
Think positive!
[signature]

The Economic Future of Hong Kong

Monograph Series in World Affairs
Graduate School of International Affairs
University of Denver

Series Editor
Karen A. Feste, *University of Denver*

Editorial Board

Steven Brams
New York University

James Caporaso
University of Washington

Jerome Clubb
University of Michigan

Catherine Kelleher
University of Maryland

Robert Jervis
Columbia University

Michael O'Leary
Syracuse University

Todd Sandler
Iowa State University

Susan Strange
*London School of Economics
and Political Science*

Kenneth Thompson
University of Virginia

John Turner
University of Minnesota

Dina Zinnes
University of Illinois

The Economic Future of Hong Kong

Miron Mushkat

GSIS Monograph Series
in World Affairs

THE UNIVERSITY OF DENVER

Lynne Rienner Publishers   Boulder & London
Hong Kong University Press

Published in the United States of America in 1990 by
Lynne Rienner Publishers, Inc.
1800 30th Street, Boulder, Colorado 80301

and in the United Kingdom
by Lynne Rienner Publishers, Inc.
3 Henrietta Street, Covent Garden, London WC2E 8LU

Published in Hong Kong in 1990 by
Hong Kong University Press
139 Pokfulam Road, Hong Kong

© 1990 by the University of Denver. All rights reserved

Library of Congress Cataloging-in-Publication Data
Mushkat, Miron.
    The economic future of Hong Kong/Miron Mushkat
    (GSIS monograph series in world affairs)
    Includes bibliographical references
        1. Economic forecasting—Hong Kong. 2. Hong Kong—Economic conditions. I. Title. II.
Series: GSIS monograph series in world affairs (unnumbered)
HC470.3.M87 1990   89-70067
330.95125'001'12—dc20   CIP

British Cataloguing in Publication Data
A Cataloguing in Publication record for this book
is available from the British Library

ISBN: 1-55587-197-6 (Lynne Rienner Publishers)
ISBN: 962-209-251-9 (Hong Kong University Press)

Printed and bound in the United States of America

The paper used in this publication meets the requirements of the American National Standard for
Permanence of Paper for Printed Library Materials Z39.48-1984

Contents

	List of Tables and Figures	vii
	Preface	ix
1	Introduction	1
2	Scenarios	19
3	Scenario Construction and Hong Kong	41
4	The Optimistic Scenario for the Hong Kong Economy	71
5	The Pessimistic Scenario for the Hong Kong Economy	111
6	The Trend Scenario for the Hong Kong Economy	137
7	Policy Implications	151
	Index	165
	About the Book and the Author	171

Tables and Figures

Tables

2.1	Characteristics of the Postindustrial Society	22
2.2	Four Basic Types of Scenario	26
2.3	Basic, Long-Term Multifold Trends Identified by Kahn and Wiener	27
2.4	New Aviation Communications Technologies	29
3.1	Roadsigns of Business, December 21, 1953	43
3.2	Leading, Coincident, and Lagging Indicators	45
3.3	A Simple Input-Output Table	48
3.4	Illustration of Cross-Impact Analysis Between Four Events	51
3.5	List of Key Informants	62
3.6	Questions Addressed to Key Informants	63
3.7	Chronology of Significant Hong Kong Events	64
4.1	Three Positions on Economic Policy in the PRC	100
7.1	Matching Organization and Environment	160

Figures

1	Economic and Political Confidence	xi
2.1	Kahn's View of Scenario Construction	21
2.2	Three-Dimensional Classification of Scenarios	27
2.3	Morphology of Scenarios	31
2.4	Scenario Construction by Means of Idealization	32
3.1	Naive Versus Causal Methods	54
3.2	The Forecasting Methodology Tree	56
7.1	Environmental States	160

Preface

Contrary to hopes previously expressed in Hong Kong, the leadership of the People's Republic of China (PRC) has opted not to treat the 1997 landmark (Table 3.7) as essentially irrelevant, but to take concrete steps towards incorporating Hong Kong into the Chinese body politic before the end of the twentieth century. After the resumption of the exercise of sovereignty by the PRC, the territory is expected to retain a measure of autonomy until 2047 as a Special Administrative Region (SAR) of China, yet the official barriers separating the two systems will be substantially lowered. The dismantling of the vestiges of British colonial power will doubtless result in greater interdependence between the capitalist enclave and the mainland—or at least in Hong Kong's greater dependence on the PRC.

With the benefit of hindsight, it is possible to argue that a more subtle approach on the part of the UK government and a more ingenious response on the part of the PRC authorities would have produced an outcome more conducive to the prosperity and stability of Hong Kong and perhaps even more beneficial to China itself. However, the argument that the outcome was basically predetermined and not subject to manipulation by political strategists and diplomatic negotiators is equally plausible. The balance of probabilities between these two arguments constitutes an issue to which contemporary analysts are ill-equipped to address themselves, and resolution thus must be left to future historians. Their task will not likely prove easy, given the difficulties of gaining access to relevant sources in the PRC, and it is conceivable that future historical reconstruction will fall short of validating any of the competing hypotheses.

Rather than dwell upon the immediate past, contemporary researchers should preferably take the "one country, two systems" formula China has devised for Hong Kong as their starting point and proceed to evaluate it from multiple perspectives. The Sino-British Joint Declaration envisages a continuing role for the territory as a capitalist centre up to the middle of the next century. PRC representatives have hailed the scheme as both generous and imaginative. They have also showed willingness to support their country's declared policies vis-à-vis Hong Kong with concrete deeds. Nonetheless, the full ramifications of the "one country, two systems" makeshift solution remain to be explored.

The present book is intended as a modest contribution in this direction. It attempts to identify in a reasonably systematic fashion possible paths along which the local economy may be propelled in the next decade or two, given the realities of the Sino-British accord. The emphasis throughout is on economic futures because, the spate of political reforms in the territory notwithstanding, I continue to perceive Hong Kong largely as a business conglomerate headed by a board of directors (rather than as a full-fledged polity) and because there is a tendency among people residing there to define welfare primarily in economic terms. However, in view of the interpenetration which exists between economic, political, and social systems, I often touch upon political and social issues.

Futurology, of course, is at best an inexact science. Therefore, no extravagant claims are made on behalf of the economic scenarios constructed in this book. The object of the exercise is not to forecast or predict, but simply to provide a better appreciation of possible future configurations and the forces likely to shape them. Such appreciation may, inter alia, result in more informed policy action, and this, in conjunction with developments difficult to foresee at present with any accuracy, could distort completely the broad picture presented here. Indeed, given the volatility of the Hong Kong environment, a substantial divergence between extrapolations based on the status quo and future events is highly probable. Be that as it may, this need not detract from the educational and practical value of the exercise.

Although the book does not have any "hidden agenda," my use of the term "status quo" above is not entirely accidental. One encounters in Hong Kong phenomena which trouble my liberal conscience and which those of a more radical (i.e., Marxist) persuasion must find unpalatable. Nonetheless, on the whole, the economic system there operates with remarkable efficiency, and the inequities it begets are generally manageable. (Most are also, sooner or later, attended to, albeit not always in earnest and successfully.) In the absence of solid evidence that an alternative system might serve better the territory's population, the status quo appears worth preserving. Thus, to some extent the book is inspired by concerns "nonacademic" in nature—a sense of curiosity as to the long-term prospects of the present system and a desire to see its principal features retained basically intact. There can be little doubt that many others who have a stake in Hong Kong share the same curiosity and desire.

This book was completed well before the tragic events of 4 June 1989 in Tiananmen Square. The reverberations of the brutal suppression of the prodemocracy movement in China's capital have impinged upon Hong Kong, rendering the uncertainties even more pronounced. It is too early as yet to come to any firm conclusions on the long-term impact of these unexpected developments.

The turmoil in the PRC and its aftermath reinforce the urgent need to continue to study the path the territory is likely to follow. The crisis of confidence expressed by some members of the community has descended upon Hong Kong with a vengeance (Figure 1). The pessimists have increased in number, with the optimists finding it markedly more difficult to justify their positions.

The realists are also under pressure, reexamining their assumptions and moving along the spectrum towards the pessimists. However, unlike those who have dismissed the territory as a viable entity in its present form, they have not completely abandoned the search for some operational solution.

There is emerging slowly in this group a feeling that if certain measures are taken internally and externally, the worst-case scenario might possibly be avoided. Those who cling to their realistic views or retain a degree of

Figure 1 Economic and Political Confidence

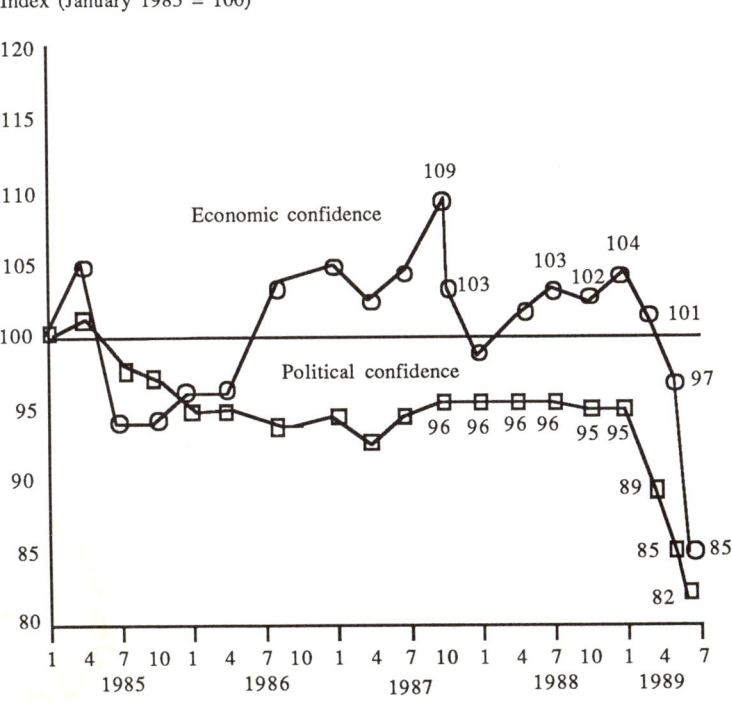

Source: Supplied by *Survey Research Hong Kong*

optimism see certain courses of action that should be embarked upon without delay. Internally, political reform (in the broad sense of the term) is regarded as a matter of priority, underlining the need for further decoupling from the authoritarian mainland system. Externally, there is clamour for the provision of passports as an insurance and for concrete steps to be taken to prevent China from acting contrary to the provisions of the Sino-British Joint Declaration. On that front, the question of the garrisoning of the People's Liberation Army (PLA) in Hong Kong assumes considerable significance—as do areas of the Basic Law such as judicial independence, emergency regulations (particularly those relating to martial law), and the relationship with the organs of the PRC central government. Some realists are also seeking ways to "internationalize" the territory (e.g., substitute UN presence in one form or another for British rule).

As always, Hong Kong's prospects and the solutions to its problems are intimately tied to developments in the PRC. A change of leadership accompanied by a policy reorientation of Beijing could lead to the reemergence of the optimistic scenario. The need for answers is acute, given the fears of the local people, but only time can tell what the future holds for the territory.

Miron Mushkat

ONE
Introduction

In an influential article published in 1965, Emery and Trist[1] coined the term "environmental turbulence." Their aim in introducing this term was to capture the essence of an emerging societal condition characterized by a high degree of complexity and rapid change and to differentiate it from more simple and stable environmental patterns (the "placid random," "placid clustered," and "disturbed reactive" categories). Subsequently, Woodward[2] sought to dispel the myth of "turbulence," but the term has generally been accepted[3] as a useful vehicle[4] for portraying the tangled stimuli and sharp discontinuities faced by a good many organized entities in the latter part of the twentieth century.

Escalating complexity and accelerating change are merely one feature of turbulent environments. (It may be said that they are necessary yet not sufficient conditions for the emergence of turbulence.) An environment is not deemed turbulent as long as a member has the requisite resources and skills to meet the demands which emanate from it. Only when such demands become truly problematic—that is, when the level of "relevant uncertainty"[5] confronting a member renders its continuing adaptation doubtful—can the label "turbulent" be legitimately assigned to an environment. Put another way, turbulence is a relative, rather than absolute, concept which hinges on adaptive capacity as well as the nature of environmental demands.[6]

Notwithstanding that British and Chinese officials insist the two sides are strongly committed to the maintenance of prosperity and stability in the territory, most observers would in all likelihood be inclined to depict as turbulent the Hong Kong environment in the period since the PRC declared its intention to resume the exercise of sovereignty over the capitalist enclave. (The colony was certainly in a state of turbulence during the Sino-British negotiations, and its environment was to all appearances potentially turbulent in the late 1980s.) The perception of turbulence probably reflects concern about both the uncertainty occasioned by the transition from British to Chinese rule and the adaptive capacity of the local system itself.

The period following Prime Minister Margaret Thatcher's controversial

1982 visit to Beijing (Table 3.7) is, of course, not the first one in Hong Kong's history that may be viewed in such pessimistic terms. It is often overlooked that the territory—which prior to the Second World War was a rather small place dependent almost entirely on quite limited entrepôt trade—emerged after four years of Japanese military occupation as a "rundown, war-damaged, pre-industrial society with no very evident future."[7] This society has overcome countless challenges (e.g., the triumph of communism in China, the influx of immigrants from the mainland, the various upheavals in the PRC, severe external recessions and price shocks, growing competition from other new industrial countries—NICs—and producers enjoying a greater comparative advantage in labour-intensive industries) and has, in spite of its rudimentary postwar infrastructure, developed into a relatively sophisticated economic entity. By implication, it may well be erroneous to regard Hong Kong's present predicament as unique and its people as incapable of continuing the previous pattern of challenge and (successful) response.

The level of development, social as well as economic, attained by the territory in the face of formidable environmental constraints can be ascertained by examining statistics produced by its Census and Statistics Department and found in both local and international publications. A more convenient source, however, is a 1983 article by Khan and Zerby.[8] These two econometricians have employed elaborate statistical procedures in order to compare Hong Kong's socioeconomic performance with that of 96 developing countries and 11 mildly developed ones. As might be expected, Khan and Zerby have come to the conclusion that the territory occupies a very respectable position in this category; to be more precise, it has climbed close to the top of the development ladder.

The socioeconomic performance of Hong Kong has not been equal in all domains. It has made impressive strides in the economic areas[9] (where it ranks seventh among the 108 countries), but its progress on the social front[10] (where it ranks eleventh) has been somewhat less spectacular. This slight imbalance notwithstanding, the territory's overall achievement is certainly creditable, for it ranks ninth in the entire sample. (Khan and Zerby have measured socioeconomic performance in terms of an aggregate index comprising 120 indicators, 54 economic and 66 social.)

These findings suggest that Hong Kong has attained considerable maturity as a socioeconomic entity. Although its economy and society have not yet reached the level of the highly developed countries, it is generally on a par with the mildly developed areas of Europe and North America and the fastest developing countries in Asia (including the Middle East). The territory is nowhere near scaling the economic peaks touched by Japan, perhaps the most remarkable example of post–Second World War industrial transformation, but along with the other Asian NICs (Singapore in particular,

South Korea, and Taiwan), it appears to be on the verge of achieving the status of a "developed country."

In fact, Khan's and Zerby's study does not fully reflect the extent of Hong Kong's progress. Because they have opted for an analysis based on cross-sectional data alone (i.e., synchronic analysis) and have not combined it with time-series (i.e., diachronic) analysis, their survey comes across as overly static; it highlights comparative socioeconomic performance at one point in time, but does not give a sense of movement. A more dynamic approach might have shown more dramatically how close Hong Kong is, given its past record, to acquiring the attributes of what the World Bank describes in its annual development reports as an "industrial market economy."

There is another point. Khan and Zerby have relied exclusively on conventional quantitative indicators as yardsticks for assessing socioeconomic performance. This approach doubtless is quite common, yet the special case of Hong Kong seems to require that quantitative model building be undertaken in tandem with some form of institutional evaluation. The territory has highly sophisticated economic institutions which perform highly sophisticated functions, and this institutional complexity is arguably not captured to a sufficient degree in conventional statistical analyses. That Hong Kong is by some criteria the world's third most important financial centre (after New York and London and ahead of Tokyo) provides perhaps the strongest evidence that the territory has truly come of age, at least economically speaking.

The corollary of this proposition presumably is that Hong Kong has a substantial capacity to adapt to environmental disturbances and thus the advent of Chinese rule should not necessarily prove more destabilizing than have previous external shocks. According to this logic, the territory's swift recovery following the "favourable" conclusion of the protracted negotiations between the UK and PRC governments concerning its future provides ample evidence of that amazing resilience and vigour. Hong Kong, it appears, would under no circumstances allow itself to be overwhelmed by environmental uncertainty; on the contrary, it would continue to repel threats to its existence and capitalize on every possible opportunity.

Such a conclusion is by no means unwarranted, but a less sanguine view is also possible. To begin with, it might be argued that the coming reunification with the mainland is likely to constitute a far greater menace than anything experienced before. Thus, the fact that environmental dislocation was brought under control on previous occasions is not entirely relevant if one assumes that future turbulence could be of a different order altogether. The enormous uncertainty which engulfed Hong Kong during various phases of the Sino-British negotiations may be indicative of the potent negative forces which external stimuli can unleash. (It is true that the territory has since more or less regained its momentum, but the disturbance was relatively short-lived and the ultimate point of no return was never actually reached.)

Extreme environmental stress occasioned by the transition from British to Chinese rule might, of course, be exacerbated by additional factors. Local commentators, for instance, often express concern about the possibility that liberalization moves in Japan could catapult Tokyo into the position of being Asia's economic capital and leading financial centre. This, they postulate, would adversely affect the status of Hong Kong and seriously impede its development. A far more ominous threat to the territory's progress is assumed to be the growing protectionist sentiment overseas. An open and externally dependent economy such as that of Hong Kong needs an environment largely free of major barriers to the mobility of factors of production and the flow of goods and services. Otherwise, problems might proliferate and compound the difficulties emanating from other sources.

Sharp escalation in the level of environmental stress is not the only potentially disruptive development looming on the Hong Kong horizon. The territory's much-vaunted adaptive capacity could also diminish as a result of a buildup of intense external and internal pressures. There is no reason to posit that the mechanisms on which Hong Kong has thus far relied successfully to absorb environmental shocks are not vulnerable to erosion and breakdowns. A confluence of externally and internally induced crises might conceivably, past performance notwithstanding, damage these mechanisms beyond repair. The almost mystical belief that the territory is destined to thrive irrespective of the circumstances is unfortunately a myth. As Woronoff has pointed out:

> Condemned to succeed? More often than not, Hong Kong seemed doomed to fail and . . . was on the brink of collapse more than once. For in its original state, it was just barren islands, with a few houses and impoverished rural districts. When it had more houses, it also had more people, far more people than could reasonably be accommodated and certainly more than could draw sustenance from its limited natural wealth. After all, what did it have going for it?
>
> The Colony is tiny. Hong Kong island itself is only about 29 square miles, the city of Kowloon across the harbour is a mere 3 square miles, while the relative vastness of the new territories only brings the total to some 404 square miles or 1,052 square kilometers. There is not much land to begin with, and far less that is usable, for the whole area is hilly and mountainous. . . .
>
> The Colony could not even feed itself from that day to this. Not until the end of the 19th century did it possess the limited arable lands of the New Territories and the somewhat backward peasant population that could hardly feed a city the size of Hong Kong. Even today, despite extraordinary efforts

> and great progress, most of the meat and vegetables, some of the poultry and fish, and almost all of the rice have to be imported. Perhaps unique in the world, Hong Kong even has to import water, otherwise supplies would run out in a dry spell. The few mineral resources are so limited in variety they are just mentioned for those who like to collect odd facts: Kaolin, feldspar and quartz. None of them are of particular value, nor are they in large quantities. There are none of the major resources that bring wealth to luckier countries and not even enough of those things like land, food, water, without which it is assumed no people can survive.[11]

Woronoff, of course, simply restates some well-known facts. Nonetheless, his account serves as a useful reminder of the limits of Hong Kong's adaptive capacity. It also reemphasizes, at a time when the local economy is defying yet again the prophets of doom and showing signs of unmistakable buoyancy, how fragile the foundations of the territory's existence really are. Given this fragility, a marked deterioration in the working of the adjustment mechanisms might possibly produce a chain reaction which could bring about a state of economic paralysis. The lack of resources to fall back on when the need arises is both an asset and a liability: It compels local entrepreneurs to be exceptionally creative, but it severely constrains the system's manoeuvrability.

In analyzing the adaptive capacity of Hong Kong, it is essential to differentiate between capacity as such and factors contributing to successful adjustment. These factors include the territory's location and the attractions of Victoria Harbour, though of primary importance are the people (i.e. human resources).[12] The locational advantage stems from the fact that Hong Kong

> lies astride the Pearl River leading to Canton, some 90 miles away, and since the river is rather shallow it provides an excellent spot for transshipment. It is also conveniently located along the South China coast, accessible to the major shipping routes to Korea and Japan, northern China, the Philippines, and Southeast Asia. But above all, it is one of the key doors to China, although far overshadowed in its day by Shanghai and less necessary when European powers or Japan had concessions all along the coast.[13]

Because it is unusually well endowed by nature, Victoria Harbour is considered to be another significant asset: "It is deep enough to allow direct entry of even the largest ships and vast enough to receive considerable numbers. It forms an excellent typhoon shelter. And, with the many inlets, bays, and islands dotting the region, a tremendous amount of traffic can be received and ships loaded, unloaded, or repaired in quick order."[14]

As indicated, however, Hong Kong's most important resource is assumed to be its people. A good many observers attribute to the Chinese, who make up the vast majority of the local population, qualities which are highly conducive to microeconomic efficiency and macroeconomic growth. Woronoff, for instance, refers to the emergence, in the modern Hong Kong context, of " 'Chineseness' . . . with those sterling virtues one recites without even thinking: Chinese are hard-working and industrious; they are frugal and put their money away for hard times; when opportunity knocks they will invest and nurse that investment until it grows; they are willing to take risks and show initiative; the close family ties and need to hold together provide a basis for cooperation. There are as many homely virtues as Confucian sayings in fortune cookies."[15]

It would, of course, be erroneous to assume that high productivity is a phenomenon with deep roots in Chinese culture. The "Protestant ethic" is more closely identified with capitalist dynamics, and China's encounter with modern capitalism is a relatively recent phenomenon unique to Chinese culture. (Furthermore, until not long ago the experience of the Chinese "was not to run their own but simply be cogs in someone else's capitalist system.")[16] It may even be argued that traditional Chinese values to some extent hamper rather than facilitate the kind of utility-maximizing behaviour that neoclassical economists ascribe to "rational" economic agents. As Topley has suggested:

> The family system put checks on the means of acquiring greater wealth. It discouraged movement into occupations bringing greater income but placing the individual outside family control. The system of inheritance led to continual division of family fortunes. The idea of mutual dependence was institutionalized in a way which tended to inhibit economic efficiency because it continually introduced personal considerations into economic relationships. The class system allotted a low social status to tradesmen and tended to discourage individuals from entering commerce on a permanent basis. . . . Acquisitiveness was discouraged by Confucianism.[17]

The "Chineseness" alluded to by Woronoff must thus be viewed as being partly a product of the modern Hong Kong milieu. (It manifests itself in other similar environments, but perhaps nowhere as strongly as within the territory's relatively unregulated confines.) This milieu to all appearances reinforces those residues of culture which encourage productive endeavour and undermines those which have the opposite effect. Indeed, the influence of the local environment is deemed so crucial by some commentators that they are inclined to dismiss the cultural factor altogether. One of them, for instance, has come to the following conclusion:

> Even if the reader still thinks that the Chinese are of naturally superior stock and that this is the explanation of Hong Kong's success, we might add that the next largest ethnic group is European, primarily British. After all, even if they are a minority, they do run the Colony, whether in administration or business, and, admired or despised, they provide most of the unconscious

models and patterns that are emulated to some extent. There are not many people today who can remember the virtues for which the British were once praised and which permitted them to rule much of America, Asia and Africa at one time. Nowadays, one hears much more of egoism, laziness, indiscipline. With the economy collapsing around them, such people hardly seem a model for anyone. Nevertheless, most of the expatriates have also made it in Hong Kong. Even the Indians and Pakistanis, looked down upon by the others, have found their niche and some have done quite well. So, the secret is not necessarily the people, at least not in their racial or cultural dimension.[18]

The question of whether culture, environment, or some combination of the two variables accounts for the drive exhibited by the territory's residents cannot, it seems, be answered authoritatively. However, irrespective of where the explanation lies, the fact is that Hong Kong is blessed with a highly disciplined and enterprising labour force which is a reliable source of growing output and sustained innovation. This "human capital" is generally seen as the most strategic of the locally available resources and one which contributes most tangibly towards smooth environmental adjustment. (It should be noted that the productive orientation highlighted here is increasingly fused with professional skills, because the territory's labour force has undergone rapid professionalization in recent years.)

Nonetheless, human assets should not be equated with adaptive capacity. The latter is inherent in what Rabushka has described as the "automatic corrective mechanism," a process rooted in the essentially free market economy that "continuously alters internal costs and prices to bring them quickly into line with costs and prices in the rest of the world. The flexible movement of internal costs and prices, with associated changes in output and employment, brings about internal and external equilibrium at all levels of world trade, and maximum economic growth."[19]

The automatic corrective mechanism outlined by Rabushka features in practically every introductory economics book. After all, market equilibria formed in the process of unobstructed interplay between the forces of demand and supply constitute both the foundation of contemporary economic analysis and the embodiment of the ideals of a good many practitioners of the art. The prices which obtain in such contexts are generally hailed as the core of an exceedingly efficient information system which guides economic agents towards "optimal" behaviour. Unfortunately for those who embrace this model—whether in its descriptive or normative aspects—it is seldom found outside of economics textbooks. Therefore, if the above characterization is valid, Hong Kong is an exception to the (empirical) rule.[20] And this, it is postulated, accounts for its adaptive capacity.

Rabushka[21] has identified a number of factors particularly conducive to the unimpeded working of the automatic corrective mechanism. They include the absence of external barriers to the flow of goods and services; the non-"stickiness" of wages (Rabushka maintains that wages in the territory move down as well as up and are not rigidly held by collective bargaining arrangements to levels above the market clearing price); the high mobility of capital and labour in Hong Kong's geographically compact and industrially light economy (the preponderance of small-scale industries operating in like premises means—in the absence of internal barriers to the mobility of factors of production—that capital can be switched from the making of one product to another, or from one industry to another, depending on external market demand); and the government's policy of noninterventionism (which manifests itself both in the microeconomic and macroeconomic spheres). Rabushka views the exercise of self-restraint on the part of the authorities as perhaps the most critical factor in the equation, and he portrays local public policy as follows:

> In Hong Kong, economic affairs are conducted in an environment of virtually unfettered free enterprise. Government policy has long dictated a virtually hands-off approach toward the private sector, an approach that seems well suited to Hong Kong's exposed and dependent economic and political situation. The philosophy that underlies government in Hong Kong can be summed up in a few short phrases: law and order, minimum interference in private affairs, and the creation of an environment conducive to profitable investment. Regulatory economic controls are held to a minimum, no restrictions are placed on the movement of capital, little protection and few subsidies are given to industry, and the few direct services provided by government are operated on a commercial basis.[22]

The picture Rabushka paints of the Hong Kong economy is not necessarily reproduced by other social scientists. For instance, Cheng,[23] in what constitutes the most comprehensive survey of the local economy, asserts that the particular genre of laissez-faire economics which has evolved in the territory is not without its drawbacks: For example, it engenders inequities, deemphasizes planned development as a valuable supplement to private market forces, and provides no sound framework for the management of economic crises and other problematic phenomena. Furthermore, both Cheng and Youngson[24] argue that the Hong Kong government has in fact adopted in recent years a more interventionist stance and that the passive posture commonly attributed to it does not conform to present-day reality. (The government itself describes its policy as one of "positive non-interventionism.")[25]

This notwithstanding, the territory has by no means jettisoned the essence of its free market economy. Nor is there evidence to suggest that the automatic corrective mechanism has lost any of its lustre. Although the government has assumed a more active role in domains such as resource allocation (i.e., production of goods and services) and economic stabilization, the modus operandi of the economy has remained basically the same. This is acknowledged even by those critics, mostly Keynesian in their orientation, who would prefer to see the government moving to display a somewhat greater initiative in the realm of macroeconomic adjustment:

> The government asserts that the Hong Kong economy is a self-regulating one; it is the classical economists' dream. There is therefore no need for the government to intervene. The essence of the argument is that nowhere else in the world is the wage/price flexibility so high as it is in Hong Kong. When a recession occurs, either from a fall in world trade or a decline in the construction industry, output and employment will fall as in the case of a recession in other countries. But, unlike other countries, the response of the Hong Kong economy to such a fall in employment and output will be fast. Such a response takes the form of a decrease in real wages followed by a decrease in prices, as predicted in the classical macroeconomic model. As most of our manufactured goods are for export, the fall in prices will make our products more competitive in overseas markets. In this way, our exports and manufacturing output can be stimulated through this automatic mechanism. Moreover, it can also be argued that the fall in prices and wages will affect the domestic sector as well. Such a fall in prices and wages has the effect of increasing the real cash balance (i.e., the cash in the hands of the public in terms of constant prices). Any increase in the real cash balance will tend to make people feel richer than before and in consequence, consumption will be stimulated and the recovery from a recession will be initiated. . . . The recent world recession in 1973–75 gave an opportunity for the theoretical model outlined above to be tested. To the great comfort of the government, it was observed that real wages and prices did indeed fall in 1974 and 1975 and that consumption rose rapidly during 1975–80. This wage/price flexibility no doubt played an important part in speeding up the recovery. Hong Kong witnessed a big increase in exports in 1976 and an extraordinarily high increase in private consumption in the following years, giving rise to double-digit growth over the period 1976–81. It seems then that the classical model does apply to Hong Kong.[26]

This statement was made during the tumultuous period the territory experienced in the wake of the realization that an ultimate takeover by the PRC was inevitable. It coincided with the pegging of the local dollar to its US counterpart and the government's assumption of control, for the first time in the territory's history, over a private commercial bank (which was on the brink of collapse because of severe liquidity problems). Nonetheless, Chen saw no reason to modify his judgement. Rather, he thought that "the present political situation in Hong Kong has made it necessary to introduce certain economic measures which serve more political than economic purposes.

There is in the minds of most people no basic change in the government's attitude towards non-intervention."[27]

To be sure, the dividing line between economics and politics in the territory is becoming increasingly blurred. Political pressures have undeniably weakened the government's resolve not to deviate from its generally neutral stance vis-à-vis the economy and have compelled it to implement some fairly radical stabilization schemes. Even the sense of acute crisis, however, has not prompted any fundamental economic restructuring. (In fact, while acting as a reluctant stabilizer, the government has been quite successful in pruning its budget and public sector employment.) The new political realities notwithstanding, the local economy remains largely free of rigid governmental controls, the absence of which observers continue to view as the principal source of its dynamism. As Woronoff has summed it up:

> One may, of course, quibble and complain that this is a weak and defective *laissez-faire*, since it has been contaminated by some of the concerns of present-day welfare. On the other hand, it is still as close to the real thing as one can come. If Hong Kong no longer boasts as much freedom as 18th century England or the free-wheeling days of 19th century Shanghai, it is still a far throw from the mixed economies of the West today, let alone socialist or communist regimes. Let us say it is early 20th century *laissez-faire* although its critics might dispute the fact that it has got so far. In some ways, it is even an improved form, as compared with the more spontaneous *laissez-faire* of earlier times, for the Hong Kong Government is following the policy consciously and purposefully, taking advantage of the benefits it does offer. But all that does not really matter. If one wishes to find a well-preserved and healthy specimen of an otherwise vanishing species, there is no other place to see and study *laissez-faire* than Hong Kong.[28]

On the whole, then, it is legitimate to conclude that economic policy in the territory is marked by continuity rather than by change. Capitalist practices there are evolving in response to external and internal events, but they remain firmly entrenched. The unshackled economy, in turn, brings into play the automatic corrective mechanism which provides Hong Kong with its remarkable adaptive capacity. Furthermore, adjustment proceeds smoothly because the territory is able to capitalize on advantages such as an attractive location, excellent harbour, and productive labour force. (The first two advantages have in fact become even more apparent in the wake of China's "open door" policy.)

Thus, as matters now stand, Hong Kong should encounter no undue difficulties in coping with a high degree of environmental stress. Short-term imbalances are doubtless unavoidable, but sooner or later they are bound to be rectified via the automatic corrective mechanism because (primarily) of its great efficiency and because (secondarily) of the considerable advantages the territory enjoys. The challenge posed by the PRC's resumption of the exercise of sovereignty, intensified by other external and internal developments, is without question a formidable one. Yet as long as the automatic corrective mechanism is allowed to function undisturbed, Hong Kong ought, on the face of it, to be capable of responding to almost any environmental pressures and moving to new equilibria.

Unfortunately, however, one cannot assume that the automatic corrective mechanism will retain its present features indefinitely. To begin with, it is not entirely clear whether the "one country, two systems" formula represents a strategic commitment on the part of China or whether it simply constitutes a shrewd tactical manoeuvre. The PRC has gone to great lengths to demonstrate its sincerity with respect to the 1997 issue. Still, doubts have been expressed that the purpose of the confidence-building measures is merely to prevent the flight of capital (financial, human, and physical) and that China will sooner or later tamper with the automatic corrective mechanism. This, in turn, will adversely affect the territory's adaptive capacity.

Even if the PRC leadership is at present firmly committed to the concept of "one country, two systems," it would doubtless modify its policy vis-à-vis Hong Kong at some later juncture. Chinese decisionmaking is not characterized by great consistency, and policy shifts, often radical in nature, are not uncommon in the PRC. Sinologists[29] refer to this elasticity of decisions as "policy oscillation." It is possible to argue, therefore, that the "one country, two systems" formula may undergo substantial changes in the future and that the automatic corrective mechanism is not immune to external interference.

The Chinese political landscape is also littered with intense factional struggles[30] which tend to have a particularly destabilizing effect on decisions. The repercussions of these struggles are felt in virtually all the major policy domains, and there is no reason to posit that the declared policy towards Hong Kong is underpinned by an unshakeable consensus. Thus, should the factional balance which has emerged in Beijing in recent years be disturbed, the concept of "one country, two systems" might be subject to partial or complete reexamination. Past experience suggests that in switching course, the PRC would not necessarily deem itself constrained by the provisions of the Sino-British Joint Declaration.

The Chinese leadership could, of course, remain unequivocally committed to the "one country, two systems" formula, but find itself unable to implement it in practice. Scholars in the field of public administration lay considerable emphasis on the distinction between policy formulation and policy implementation and maintain that decisions in the public sector are often implemented in a way which does not reflect the intentions of those who make them. The divergence between policy formulation and policy implementation—apparently a widespread phenomenon—is without question prevalent in the PRC because of its size, geographic and cultural complexity, poor communications system, bureaucratic inertia, and dysfunctional political controls.[31] The point is that China simply might be unable to bring the "one country, two systems" concept to fruition.

Another factor which should be taken into account are developments within Hong Kong itself. The PRC has resisted any attempts to promote the "three-legged stool" notion, insisting that the 1997 question is a bilateral matter involving only China and the UK (in fact, primarily the former). There can be little doubt, however, that the success of the "one country, two systems" formula hinges *in part* on the willingness and ability of the local people to infuse it with life. As noted previously, Hong Kong is endowed with a wealth of human talent, but the long-term commitment of its business and professional classes remains somewhat tenuous,[32] and their members might grow even more dispirited in the face of heavy-handed external manipulation. Factional conflict in the territory could also escalate in the future, possibly detracting from the efficiency of the automatic corrective mechanism.

An additional cause for concern is the attitude of third parties towards the Hong Kong SAR. The PRC has opposed any moves to internationalize the 1997 issue and has concentrated on forging an agreement with the UK. Such a strategy was to be expected, but given the great importance that China attaches to the symbolic aspects of sovereignty, the upshot is that third parties have no stake in the arrangement worked out by the two signatories. Several countries have substantial investments in the territory and an interest in preserving the status quo there, but in the present competitive climate, many trading nations could welcome Hong Kong's decline. They might, individually or collectively, take steps contrary to the spirit of the Sino-British Joint Declaration (e.g., treat the territory as an integral part of the PRC), which doubtless would render adjustment exceedingly difficult.

Sharp deterioration in adaptive capacity is, therefore, a possibility which cannot be ruled out. Of course, it might be argued that Hong Kong would for the foreseeable future continue to capitalize on its location, harbour facilities, and human energy. Neither the location nor the harbour, however, are of real advantage without the economic dynamism which is at present the hallmark of the territory. Furthermore, human resources could be depleted through immigration and environmental change because an environment bereft of the incentives currently available to maximize effort and performance is bound to produce markedly different patterns of economic behaviour.

Significant decline in adaptive capacity, coupled with externally induced stress, might in turn precipitate environmental turbulence, as suggested earlier. This gloomy prospect need not necessarily materialize, but it would be erroneous to adopt an ostrichlike attitude (such as that seemingly advocated by the British, Chinese, and Hong Kong governments) and assume that prosperity and stability are to all intents and purposes guaranteed. If the analysis offered here is valid, a number of potentially worrisome developments loom on the horizon; it behooves those with the motivation, interest, and expertise to try to determine the direction in which the local economy may be heading in the next decade or two.

Indeed, the task of the social scientist is not merely to dissect historical and contemporary patterns but also to highlight further trends.[33] Given the dangers inherent in environmental turbulence, the need for crystal-ball gazing is particularly acute in Hong Kong. This book constitutes an attempt to satisfy this need, at least in part, by constructing long-term economic scenarios for the territory. Although futures research is fraught with considerable difficulties, the educational value of the undertaking lies in the fact that it may heighten awareness of the forces likely to impinge on the local economy and their possible effects.

Scenario construction has a practical value as well. Specifically, it can serve as a basis for a sophisticated type of planning alluded to as "scenario- (or environmentally) driven planning."[34] This planning mode revolves round the evaluation of options generated in response to an array of environmental constructs (scenarios). Because planning is more common in Hong Kong than is officially acknowledged,[35] the availability of a range of reasonably well-researched scenarios could facilitate efforts directed towards developing appropriate contingency plans.[36] The production of such a range of scenarios is the principal objective of this book.

Notes

1. F.E. Emery and E.L. Trist, "The Causal Texture of Organizational Environments, *Human Relations* 18 (February 1965): 21–32. See also R.L. Ackoff and F.E. Emery, *On Purposeful Systems* (Chicago: Aldine-Atherton, 1972); F.E. Emery, *Towards a Social Ecology* (London: Plenum, 1972); F.E. Emery and M. Emery, *A Choice of Futures* (Leiden: Nijhoff, 1976); F.E. Emery, *Futures We Are In* (Leiden: Nijhoff, 1977); E.L. Trist, "The Environment and System-Response Capability," *Futures* 12 (April 1980): 113–127.

2. S.N. Woodward, "The Myth of Turbulence," *Futures* 14 (August 1982): 266–279.

3. See, for example, S. Terreberry, "The Evolution of Organizational Environments," *Administrative Science Quarterly* 12 (March 1968): 590–613; D.C. Basil and C.W. Cook, *The Management of Change* (New York: McGraw-Hill, 1974); L. Metcalfe, "Systems Models, Economic Models and the Causal Texture of Organizational Environments," *Human Relations* 27 (July 1974): 639–663; L. Metcalfe, "Policy Making in Turbulent Environments," in *Interorganizational Policy Making*, ed. K. Hanf and F.W. Scharpf (Beverly Hills, Calif.: Sage, 1978), pp. 37–55;

H. Nystrom, *Creativity and Innovation* (New York: Wiley, 1979); K.B. De Greene, *The Adaptive Organization* (New York: Wiley, 1982); G.L. Wamsley and M.N. Zald, "The Environment of Public Managers," in *Handbook of Organization Management*, ed. W.B. Eddy (New York: Dekker, 1983), pp. 501–529; J.E McCann and J. Selsky, "Hyperturbulence and the Emergence of Type 5 Environments," *Academy of Management Review* 9 (July 1984): 460-470.

4. Some writers, however, prefer the term "environmental stress." See, for example, B. Bozeman and E.A. Slusher, "Scarcity and Environmental Stress in Public Organizations," *Administration and Society* 11 (November 1979): 335–355.

5. See Emery and Trist, "The Causal Texture of Organizational Environments."

6. See McCann and Selsky, "Hyperturbulence and the Emergence of Type 5 Environments."

7. See A.J. Youngson, *Hong Kong* (Hong Kong: Oxford University Press, 1982), p. 2.

8. M.H. Khan and J.A. Zerby, "The Position of Hong Kong on International Scales of Socioeconomic Development," *Asian Profile* 11 (October 1983): 447–453.

9. The specific areas are agriculture, industry, labour, transport and communications, international trade, and general economy.

10. In demography, health and nutrition, education, housing, culture, and politics.

11. J. Woronoff, *Hong Kong* (Hong Kong: Heinemann Asia, 1980), pp. 10–11.

12. Ibid.

13. Ibid., p. 11.

14. Ibid., p. 12.

15. Ibid., p. 14. Woronoff, however, also contends (ibid.) that those qualities:

> should not keep us from remembering the underside of the virtues, things resembling vices. Chinese who are hard-working often also drive their underlings particularly hard, sometimes more than is good for them. They do save money, but not always for productive investments or charity. There is a disconcerting tendency to use money for non-economic social purposes, to engage in conspicuous consumption to gain "face" or to make ostentatious purchases in the hope of rising in social ranking. The family or clan provides strong bonds, so strong that there is little room for outsiders. Doubtlessly many are daring; some are outright gamblers. Whichever Chinese are traditionally disciplined, few of them can be encountered walking the streets of Hong Kong.

16. Ibid., p. 13.

17. M. Topley, "The Role of Savings and Wealth Among Hong Kong Chinese," in *Hong Kong*, ed. I.C. Jarvie (London: Routledge and Kegan, 1969), p. 185.

18. See Woronoff, *Hong Kong*, p. 14.

19. A. Rabushka, *Hong Kong* (Chicago: University of Chicago Press, 1979). See also A. Rabushka, *The Changing Face of Hong Kong* (Washington, D.C.: American Enterprise Institute, 1973); A. Rabushka, *Value for Money* (Stanford, Calif.: Hoover Institution Press, 1976). Rabushka in *Hong Kong*, pp. 3–5, provides this example of how the automatic corrective mechanism operates:

Hong Kong's experience between 1973 and 1976 illustrates the automatic corrective mechanism adjusting through one full cycle of boom, recession, and recovery. Hong Kong's boom reflected a peak of activity in the world economy in 1973, when real per capita gross domestic product in the territory increased 10 percent. . . . Boom, however, gave way to recession. The previous year had witnessed a domestically generated monetary squeeze. A large net inflow of funds through the foreign exchange market in 1971 and 1972, associated with investment on the stock market, sharply increased the money supply and rapidly drove up property prices and rents. An equally rapid decline in stock market prices . . . and the consequent outflow of foreign exchange resulted in a sharp deceleration in the growth of the money supply. But the full impact on the economy did not appear until the oil price increase late in 1973 diminished world economic activity and overseas demand for Hong Kong products. Reductions in output and employment in the manufacturing sector followed, which in turn reduced demand for imports. . . . The sharp recessionary forces of late 1973 through 1975 induced a severe squeeze on costs and prices, which led to a rapid and marked recovery in Hong Kong's competitive position in overseas markets. The elimination of inflation in Hong Kong's economy was accompanied by a very large inflow of funds from overseas, yielding a surplus in the overall balance of payments. The effect was to increase the assets of the banking system and leave it liquid and able to expand lending as demand recovered. . . . Throughout 1976 the economy recovered briskly. . . . By the end of 1976, real wages had almost returned to the peak level of March 1973, and have since steadily risen.

20. Such a view is expressed in M. Friedman and R. Friedman, *Free to Choose* (Harmondsworth: Penguin, 1980); M. Friedman with R. Friedman, *Capitalism and Freedom* (Chicago: University of Chicago Press, 1982). See also Woronoff, *Hong Kong*; E. Szczepanik, *The Economic Growth of Hong Kong* (London: Oxford University Press, 1958); W.F. Beazer, *The Commercial Future of Hong Kong* (New York; Praeger, 1978).

21. Rabushka, *Value for Money*, p. 84.

22. Rabushka, *Hong Kong*, p. 44.

23. T.Y. Cheng, *The Economy of Hong Kong* (Hong Kong: Far East Publications, 1982).

24. Youngson, *Hong Kong*.

25. See, for example, P. Haddon-Cave, "Introduction," in *The Business Environment in Hong Kong*, ed. D.G. Lethbridge (Hong Kong: Oxford University Press, 1984), pp. xiii–xx.

26. See E.K.Y. Chen, "The Economic Setting," in *The Business Environment in Hong Kong*, ed. Lethbridge, p. 40. Chen, however, proceeds to offer at pp. 40–41 the following assessment:

But even if there is an automatic mechanism inherent in the Hong Kong economy, there should still be room for macroeconomic policy to speed up the adjustment process, which can be long and painful. Past experience has shown that the speed of the adjustment process might have been due to the fact that the Hong Kong Government followed Keynesian policy in practice, though this was not its intention because it always publicly claimed that it rejected the applicability of such policy to Hong Kong. If we examine the government revenue and expenditure account in the post-war period, some support for the assertion can be found. During periods of fast growth, say 1960–1966 and 1969–1973, there was a considerable surplus in each year's budget. Such surpluses had the effect of cooling the overheated economy, and severe inflation was thus avoided. On the other hand, during the trade recession in 1957–1959, the collapse of the housing boom in 1965, and the world recession in 1974–1975, deficits appeared in the budget in 1959–1960, 1965–1966, and 1974–1975, corresponding to the periods of low levels of economic activity. These deficits had the effect of stimulating the recovery of the economy. Thus, despite the consistent denial of adherence to Keynesian philosophy, there have been indications that the Hong Kong Government has in practice had a stabilizing budgetary policy. . . . Another argument put forth by the government to support a non-intervention policy is the openness of the Hong Kong economy. The government has repeated many times that because of the openness of the Hong Kong economy and the high marginal propensity to import (which measures the increase in imports resulting from a given increase in income) any increase in government expenditure will largely be spent on imported goods and hence an expansionary budget policy will only increase output and employment in other countries but not in Hong Kong. There is certainly some truth in this argument, but it is doubtful whether fiscal policy is as ineffective as the government asserts. The effectiveness of fiscal policy can be indicated by the magnitude of the multiplier, which shows the number of dollars of income generated from a dollar increase in government expenditure. The government believes that the multiplier for Hong Kong is almost zero, namely that any increase in government expenditure will be entirely dissipated abroad and will contribute nothing to the increase of income within Hong Kong. However, based on the available income and trade statistics, we find that the multiplier could be in the range of 1.5 to 2, rather than zero. A multiplier of this size is not very large, but should be large enough to refute the proposition that fiscal policy is totally ineffective in Hong Kong.

27. See ibid., p. 43.
28. Woronoff, *Hong Kong*, p. 41.
29. See in particular G.W. Skinner and E.A. Winckler, "Growth and Decline Processes in Organizations," in *A Sociological Reader on Complex Organizations*, ed. A. Etzioni (New York: Holt, Rinehart and Winston, 1980), pp. 401–423. See also A.J.

Nathan, "Policy Oscillations in the People's Republic of China," *China Quarterly* 68 (December 1976): 720–733; E.A. Winckler, "Policy Oscillations in the People's Republic of China," *China Quarterly* 68 (December 1976): 734–750.

30. See in particular L. W. Pye, *The Dynamics of Chinese Politics* (Cambridge, Mass.: Oehgeschler, Gunn and Hain, 1981).

31. See in particular M.D. Lampton, ed., *Policy Implementation in the Post-Mao Era* (Berkeley: University of California Press, 1985).

32. See, for example, I. Scott, "Sino-British Agreement and Political Power in Hong Kong," *Asia Pacific Community* 31 (Winter 1986): 1–18.

33. See, for example, O. Helmer, *Looking Forward* (Beverly Hills, Calif.: Sage, 1982).

34. See R. Amara and A.J. Lipinski, *Business Planning for an Uncertain Future*, (Oxford: Pergamon, 1983).

35. See, for example, R. Bristow, *Land-Use Planning in Hong Kong* (Hong Kong: Oxford University Press, 1984).

36. See, for example, P. Strangert, "Adaptive Planning and Uncertainty Resolution," *Futures* 9 (February 1977): 32–44.

TWO
Scenarios

The economic future of Hong Kong may be explored by means of a number of methods.[1] The one relied upon in this book is scenario construction—perhaps the most widely used and best known of the tools developed by futurologists. The popularity of this method among researchers and the general familiarity with it, however, pose something of a problem. As Schwartz, Svendin, and Wittrock[2] have pointed out, scenario construction has consequently become almost synonymous with the whole field of futures studies and the term no longer conveys precisely what is entailed in the activity to which it refers. Therefore, an attempt to clarify the meaning of the concept of "scenario" should ideally precede the presentation of images of the territory's future. Such an attempt is made in this chapter.

Its contemporary connotations notwithstanding, the word "scenario" is not new. Carney[3] has traced its origins to the Middle Ages when, according to him, it was invented by Italian actors. He has established that they employed the word to describe a type of comedy with a written plot but no written dialogue, which was improvised by the actors themselves when they staged the comedy. Carney has noted that subsequently the term "scenario" was embraced by Hollywood and given a somewhat different meaning. The movie moguls used it rather loosely to denote a plot, that is, staging directions for a single scene or an entire shooting script.

At present the term is associated primarily with the work of the think tanks which have proliferated in the United States since the Second World War, rather than the products, whether intermediate or final, of the entertainment industry. In particular, scenarios featured prominently in the investigations conducted by Kahn under the auspices of the Rand Corporation and the Hudson Institute. He employed them as analytical devices in order to gain insight into the dynamics of phenomena such as military conflict,[4] socioeconomic change,[5] and national development.[6] Although Kahn's books do not contain elaborate discussions of the concept of "scenario" (his primary focus was reporting his substantive findings), he often touched upon the subject and offered definitions which are deemed authoritative.[7]

In his analysis of military conflict, Kahn used the word "scenario" to mean the detailed representation of the future outcomes of a given policy. His aim, and that of other think-tank denizens,[8] was presumably to compel decisionmakers to consider alternatives in terms of their likely impacts. He worked towards this aim by examining the consequences of the courses of action open to those responsible for national defence in the United States. Because of the applied nature of the research which Kahn undertook for military clients, he tended to confine the scope of scenarios, at least in that context, to the results of policies.

While dissecting socioeconomic processes, however, Kahn was inclined to adopt a somewhat broader definition. Thus, in his classic *The Year 2000*, he has stated that "[s]cenarios are hypothetical sequences of events constructed for the purpose of focusing attention on causal processes and decision-points."[9] In the same book, Kahn has further explained that "[t]hey answer two kinds of questions: (1) Precisely how might some hypothetical situation come about, step by step? and (2) What alternatives exist, for each actor, at each step, for preventing, diverting, or facilitating the process?"[10] Here the policy relevance of scenarios is still underlined, but they are not portrayed as a vehicle for the representation of decision outcomes alone (Figure 2.1).

Kahn's definition has been accepted by most futurologists. Nonetheless, some find it unduly restrictive. Those who have expressed reservations maintain that scenarios need not focus on sequential development and causal dynamics and be geared to policy action (although such features are doubtless desirable). Put another way, they argue that it is legitimate to construct models of the future which are static, fall short of determining cause-effect relationships, and serve purposes other than decisionmaking. Indeed, a number of scholars have produced definitions far more elastic than that of Kahn.

For instance, after surveying relevant work in the area of military systems analysis, Brown has come to the conclusion that the various notions of "scenario" he has encountered

> all refer to descriptions of the *conditions under which* the systems they are analyzing, designing, or operating are assumed to be performing. The system may be a weapon, it may be a component of a weapon, it may be a vast complex of weapons and support facilities (such as NORAD), it may be an organization (such as the National Military Command and Control System), it may even be the entire national security establishment. Whatever the scope and properties of the specific system, a scenario—in systems analysis—can be defined as a statement of assumptions about the operating environment of the particular system we are analyzing.[11]

Figure 2.1 Kahn's View of Scenario Construction

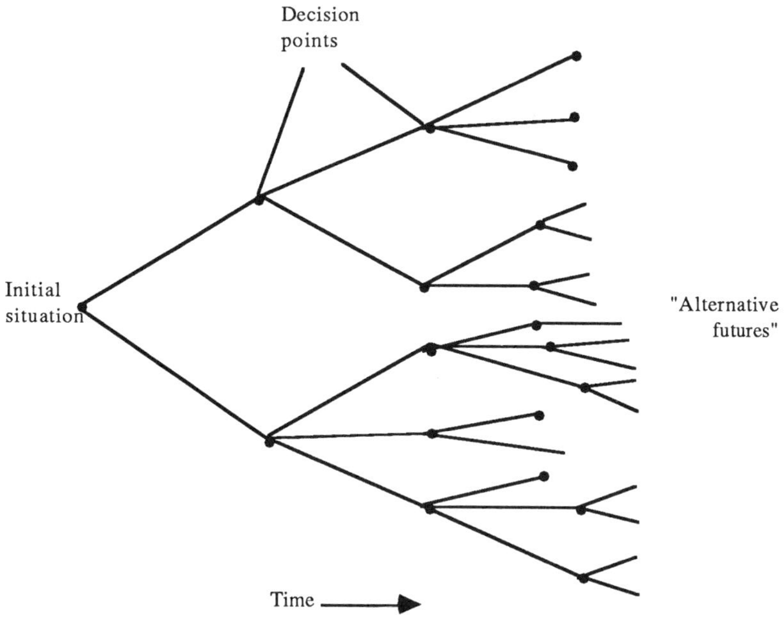

Source: Adapted from H. Kahn and A. J. Wiener, *The Year 2000* (New York: Macmillan, 1967).

Brown has conceded this definition is so widely cast that "the net could drag up a wide assortment of fish." He has, however, countered this argument with the suggestion that the problem might be circumvented by developing a typology of scenarios (i.e., "classifying the fish"). The advantage of starting initially from a broad base, according to Brown, lies in the fact that it serves as a safeguard against possible entanglement in a narrow definitional net that "lets some of the more interesting catches swim away." A similar position has been adopted by other researchers.

One of those who have consciously opted for a broad definition is Gershuny. In an influential article, he has equated scenarios with "general descriptions of future conditions and events.[12] Wilson and Rivett have also chosen not to be overly specific in defining the concept: Wilson has stated that a scenario is "an outline of one conceivable state of affairs, given certain assumptions."[13] Rivett has put forward the case that scenarios "give a qualitative or quantitative description of the world at a particular future time."[14]

All the preceding definitions appear to be workable (particularly Rivett's, for it contains no terms—e.g., "systems," "conditions," "events," and "assumptions"—which may require further elaboration). Nonetheless, in the present context[15] it is desirable to simplify matters to a greater extent and regard a scenario as a future picture, in whatever form, of the environment. The word "picture" is preferable to the expression "qualitative or quantitative description" because it does not have the same rigorous connotations. In addition, because the term "world" is perhaps on the vague side, one is inclined to seek a substitute (ideally "environment," but additional alternatives are available).

Table 2.1 Characteristics of the Postindustrial (or Post–Mass Consumption) Society

1. Per capita income about fifty times the preindustrial.
2. Most "economic" activities are tertiary and quaternary (service-oriented), rather than primary or secondary (production-oriented).
3. Business firms no longer the major source of innovation.
4. There may be more "consentives" (vs. "marketives").
5. Effective floor on income and welfare.
6. Efficiency no longer primary.
7. Market plays diminished role compared to public sector and "social accounts."
8. Widespread "cybernation."
9. "Small world."
10. Typical "doubling time" between three and thirty years.
11. Learning society.
12. Rapid improvement in educational institutions and techniques.
13. Erosion (in middle class) of work-oriented, achievement-oriented, advancement-oriented values.
14. Erosion of "national interest" values.
15. Sensate, secular, humanist, perhaps self-indulgent criteria become central.

Source: H. Kahn and A.J. Wiener, *The Year 2000* (New York: Macmillan, 1967).

An example of a future picture of the environment is Kahn's portrayal of the postindustrial (or post–mass consumption) society. He has observed that the transition to such a condition is likely to be as significant as the metamorphosis which accompanied the process of industrialization in the eighteenth and early nineteenth centuries and has proceeded to outline its possible characteristics. Fifteen of these have been identified, which Kahn has combined to form a scenario of a postindustrial society—incorporating cultural, cybernetic, economic, and educational attributes (Table 2.1).

Another example of a future picture of the environment is Palmer's and Schmid's[16] description of events (favourable and unfavourable) which might impinge on the performance of the New York banking industry and the conditions (favourable and unfavourable) that could result if various sets of events envisaged by them materialize. They first listed 110 key events and then attempted to establish whether the different chains of interrelated events[17] are likely to increase the opportunities for gaining market shares or increase the risks of losing those. (For example, the following factors would probably create a low-risk climate for large New York banks: high GNP growth, low inflation, positive balance of payments, high corporate profits, balanced government budget, retention by New York City of its status as a commercial/financial centre, relaxation of branching and bank–holding company laws, general regulatory climate stressing increased competition, few technological breakthroughs in banking, implementation of new systems proving expensive, and existence of security problems.)

An additional example of a future picture of the environment is Brecher's[18] discussion of the broad options available to American educational planners. She has approached the problem in terms of the following questions: "Who should control educational policy? What are the goals of American education? What curricula are necessary? Should schooling be mandatory? Finally, who should finance educational programs?"[19] The choices which have emerged in the wake of her multidimensional probing are said to reflect closely historical phases in policy development and debates over educational strategies. They fall into three categories:

Scenario One: Education is controlled by the federal government. All standards are established by Congress and federal administrative agencies. The goal of education is to provide upward mobility in a democratic society.
. . .
Scenario Two: Schools are state controlled. Each state sets its own goals and educational standards. Each state determines whether there should be compulsory attendance or state financing of private schools. . . .
Scenario Three: Education is a private matter. Parents are free to determine whether any schooling is necessary for their children. Neither the federal nor the state governments are involved in the educational process.[20]

An examination of examples such as the ones provided here[21] reveals that scenarios share certain common characteristics.[22] In the first place, it is evident that they are hypothetical, a fact that stems from the elusive nature of the future and the inherent limitations of futures research. As Wilson has commented: "However good our futures research may be, we shall never be able to escape the ultimate dilemma that all of our knowledge is about the past, and all our decisions are about the future."[23] The point is that futures research constitutes a useful vehicle for exploring alternative possible futures (and scenarios are ideally suited to the task), but given the considerable uncertainty surrounding the future, it would be inappropriate to claim that scenarios can serve as an instrument for reliable prediction.

Second, a scenario does not normally amount to more than a sketch—an outline. In the theatre and the motion picture industry, it furnishes a synopsis of the action and brief descriptions of the principal characters, without going into the full details that are to be found in the actual script. Similarly, in futures research, a scenario "seeks only to map out the key 'branching points' of the future, to highlight the major determinants that might cause the future to evolve from one 'branch' rather than another, and to sketch in the prime consequences of a causal chain. Selectivity is, therefore, of the essence in developing a scenario—selectivity and, as in the theater, a degree of dramatic ability in highlighting the flow of action and making it interesting."[24]

Third, scenarios are (or should be) multifaceted and holistic in their approach to the future. In the early days of futures research, it was the isolated event, the specific forecast, that riveted attention ("By 1990 more than half the homes in the country will have picture-on-the-wall television"); there was also an inexplicable fascination with particular dates in the future (e.g., 1984, 2000, or the tricentennial 2076 in the United States). The preoccupation with isolated events and particular dates is still a feature of the popular literature on the subject. Wilson maintains that this preoccupation is unwarranted:

> History is a "booming, buzzing confusion" of events, trends, and discontinuities; it is constantly in motion and so is more accurately represented by a motion picture than by a snapshot. Scenarios have a special ability to represent this multifaceted, interacting flow process, combining (when appropriate) demographic changes, social trends, political events, economic variables and technological developments. Of course, the scope of a scenario's approach varies with its topic; a scenario of the future of U.S. society must encompass more variables than one dealing with, shall we say, a particular community or product. But the principle of holism remains as a guiding tenet in the development of scenarios, for it is the cross-impact of events and trends that gives history (and the future) its dynamics. It is this dynamism that we must try to reproduce in our futures research.[25]

Examples such as those given here illustrate that scenarios not only share certain common characteristics, but also that they differ in several respects. For instance, some are "descriptive" in nature (e.g., that of Kahn), whereas others display a "normative" orientation (e.g., that of Brecher).[26] The descriptive types simply depict possible future occurrences, irrespective of their desirability or undesirability. (Descriptive scenarios may include statements concerning the reality or probability of such occurrences, in which case they are referred to as "plausible.")[27] Normative scenarios, on the other hand, embody values by portraying developments which should occur in order to attain given goals.

Scenario construction in the descriptive mode is often perceived as an essentially passive type of activity. To describe it as such, however, might be inaccurate. Gerardin[28] has identified four attitudes towards the future: "totally passive," "opportunist," "adaptive," and "creative." The totally passive attitude was typical of the preindustrial society when the future was largely seen as a repetition of the past. The opportunist attitude, which is prevalent today, is cognizant of environmental change, but it is predicated on a short-term logic that prompts people to seek adjustment by organizing their activities with a view to avoiding daily dangers and capitalizing on daily opportunities. The adaptative attitude manifests itself in a quest "to optimize the today actions in order that their consequences are better adapted to the foreseeable future."[29] The creative attitude entails "futures creative planning,"[30] or an attempt to redesign the environment in accordance with policy goals. (The difference between the third and fourth attitude is tantamount to the difference between adapting [with delay] to the external change and causing [in advance] the desired change.) Contrary to what may be generally thought, descriptive scenario construction is by no means indicative of a passive or an opportunist outlook.

Successful adaptation, after all, hinges on the ability to describe the future. Moreover, it is inadvisable to engage in creative redesign without undertaking first a thorough descriptive analysis, a tenet explicitly acknowledged in the planning literature. Corporate planners,[31] in particular, lay considerable emphasis on describing the future prior to prescribing courses of action. Public planners[32] are also increasingly inclined to produce descriptions of the future as part of the overall planning effort. Descriptive and normative scenario construction may thus be viewed as complementary activities which serve the purpose of both illuminating the future and shaping it.

The distinction between descriptive and normative scenarios is deemed to be the most fundamental, but it is not necessarily the only one in vogue. A good many writers,[33] for instance, differentiate between "exploratory" and "anticipatory" scenarios. Exploratory construction seeks to establish "causality," whereas the anticipatory mode focuses on "effectuality." Thus the questions asked are framed in opposite fashion (Table 2.2). Exploratory and anticipatory scenarios may be either descriptive (linking causes and effects) or normative (linking means and goals).

The scenarios constructed by Palmer and Schmid provide an example of

Table 2.2 Four Basic Types of Scenario

	Exploratory	Anticipatory
Descriptive	Given the causes, what are the effects?	Given the effects, what are the causes?
Normative	Given the means, what goals can be reached?	Given the goals, what means can be used?

Source: C. Ducot and G.J. Lubben, "A Typology for Scenarios," *Futures* 12 (February 1980), p. 53.

exploratory research. The exploratory nature of their endeavour stems from the fact that they have identified chains of events (i.e., causes) which could lead to an expansion or a contraction in the market share of large New York banks (i.e., effects). Clearly, Palmer and Schmid have proceeded from causes to effects. Had they specified the effects first and then attempted to trace the causes, their scenarios would qualify as "descriptive-anticipatory" rather than as "descriptive-exploratory." Palmer's and Schmid's approach is typical—future researchers are normally concerned with causality and exploration, not with effectuality and anticipation. This is particularly true in the case of exploratory forecasting because in normative work it is quite common to tackle problems from an anticipatory perspective (i.e., to ask "Given the goals, what means can be used?")[34]

Ducot and Lubben[35]—who have elaborated the distinctions between descriptive, normative, exploratory, and anticipatory futures research—have suggested that scenarios should also be differentiated on the basis of their probabilities. Specifically, they have termed a highly probable future picture of the environment a "trend scenario" and one much less likely to materialize a "peripheral scenario." In studying the future, according to Ducot and Lubben, one inevitably gravitates towards emerging trends, but it is desirable not to overlook peripheral developments. (It is also important to stress that a trend scenario, contrary to what is implied by its name, does not necessarily correspond to a pure and simple extrapolation of trends.) As Godet has remarked: "Certainly, in the recent past, when the world changed less rapidly than today, the most likely development was the continuation of trends. For the future, however, the most likely often appears to entail a clean break with present trends."[36]

Ducot and Lubben have considered the trend-peripheral dichotomy to be of sufficient significance to incorporate it into their three-dimensional classification of scenarios (Figure 2.2). This approach is in line with the method originally proposed by Kahn.[37] He sought to identify basic, long-term multifold trends (Table 2.3) and relied on these to generate "surprise-free" projections and to specify one or more "standard" worlds consistent

Figure 2.2 Three-Dimensional Classification of Scenarios

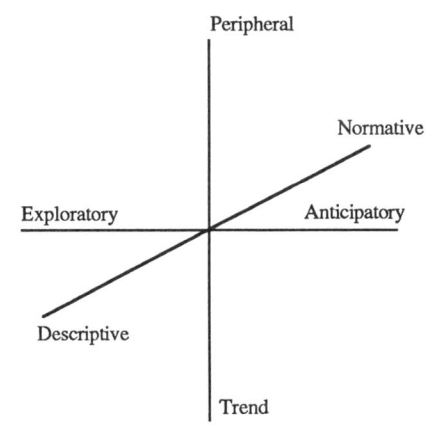

```
                    Peripheral
                        |
                        |        Normative
                        |       /
       Exploratory      |      /    Anticipatory
       ─────────────────┼─────/──────────────
                       /|
                      / |
          Descriptive   |
                        |
                        | Trend
```

Source: Adapted from C. Ducot and G.J. Lubben, "A Typology for Scenarios," *Futures* 12 (February 1980).

Table 2.3 Basic, Long-Term Multifold Trends Identified by Kahn and Wiener

1. Increasingly sensate (empirical, this-worldly, secular, humanistic, pragmatic, utilitarian, contractual, epicurean, hedonistic, and the like) cultures.

2. Bourgeois, bureaucratic, meritocratic, democratic (and nationalistic?) elites.

3. Accumulation of scientific and technological knowledge.

4. Institutionalization of change, especially research, development, innovation, and diffusion.

5. Worldwide industrialization and modernization.

6. Increasing affluence and (recently) leisure.

7. Population growth.

8. Urbanization and (soon) the growth of megapolises.

9. Decreasing importance of primary and (recently) secondary occupations.

10. Literacy and education.

11. Increasing capability for mass destruction.

12. Increasing tempo of change.

13. Increasing universality of the multifold trend.

Source: H. Kahn and A.J. Wiener, *The Year 2000*, (New York: Macmillan, 1967) p. 7.

with them. ("While the surprise-free projection," Kahn has explained, "is similar in spirit to the 'naive projection' of the economist, which assumes a continuation of current tendencies, it is more complex in that it also includes the implications of whatever empirical and theoretical considerations affect our expectations. For example, a 'naive' projection of world population to 2000 would be about 7.2 billion, but our 'surprise-free' projection would be 6.4 billion, and a persuasive case could be made for a somewhat lower figure.")[38]

Kahn concentrated in his investigations on standard worlds (i.e., trend scenarios). However, he also explored alternative future pictures of the environment (i.e., peripheral scenarios or their equivalents), referred to by him as "canonical variations." Kahn claimed that this enabled him to gain a better appreciation of the interplay of environmental forces and to produce a fairly comprehensive set of forecasts. An interesting characteristic of his canonical variations was their wide range. He did not confine himself to one or two peripheral possibilities, but examined a large number of nearly surprise-free and far less likely patterns.

The emphasis on the construction of multiple scenarios is perhaps even stronger in the more recent literature on futures research. Although it is no longer common to focus on truly peripheral cases, several probable scenarios are normally considered, and the likelihood of their occurrence is assessed either formally or informally. Some scholars[39] still employ a trend, or a "reference," scenario as their baseline and scrutinize it in conjunction with two or more somewhat less probable and contrasting (e.g., "optimistic" versus "pessimistic") possibilities. Most of those engaged in long-range work, however, adopt a slightly less structured approach and simply generate a range of likely scenarios together with some indication of their respective probabilities.

The educational options outlined by Brecher constitute an example of multiple futures. The alternatives she has chosen to illustrate the dilemmas faced by American planners in this particular sector may be regarded as a vehicle to facilitate normative decisionmaking; one would normally evaluate the issues in terms of feasibility and desirability rather than probability. Another example of multiple scenario construction—but with a descriptive and probabilistic orientation—is to be found in the study by Chen, Jarboe, and Wolfe.[40] Their objective has been to develop models of the future socioeconomic environment in the United States which could provide a framework for the assessment of new aviation communications technologies. They have concluded that three scenarios merit careful consideration:

> The *Balanced Growth* (Theme X) scenario takes as its starting point the Federal Aviation Administration's Baseline Scenario. The dominant themes of "Balanced Growth" are the gradual transformation of the United States from an industrial society to an information society with controlled

Table 2.4 New Aviation Communications Technologies: Comparative Summary of Three Scenarios

	Theme X: Balanced Growth	Theme Y: Rapid Growth	Theme Z: Stagflation
Society and technology	Social control of technology	Technological dominance	Antitechnology backlash
Societal characteristics	Mature, stable information society	Continually expanding information society	Decaying industrial society
Population by 2000 (millions)	294	362	281
Population distribution	Decentralized to medium and small cities; balanced regional distribution	Megapolises along coasts and in Sun Belt	Congested metropolises; high growth in Sun Belt
Growth of GNP	Moderate (3%)	High (4.5%)	Low (1.5%)
Inflation	Moderate (4%)	Low (2%)	High (8%)
Productivity	Moderate	High	Low
Regulation	Moderate regulation	Deregulation	Reregulation
Communications technology innovation lag (years)	1.8	3	5.7
Total aircraft flights by 2020 (millions)	161	250	90

Source: Adapted from K. Chen, K. Jarboe, and J. Wolfe, "Long-Range Scenario Construction for Technology Assessment," *Technological Forecasting and Social Change* 20 (January 1981), p. 31.

development of technology. The balancing of economic and technological growth with social and environmental needs results in a modest rate of economic growth, carrying forward the general rate of economic growth forecasted for the years between 1979 and 1990 in the FAA's Baseline scenario. . . .

The major theme of the *Rapid Growth* scenario (Theme Y) is the transformation of the United Sates to an information society by way of technological determinism. Technological development is the driving force behind the societal transformation. Rapid technological development leads to rapid economic growth. This rapid economic growth is a continuation of the growth rate used for the years 1979-1990 in the FAA's High Prosperity scenario, which serves as the starting point for the Rapid Growth scenario. . . .

The *Stagflation* scenario (Theme Z) is prolonged economic stagnation combined with excessive inflation. This scenario is built upon the motif of acute tension within society combined with an antitechnology backlash. The result is that the United States becomes a decaying industrial country rather than an information society. Tension among groups over entitlements, a growing antitechnology mood within the body politic, and rising energy prices lead to stagflated economic conditions. The economic conditions of the FAA's Slow Growth scenario, which is used by the Stagflation scenario as the starting point, are therefore carried forward past the year 1990 to the year 2020.[41] (See also Table 2.4.)

This conception of the future is representative in form of those encountered in similar scholarly products of the 1970s and 1980s. The authors envisage a number of possible environmental patterns which differ in their probabilities. It is clear that they view Theme X as their trend scenario and that Themes Y and Z are not perceived by them as equally likely to materialize at some point in time. Nonetheless, it would be erroneous to describe the latter two constructs as peripheral scenarios. Both are sufficiently realistic to warrant scrutiny by planners. Chen and his associates can hardly be said to have ventured beyond the realm of surprise-free and nearly surprise-free projections. Thus their approach reflects contemporary futures research in general: As previously mentioned, although remote possibilities are not necessarily ruled out, the focus nowadays is on a range of probable outcomes. The corollary presumably is that the distinction between trend and peripheral scenarios is not as useful as that between descriptive and normative or exploratory and anticipatory ones.

The three-dimensional typology of Ducot and Lubben (Figure 2.2) has not been the only attempt at a systematic classification of scenarios. Hirschhorn[42] has also devised an elaborate scheme which has attracted considerable attention. His first step has been to differentiate between "state" scenarios, which merely posit a future environment without indicating how it may evolve in the assumed direction, and "process" scenarios, which specify the sequence or chain of events that lead up to a particular future state. As Hirschhorn has elucidated: "The statement, 'there will be human colonies on the moon in the year 2025' is a simple state scenario. A story that tells how human colonies will be established by the year 2025 is a process scenario."[43] (Figure 2.3.)

Figure 2.3 Morphology of Scenarios

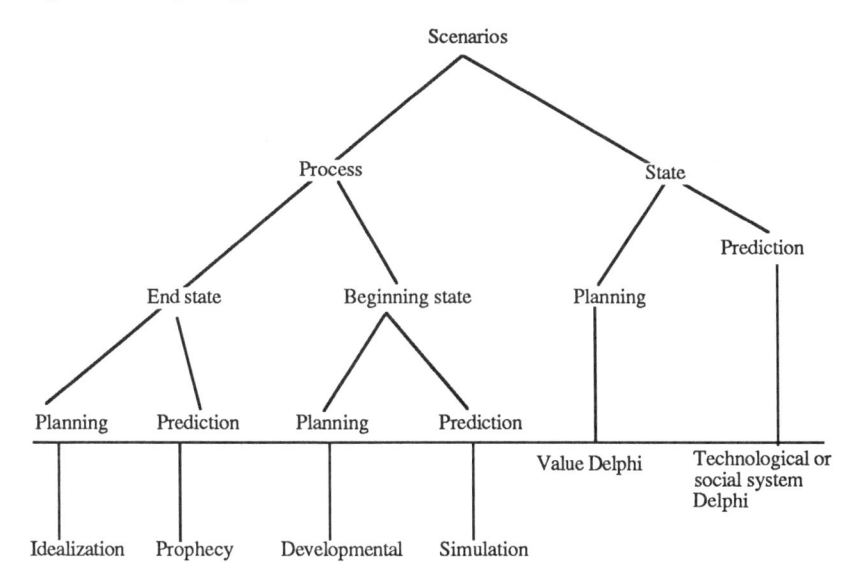

```
                           Scenarios
                          /         \
                    Process           State
                   /     \           /     \
                  /       \         /       Prediction
            End state   Beginning state  Planning
            /    \       /     \            |
       Planning Prediction Planning Prediction
           |       |        |        |
           |       |        |     Value Delphi    Technological or
           |       |        |                     social system
           |       |        |                     Delphi
      Idealization Prophecy Developmental Simulation
```

Source: Adapted from L. Hirschhorn, "Scenario Writing,"*Journal of the American Planning Association* 46 (April 1980).

The second distinction highlighted by Hirschhorn is whether the scenario is driven by the "end state" or the "beginning state." In the former case, some predetermined conception of the future (however that might be developed) dictates how the scenario is constructed (i.e., the end state is specified prior to any other analytical steps). In the latter case, the beginning state serves as the starting point or benchmark for the scenario, and the emphasis is on demonstrating how or why future states emerge from the beginning state. (Figure 2.3.)

Hirschhorn's third and final point is that scenarios may be differentiated on the basis of whether they are used for the purpose of prediction or for planning and decisionmaking. If prediction is the aim of the exercise, the scenario writer is concerned primarily with accuracy, validity, and (where meaningful) statistical significance. By contrast, if the objective is to facilitate planning and decisionmaking, the writer is more preoccupied with usefulness, richness, and the power of the scenario to provoke unexpected ideas (Figure 2.3). As suggested earlier, the dividing line between prediction and planning often becomes blurred in practice, but the distinction is deemed to be of considerable heuristic value.

Hirschhorn has relied on the above dichotomies to form a morphology of scenarios (Figure 2.3). In theory, his scheme allows for $8(2^3)$ configurations. However, state scenarios cannot be effectively classified according to how they are driven—they are, by definition, driven by the end state (i.e., they focus on some imagined or desired future state of a particular system). Therefore, one is left with only six possibilities: idealization, prophecy, developmental scenario, simulation, value Delphi, and technological or social system Delphi.

The first of these methods of scenario construction, idealization, entails three steps. The planner first develops a reference projection, which shows how the system under study will look "X" number of years from the present, under the assumption that no new actions or plans are undertaken. The next step is to specify an ideal state for the system "X" number of years from now. Finally, the planner contrasts the reference projection with the ideal state description and writes a scenario or a plan of action for moving the system from its projection curve to its ideal state (Figure 2.4). This procedure is end state–driven (i.e., the ideal state is specified a priori and then employed to anchor the plan of action or scenario), process-oriented (i.e., a plan of action has to be specified to move from the reference projection to the ideal state), and has the greatest utility for planning. While idealization involves

Figure 2.4 Scenario Construction by Means of Idealization

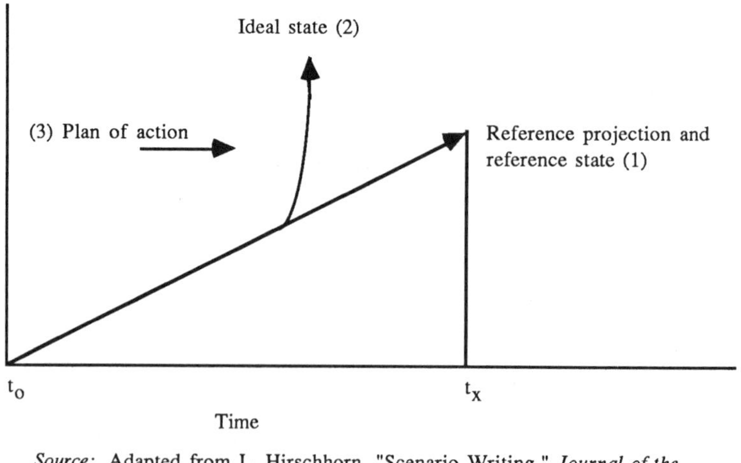

Source: Adapted from L. Hirschhorn, "Scenario Writing," *Journal of the American Planning Association* 46 (April 1980).

prediction—the reference projection is prediction under the assumption that all exogenous variables (environmental as well as value and action variables) remain unchanged—the prediction is subservient to plan development. As a corollary, the usefulness of this method lies in the quality of the plans it produces, not the reliability of the predictions themselves.

Prophecy is also end state–driven and process-based, but it constitutes a vehicle for prediction rather than planning. The prophet has a compelling vision of how the environment will or must be in the future. The roots of that vision are found less in a conception of laws of growth, change, or social motion, and more in some view of the best or worst possible environmental states. For instance, the religious prophet might embrace a vision of the inevitable "kingdom of God" that must be established on earth, and all present states would be judged relative to that ideal. Similarly, a social utopian might adopt a communalistic vision of social organization and could consequently predict "doom" for all forms of social organization which embody different principles. Many ecological-disaster scenarios conform to this pattern. A golden-age state is postulated (e.g., the resource-steady state), the prevailing models of resource consumption are depicted in bleak terms, and a scenario of doom is then constructed to demonstrate how the world would collapse if current practices persist. Although prophecies may be employed to modify present behaviour and as such serve planning purposes, prophets are normally ambivalent about the desirability for change.Rather, they tend to insist that doom alone can pave the way for a drastic environmental transformation. Prophecies thus are end state–driven (i.e., visions guide the construction of the future), they predict a future which to all appearances is not amenable to human intervention, and they portray the process through which the present evolves into the future.

Simulation is a far more rigorous analytical procedure than prophecy. It is beginning state–driven, process-based, and oriented towards prediction, In a typical computer simulation of a particular system, the researcher usually builds a model of that system, specifies initial state values for exogenous variables, and then programs a computer to generate a time series of future values for all the relevant endogenous variables.[44] Simulations differ markedly from conventional "growth law" models (e.g., time paths based on the assumption that change follows a linear, exponential, or sigmoid pattern) because in this case time paths are obtained by constructing and employing a theory which encapsulates the interrelationships between the endogenous variables of the system. Put another way, the time paths that are the product of simulation exercises are not merely projections but in fact genuine process scenarios which show both how and why the system is transformed from one state to another.

Scenario writing in the developmental mode does not call for the kind of mathematical and statistical versatility that is expected of those who resort to simulation. Here one simply begins with an initial state and proceeds to describe quite informally processes through which a given system can arrive at one or a series of end states that are not specified prior to the construction of the scenario itself. However, the object of developmental work in the context of futures studies is not prediction in the strict sense of the word, but planning. The idea is to enhance planners' understanding of the dynamics of the system so that they might be better equipped to steer it towards desired goals.

Developmental scenarios are similar in terms of underlying logic and procedure to normative-exploratory ones. Their exploratory nature manifests itself in the fact that they purport to offer insights into the "history of the future" by linking events in a chain of cause-and-effect sequences. The analyst basically engages in exploration by progressing from causes to effects. Nonetheless, the events which constitute the chain include discretionary actions by the decisionmakers who largely determine the outcome by opting to follow routes that hold the promise of value maximization. The corollary is that developmental scenarios serve essentially as normative rather than descriptive tools of inquiry.

The same is true of value Delphis, which are often relied upon by planners as a basis for setting objectives. In this case, a panel of experts or interested persons are normally asked to indicate what state they think the system should attain at some future date or, more generally, in the best of all possible worlds. One might, for instance, seek the views of residents on the size—in terms of population and physical parameters—that their city ought to reach by the year 2000. Such information-gathering efforts play an important role in ascertaining public preferences and enable planners to adopt acceptable growth targets.

Technological or social system Delphis, on the other hand, are concerned with description rather than prescription. The procedure employed here is similar to that utilized in value Delphis because the opinions of a panel of respondents form the principal input to the forecast. Thus, a panel of experts might be asked by what date they expect 50 percent of all households to own an electrically powered automobile. Their predictions are combined through an iterative process (explained in the next chapter) to generate a distribution of estimated dates which, in turn, determine the model date and the dispersion around it. The panelists are seldom queried about the implicit models of change or growth that guide them, and Delphi exercises therefore lack a process orientation.

As stated previously, the aim of this book is to describe/predict rather than to prescribe/plan. Consequently, scenarios which fall into the normative-exploratory, normative-anticipatory, idealization, developmental, and value Delphi categories lie by definition outside its domain. The descriptive-normative/prediction-planning distinction need not always be rigidly adhered to, but the nature of the study clearly dictates a strong emphasis on description/prediction. The types of scenarios, then, that might be most relevant include the descriptive-exploratory and descriptive-anticipatory variants, prophecy, simulation, and technological or social system Delphi.

Of these possibilities, prophecy has doubtless to be ruled out on the ground that it is not sufficiently systematic. Simulation also appears unsuitable in the present context because the question of Hong Kong's economic future is far too complex to lend itself to meaningful analysis by means of such a powerful modelling technique. To identify all the factors that may propel the local economy from the status quo to some future state(s), and specify the relationships between them, is a daunting task which can hardly be recommended. Reliance on descriptive-exploratory scenarios,[45] the descriptive-anticipatory method, or something akin to the technological or social system Delphi would seem to constitute a more practical option.

The drawback of the Delphi alternative, however, is that it produces an overly static picture. True, the primary objective of this book is to portray the likely state(s) of the Hong Kong economy in a decade or two from now, or to construct state scenarios. But this is by no means the sole objective; the analytical scope here is somewhat broader than that of a conventional technological or social forecast. The purpose is not merely to generate pictures of the economic environment at some point in time, but also to shed light on why, and possibly even how, the various states might materialize. For this purpose, a technological or social system Delphi is not well suited.

Thus, although the problem at hand could theoretically be tackled from a number of different methodological perspectives, in practice the choice is confined to constructing descriptive-exploratory scenarios or descriptive-anticipatory ones. The former approach seems particularly promising—it is usually preferable to use the status quo as the starting point and explore future states by converting causes into effects—but the exploratory mode requires a more solid data base than is presently available to futures researchers in Hong Kong. In addition, it may be quite difficult to handle conceptually in long-range contexts. As a consequence, I have followed the descriptive-anticipatory route in this book.

Put another way, the starting point here is not the status quo but the future state(s) of the Hong Kong economy. Of course, this in itself does not render the scenarios anticipatory, for it simply implies that they are driven by the end state rather than the beginning state. Their anticipatory nature may be attributed to the fact that I endeavour to identify the effects (or economic end states) first and then proceed to seek possible causes. The corollary is that the resultant scenarios extend beyond end-state description and seek to provide insight, in an anticipatory fashion, into cause-effect relationships.

In certain respects, the scenarios extend perhaps even further. Specifically, although they belong to the state category (and as such cannot be combined with a dynamic type of analysis in the formal sense of the term), an attempt has been made to give at least an indication of how, as well as why, the environmental patterns depicted by each might evolve. This does not necessarily mean that they qualify as process scenarios (or even constitute a hybrid of state and process elements) but rather that the future Hong Kong economic environment is not portrayed in purely static terms. The reader is presented with a number of possible scenarios—some of which are more likely than others—within a framework which stresses causality and evolutionary sequence.

Notes

1. See, for example, D. Bell, "Twelve Modes of Prediction—A Preliminary Sorting of Approaches in the Social Sciences," *Deadalus* 93 (Summer 1964): 845–880; J.F. Coates, "Some Methods and Techniques for Comprehensive Impact Assessment," *Technological Forecasting and Social Change* 6 (4/1974): 341–357; D. Runyan, "Tools for Community-Managed Impact Assessment," *Journal of the American Institute of Planners* 43 (January 1977): 125–135; H. Jones and B.C. Twiss, *Forecasting Technology for Planning Decisions* (London: Macmillan, 1978).

2. B. Schwartz, U. Svendin, and B. Wittrock, *Methods in Futures Studies* (Boulder, Colo.: Westview, 1982).

3. T.F. Carney, *No Limits to Growth* (Winnipeg: Harbeck, 1976).

4. H. Kahn, *On Thermonuclear War* (Princeton, N.J.: Princeton University Press, 1961); H. Kahn, *Thinking About the Unthinkable* (London: Weidenfeld and Nincolson, 1962); H. Kahn, *On Escalation* (London: Pall Mall Press, 1965); H. Kahn, *Thinking About the Unthinkable in the 1980's* (New York: Simon and Schuster, 1984).

5. H. Kahn and A.J. Weiner, *The Year 2000* (New York: Macmillan, 1967); H. Kahn et al., *The Next Two Hundred Years* (New York: Morrow, 1976); H. Kahn et al., *World Economic Development* (Boulder, Colo.: Westview, 1979); H. Kahn, *The Coming Boom* (New York: Simon and Schuster, 1983).

6. H. Kahn, *The Emerging Japanese Super State* (Englewood Cliffs, N.J.: Prentice Hall, 1970); H. Kahn and T. Pepper, *Will She Be Right? The Future of Australia* (Brisbane: University of Queensland Press, 1981).

7. See E. Jantsch, *Technological Forecasting in Perspective* (Paris: OECD, 1967); E. Jantsch, *Technological Planning and Social Futures* (London: Associated Business Programmes, 1972).

8. See, for example, R.U. Ayers, *Technological Forecasting and Long-Range Planning* (New York: McGraw-Hill, 1969); H.A. DeWeerd, "A Contextual Approach to Scenario Construction," *Simulation and Games* 5 (December 1974): 403–414; P. DeLeon, "Scenario Designs," *Simulation and Games* 6 (March 1975): 39–60; W.B. Clapham, R.F. Pestel, and H. Arnaszus, "On the Scenario Approach to Simulation Modeling for Complex Policy Assessment and Design," *Policy Sciences* 11 (November 1979): 157–177.

9. Kahn and Weiner, *The Year 2000*, p. 6.

10. Ibid.

11. S. Brown, "Scenarios in Systems Analysis," in *Systems Analysis and Policy Planning*, ed. E.S. Quade and W.I. Boucher (New York: North Holland, 1968), pp. 299–300.
12. J. Gershuny, "The Choice of Scenarios," *Futures* 8 (December 1976): 496.
13. I.H. Wilson, "Scenarios," in *Handbook of Futures Research*, ed. J. Fowles (Westport, Conn.: Greenwood Press, 1978), p. 225.
14. B.H.P. Rivett, "Futures Literature and Futures Forecasting—A Critical Review," *Omega* 7 (1/1979): 35.
15. See also Jones and Twiss, *Forecasting Technology for Planning Decisions*.
16. M. Palmer and G. Schmid, "Planning with Scenarios," *Futures* 8 (December 1976): 472–484.
17. Both serial and simultaneous.
18. S.W. Brecher, "Judicial Input into Policy Formulation," *Case Western Reserve Law Review* 28 (Spring 1978): 739–765.
19. Brecher, "Judicial Input into Policy Formulation," p. 743.
20. Ibid., pp. 742–743.
21. See also Gershuny, "The Choice of Scenarios"; Schwartz, Svendin, and Wittrock, *Methods in Futures Studies*; R. Amara and A.J. Lipinski, *Business Planning for an Uncertain Future* (Oxford: Pergamon, 1983); R. Brech, *Britain 1984* (London: Longman and Todd, 1963); D.H. Meadows et al., *Limits to Growth* (New York: Universe Books, 1972); H.S. Cole et al., *A Critique of the Limits to Growth* (New York: Universe Books, 1973); C.C. Abt, R.N. Foster, and R.H. Rae, "A Scenario-Generating Methodology," in *A Guide to Practical Technological Forecasting*, ed. J.R. Bright and M.E.F. Schoeman (Englewood Cliffs, N.J.: Prentice-Hall, 1973), pp. 191–214; K.L. Kraemer, *Policy Analysis in Local Government* (Washington, D.C.: International City Management Association, 1973); B. Cazes, "The Future of Work," *Futures* 8 (October 1976): 405–410; T.L. Saaty and P.C. Rogers, "Higher Education in the United States (1985–2000)," *Socio-Economic Planning Sciences* 10 (6/1976): 251–263; S. Hellman, "Swedish Defence Planning," *Futures* 9 (February 1977): 79–86; R.E. Linneman and J.D. Kennell, "Short-Sleeve Approach to Long-Range Plans," *Harvard Business Review* (March-April 1977): 141–150; K.J. Radford, *Complex Decision Problems* (Reston, N.J.: Reston, 1977); C.A. Ralph MacNulty, "Scenario Development for Corporate Planning," *Futures* 9 (April 1977): 128–138; G. Chadwick, *A Systems View of Planning* (Oxford: Pergamon, 1978); M. Godet, *The Crisis in Forecasting and the Emergence of the "Prospective" Approach* (Oxford: Pergamon, 1979); K. Nair and R.K. Sarin, "Generating Future Scenarios—Their Use in Strategic Planning," *Long Range Planning* 12 (June 1979): 57–61; L. Hirschhorn, "Scenario Writing," *Journal of the American Planning Association* 46 (April 1980): 172–183; R.E. Linneman, *Short-Sleeve Approach to Long-Range Planning* (Englewood Cliffs, N.J.: Prentice-Hall, 1980); K.J. Radford, *Strategic Planning* (Reston, N.J.: Reston, 1980); K. Chen, K. Jarboe, and J. Wolfe, "Long-Range Scenario Construction for Technology Assessment," *Technological Forecasting and Social Change* 20 (1/1981): 27–40; K.J. Radford, *Modern Managerial Decision Making* (Reston, N.J.: Reston, 1981); A.W. Smith, *Management Systems* (Chicago: Dryden Press, 1982); B. Taylor and D. Hussey, *The Realities of Planning* (Oxford: Pergamon, 1982); T.F. Mandel, "Future Scenarios and Their Uses in Corporate Strategy," in *The Strategic Management*

Handbook, ed. K.J. Albert (New York: McGraw-Hill, 1983), pp. 10-1 to 10-21; J.L. Morrison et al., *Applying Methods and Techniques of Futures Research* (San Francisco: Jossey-Bass, 1983); M.P. Sloan, "Strategic Planning by Multiple Political Future Techniques," *Management International Review* 24 (1/1984): 4–17; J.P. Leemhuis, "Using Scenarios to Develop Strategies," *Long Range Planning* 18 (April 1985): 30–37; R.E. Linneman and H.E. Klein, "Using Scenarios in Strategic Decision Making," *Business Horizons* 28 (January-February 1985): 64–74; R.G. Hoffman, "Economic Scenarios for Project Evaluation," *Journal of Business Strategy* 5 (Spring 1985): 66–74; B.J. Simson, *Quantitative Methods for Planning and Urban Studies* (Aldershot, England: Gower, 1985); P. Wack, "Scenarios," *Harvard Business Review* 85 (September–October 1985): 73–89; P. Wack, "Scenarios," *Harvard Business Review* 85 (November-December 1985): 139–150; B.R. Witkin, *Assessing Needs in Educational and Social Programs* (San Francisco: Jossey-Bass, 1985); M. Godet, *Scenarios and Strategic Management* (Seven Oakes, UK: Butterworths, 1987); W.R. Huss and E.Y. Honton, "Scenario Planning—What Style Should You Use," *Long Range Planning* 20 (August 1987): 21–29; S.P. Schnaars, "How to Develop and Use Scenarios," *Long Range Planning* 20 (February 1987): 105–114; G. Wills, *Technological Forecasting* (Herdondsworth: Penguin, 1972).

22. See in this connection Wilson, "Scenarios."
23. Ibid., p. 226.
24. Ibid.
25. Ibid., p. 227
26. See Jantsch, *Technological Forecasting in Perspective*; Ayers, *Technological Forecasting and Long-Range Planning*; Jantsch, *Technological Planning and Social Futures*; Wills, *Technological Forecasting*; Chadwick, *A Systems View of Planning*; Jones and Twiss, *Forecasting Technology for Planning Decisions*; O. Helmer, *Looking Forward* (Beverly Hills, Calif.: Sage, 1982).
27. C. Ducot and G.J. Lubben, "A Typology for Scenarios," *Futures* 12 (February 1980): 51–57.
28. L. Gerardin, "A Study of Alternative Futures," in *A Guide to Practical Technological Forecasting*, ed. Bright and Schoeman, pp. 276–288.
29. See ibid., p. 277.
30. See H. Ozbekhan, "Toward a General Theory of Planning," in *Perspectives on Planning*, ed. E. Jantsch (Paris: OECD, 1969), pp. 47–155; H. Ozbekhan, "The Future of Paris," in *Management Handbook for Public Administrators*, ed. J.W. Sutherland (New York: Van Nostrand Reinhold, 1978), pp. 542–567.
31. See, for example, Amara and Lipinski, *Business Planning for an Uncertain Future*; R.E. Linneman and H.E. Klein, "The Use of Multiple Scenarios by U.S. Industrial Companies," *Long Rang Planning* 12 (February 1979): 83–90; H.E. Klein and R.E. Linneman, "The Use of Scenarios in Corporate Planning—Eight Case Histories," *Long Range Planning* 14 (October 1981): 67–77; R.L. Ackoff, E. Vergara Finnel, and J. Gharajedaghi, *A Guide to Controlling Your Corporation's Future* (New York: Wiley, 1984).
32. See, for example, Chadwick, *A Systems View of Planning*.
33. See in particular Ducot and Lubben, "A Typology for Scenarios." See also Jantsch, *Technological Forecasting in Perspective*; Ayers, *Technological Forecasting and Long-Range Planning*; Jantsch, *Technological Planning and Social Futures*;

Wills, *Technological Forecasting*; Chadwick, *A Systems View of Planning*; Jones and Twiss, *Forecasting Technology for Planning Decisions*.

34. See, for example, Saaty and Rogers, "Higher Education in the United States (1985–2000)."

35. Ducot and Lubben, "A Typology for Scenarios."

36. Godet, *The Crisis in Forecasting and the Emergence of the "Prospective" Approach*, p. 51.

37. See in particular Kahn and Wiener, *The Year 2000*.

38. Ibid., p. 8.

39. See, for example, Godet, *The Crisis in Forecasting and the Emergence of the "Prospective" Approach*.

40. Chen, Jarboe, and Wolf, "Long-Range Scenario Construction for Technology Assessment."

41. Ibid., pp. 30–32.

42. Hirschhorn, "Scenario Writing."

43. Ibid., p. 173.

44. Two types of variables may be distinguished: Those determined within the model are referred to as "endogenous," whereas variables whose values are determined outside the model are called "exogenous."

45. Simulation may, in fact, be regarded as a sophisticated variant of the descriptive-exploratory procedure.

THREE
Scenario Construction and Hong Kong

Conceptual diversity is only the first problem confronting futures researchers who resort to scenario writing in order to examine unplanned or planned environmental change. An even more serious hurdle is the lack of an established method for generating scenarios, particularly the kind which feature in this book. One may state one's intention to offer a picture of the Hong Kong economy in a decade or two, and elaborate the concept of "scenario" in the process, but this is not where the real challenge lies. That largely stems from the uncertainty which prevails regarding the actual mechanics of scenario development.

The Choices Available

The longer the time horizon of the study and the broader its scope, the greater the uncertainty. The reason is that there exists a measure of professional consensus with respect to the potential and limitations of the various short-term and narrowly based forecasting techniques, whereas the merits and demerits of their longer-term and more wide-ranging counterparts appear to be subject to considerable disagreement. In addition, the former are fairly robust, while the latter must be viewed as essentially experimental in nature. Researchers undertaking long-term projects which focus on macroscopic issues need, therefore, to be very careful insofar as method selection is concerned. That is, they should consider all the available options, weigh their pros and cons, and choose one which is basically sound and seems to serve best their objectives. Because scenario construction is such a tentative enterprise, it is also incumbent upon researchers to provide an account of the factors that tipped the scale in favour of a particular technique and highlight its operational characteristics. This chapter addresses itself to both methodological requirements.

A number of writers have surveyed and classified forecasting techniques in a way which can facilitate to some extent the task of method selection for the prospective scenario writer. The first ones to have done so have been Spencer, Clark, and Hoguet.[1] They have grouped forecasting techniques into four categories: (1) naive methods, (2) barometric techniques, (3) opinion polling, and (4) econometric methods. The typology constructed by them reflects the state of the art in the early 1960s, but it still constitutes a useful starting point for exploring the technical aspects of economic forecasting.

Naive methods as defined by Spencer, Clark, and Hoguet are "unsophisticated and unscientific projections based on guesses or on mechanical extrapolations of historical data."[2] As a method of prediction, they can include procedures ranging from simple coin tossing to determine an upward or downward movement to the projection of trends, seasonal and cyclical patterns, and seemingly even more complex mathematical models. What distinguishes the relatively rigorous variants of naive forecasting from other systematic techniques is the fact that they are essentially mechanical and are not closely integrated with relevant economic theory and statistical data.

Spencer, Clark, and Hoguet have singled out two naive methods for purposes of illustration—one "purely subjective" and one characterized by a greater degree of "objectivity." In employing the former, which is referred to as the "factor-listing technique," the analyst simply enumerates the favourable and unfavourable conditions that are likely to affect economic activity as the analyst perceives them and then concludes with little or no explanation that business will either be good, bad, or the same in the future (e.g., next year). The list normally makes no provisions for the quantitative assessment of each of the factors and their role in influencing economic change, thus furnishing no basis for the weighting of the forces that appear to have a bearing on business dynamics. Table 3.1 is an example of this technique in the context of the business outlook for the United States in 1954.

The more objective form of naive forecasting identified by Spencer, Clark, and Hoguet is time-series analysis. A time series consists of a sequence of values corresponding to particular points or periods of time. Data such as prices, production, and sales figures—when arranged chronologically—are thereby ordered in time and hence alluded to as "time series." The simple line chart is the most common graphic device for depicting a time series, with the dependent variable—e.g., price, production, or sales—scaled on the vertical axis, and the independent variable—time, expressed in years or any other temporal measure—scaled on the horizontal axis.

In time-series analysis the objective is to discover and measure forces which have caused a series to exhibit its particular fluctuations, in the hope that the causal factors may be projected into the future and the series thus extended beyond its historical data base. The simplest type of naive projection is a continuity model in which the last-observed variable serves as

Table 3.1 Roadsigns of Business, December 21, 1953

The major forces affecting the general business outlook for the first quarter of 1954 include:

Favourable	Unfavourable
1. *Lower Taxes* On January 1st individual and corporate taxes are to be reduced by $4 billion (annual rate).	1. *Farm Income Off* Farm income is likely to be 10% lower in the first quarter than in the same period this year.
2. *Construction Up* Contracts awarded indicate that construction expenditures in the first quarter are likely to total about $175 billion and set a new record high for that quarter.	2. *Inventory Investment Down* Spending on inventory accumulation is likely to decrease by $2 to $3 billion in the first quarter.
3. *Government Spending High* Total government spending is expected to continue high, with a decrease in federal expenditures to be offset by increased state and local government outlays.	3. *Overtime to Decrease* Manufacturing workers are likely to experience a 2% to 3% decline in the work week.
4. *Big Savings Base* Liquid assets owned by consumers have grown by $10 billion, or 5%, in the past year and now total over $200 billion.	4. *Debt Repayment Absorbing More Purchasing Power* Repayments on installment debt in the first quarter are likely to be $2 to $3 billion greater than in the same period this year.

Conclusions: The favourable factors appear to be as strong as the unfavourable; consequently, consumer disposable income is expected to continue at its present record high level of $250 billion.

Source: M.H. Spencer, C.G. Clark, and P.W. Hoguet, *Business and Economic Forecasting* (Homewood, Ill.: Irwin, 1961), p. 5.

a prediction of the future. This occurs, for instance, with a forecast which states that next year's prices will be the same as this year's prices (plus or minus, perhaps, a random factor). The underlying assumption, therefore, is that there will be a steady movement of the variable in question.

Continuity models may afford an inexpensive method for arriving at reliable predictions. (For example, in certain geographical areas where climatic conditions change very slowly, weather forecasts can perhaps be made on a short-term basis by means of this technique.) But their scope is exceedingly limited. For this reason, time-series analysts normally rely on more than just the last observation and manipulate their data sets in a fairly systematic manner. Spencer, Clark, and Hoguet have paid special attention to a rather elaborate procedure known as "classical decomposition analysis" or "traditional time-series analysis."

Classical decomposition analysis focuses on four sources of variation that are assumed to be at work in economic time series: trend, seasonal variation, cyclical variation, and irregular factors. Trend represents the long-term growth or decline of a series. Seasonal variations—e.g., caused by weather conditions—manifest themselves during approximately the same time periods each year. Cyclical variations, covering usually several years at a time, reflect swings from prosperity to recession and vice versa. And finally, irregular factors—e.g., boycotts, strikes, and war—are events deemed to be largely unforeseen but which nonetheless must be taken into account.

Of these four sources of variation, the seasonal one is quite easy to measure and predict. The irregular factor is often unpredictable, although it can be adjusted by a smoothing-out process or some other means. Hence the trend, which represents persistent growth or decline, and cyclical variations, which are presumably recurrent, are the forces that have tended to occupy the attention of forecasters employing classical decomposition analysis. The methods used to dissect economic trends and cycles have been refined considerably over the years, and it is perhaps no longer appropriate to describe them as "unsophisticated." Yet because of its mechanical nature or its historical bias and narrow range, a good many social scientists continue to view classical decomposition analysis as a form of naive forecasting.

Unlike naive methods, particularly time-series analysis, which presuppose that the future is essentially an extension of the past, barometric techniques are grounded on the idea that the future may be predicted from certain occurrences in the present. Specifically, the barometric mode entails the use of clusters of statistical indicators—selected quantitative data which, when used in conjunction with one another or when combined in certain ways, provide a signal about the direction in which the economy or particular sectors thereof are heading. The indicators chosen thus serve as barometers of economic change. Spencer, Clark, and Hoguet have reviewed two variants of the barometric approach: leading series and pressure indexes.

Leading series are sets of current data which signal in advance, and with substantial regularity, turns in economic activity. Two early attempts to develop leading series were by the Brookmire Economic Service—an American firm which utilized as early as 1911 an array of commodity, money, and stock market indicators to forecast changes in the economy—and the Harvard Business School—whose experts relied on similar barometers (the now defunct Harvard Index Chart) to predict turns in business and financial conditions. Spencer, Clark, and Hoguet, however, credit Geoffrey Moore and his associates at the US National Bureau of Economic Research with making the most significant contribution in this area. He and his team examined over 800 time series collected by the bureau and covering the pre–Second World War period. They found that twenty-one series had exhibited great consistence in leading the "reference cycle," running coincidently with it, or lagging behind it at the turning points (peaks and troughs). In forecasting, of course, the leading and coincident indicators, particularly the former, are the most useful, but all three subsets are presented here for the sake of completeness (Table 3.2).

Pressure indexes are a more limited tool than barometric techniques.

Table 3.2 Leading, Coincident, and Lagging Indicators

Leading Indicators

1. New incorporations (Dun and Bradstreet).
2. Business failures (Dun and Bradstreet).
3. Residential building contracts awarded (F.W. Dodge Corporation).
4. Commercial and industrial building contracts awarded (F.W. Dodge Corporation).
5. Common stock prices, industrial (Dow Jones).
6. Wholesale commodity price index (Bureau of Labor Statistics).
7. Average hours worked per week in manufacturing (Bureau of Labor Statistics).
8. New orders for manufacturers' durable goods (Department of Commerce).

Coincident Indicators

1. Gross national product, quarterly (Department of Commerce).
2. Corporate profits, quarterly (Department of Commerce).
3. Unemployment, inverted (Bureau of Labor Statistics).
4. Nonagricultural employment (Bureau of Labor Statistics).
5. Nonfood wholesale price index (Bureau of Labor Statistics).
6. Industrial production index (Federal Reserve Board).
7. Bank debits outside of New York City (Federal Reserve Board).
8. Freight carloadings index (Association of American Railroads).

Lagging Indicators

1. Personal income (Department of Commerce).
2. Retail sales (Department of Commerce).
3. Manufacturers' inventories (Department of Commerce).
4. Consumer installment debt (Federal Reserve Board).
5. Bank rates on business loans (Federal Reserve Board).

Source: M.H. Spencer, C.G. Clark, and P.W. Hoguet, *Business and Economic Forecasting*, (Homewood, Ill.: Irwin, 1961), p. 11.
Note: Organizations in parentheses are source of statistic.

They normally assume the form of differences or ratios and are favoured by economists who subscribe to the view that amplitude differences provide insight into the dynamics of business cycles. A typical example is the difference between the rate of family formation and the rate of housing inventory growth; the gap may serve as a pressure indicator of the long-term demand for new housing. (In the short run, of course, factors such as disposable income and credit conditions often exert a far greater influence on the rate of construction.) Another case in point is the ratio of durable to nondurable goods production, the reason being that durable goods production fluctuates much more widely than nondurable goods production over the course of the business cycle, generally causing the ratio to increase in periods of prosperity and to decline before an economic downturn.

The opinion polling or sample survey method of forecasting differs markedly from both leading series and pressure indexes. It is a largely subjective technique (although perhaps less so than some rudimentary forms of naive prediction), consisting primarily of inferences drawn from attitudinal data. The underlying assumption is that certain key attitudes may be defined and measured in advance, thus enabling forecasters to identify possible business trends. Survey data are obtained by asking economic decisionmakers about their intentions and/or expectations. The results are processed and subjected to statistical analysis.

Spencer, Clark, and Hoguet[3] have discussed two types of opinion polling: economic forecasting and sales forecasting. The former concerns changes in the economy as illustrated by the surveys conducted by McGraw-Hill of what American businesses intend to spend on plant and equipment. In the early 1960s, these surveys covered nearly 500 companies which accounted for about 60 percent of the investment of the important capital-consuming industries. The McGraw-Hill forecasts served as good predictors of actual expenditures in the period preceding the publication of Spencer's, Clark's, and Hoguet's book—except for a few scattered years where the errors stemmed from an unexpected reduction in personal income taxes, which stimulated demand (1948), and from a failure to anticipate the Korean War (1951).

Sales forecasting is narrower in scope than its economic counterpart in that it seldom extends beyond the confines of the market of a single business entity (although such entity may, of course, be a large multinational company). Spencer, Clark, and Hoguet differentiate between three forms of sales forecasting: executive polling, sales force polling, and consumer intentions surveys. The first category refers to surveys of executives who act as a panel of experts and provide indications of the sales outlook for, say, the coming year. Sales force polling is another version of the survey method whereby a composite outlook is constructed on the basis of information derived from those closest to the market. (Here, the sales forecast may be built up from estimates provided by sales personnel in cooperation with branch or regional managers, or by going directly to distributors, jobbers, and major customers in order to discover their needs.) Last, consumer intentions surveys centre on potential buyers and purport to ascertain their plans with respect to specific products.

Econometric model-building is the most sophisticated forecasting technique of those identified by Spencer, Clark, and Hoguet. As the combined term ("econo" and "metrics") implies, this branch of applied science deals with economic measurement. It seeks to explain past economic activity and to predict future economic activity by constructing mathematical equations that express the most probable interrelationships between a cluster of economic variables. The variables may include disposable income, foreign trade, government revenues and expenditures, inventories, money stock, and so forth. By combining the relevant variables—each of which constitutes a separate series covering some previous period of time—into what appears to be the best mathematical arrangement, econometricians proceed to predict the future course of one or more of these variables on the basis of the established relationships.

The "best mathematical arrangement" is thus a model which takes the form of an equation (or a system of equations) portraying as accurately as possible a set of past relationships within a framework determined by economic theory and statistical analysis. The model employed as a prediction instrument to yield numerical results is, of course, a highly simplified abstraction of complex reality. Nonetheless, to the extent that economic theorems and relationships lend themselves to verification by subjecting historical data to statistical testing, then, at least in principle, econometrics as a system of measurement stands as a useful compromise between pure "ivory tower" economic theory on the one hand and sheer description of facts on the other.

A decade after the book by Spencer and his colleagues was published, two other scholars undertook a systematic survey of forecasting methods. Chisholm and Whitaker[4] have classified techniques of economic prediction into six categories: naive forecasting methods, barometric or indicator forecasts, survey methods of forecasting, input-output analysis, regression analysis, and opportunistic forecasting. The first three of these categories are identical to those suggested by Spencer, Clark, and Hoguet. Furthermore, both regression analysis and time-series analysis feature prominently in econometric model-building. Only input-output analysis and opportunistic forecasting, therefore, qualify as new approaches in the present context—although Chisholm and Whitaker have introduced some rather complex naive models, and their discussion of regression analysis encompasses sophisticated extensions of the technique not highlighted in the earlier book.

Input-output analysis, one of the two new methods reviewed by Chisholm and Whitaker, constitutes an important device for relating production and distribution of goods throughout the economy. Specifically, the output of each industry is traced in considerable detail through intermediate stages to final destinations, as is the source of raw materials and components as inputs to this industry. The interindustry (as well as intraindustry) flows are arrayed in a large matrix (Table 3.3) converted into technical coefficients, consequently enabling planners to determine the

Table 3.3 A Simple Input-Output Table

	Agriculture	Steel	Mining	Information Processing	
Agriculture	10	5	2	1	
Steel	1	6	11	9	Outputs
Mining	3	7	3	8	
Information processing	4	9	5	4	
		Inputs			

Source: M.L. Hatten, *Macroeconomics for Management* (Englewood Cliffs, N.J.: Prentice-Hall, 1984), p. 42.

repercussions of a change in demand for the finished goods of a particular industry upon other industries. As Lindsay has elaborated:

> Basic to input-output analysis is a unique set of input-output ratios for each production and distribution process. For example, the inputs of coal, ore, limestone, electrical power, etc., all enter into the production of pig iron in fixed ratios. Thus, if the ratios of inputs per unit of output are known for all production processes, and if the total production of each end product of the economy—or of that section being studied—is known, it is possible to compute precisely the production levels required at every intermediate stage to supply the total sum of end products. Further, it is possible to determine the effect at every point in the production process of a specified change in the volume and mix of end products.[5]

Opportunistic forecasting is a more flexible approach than input-output analysis. In fact, it is not based on any particular source, nor does it revolve around any particular procedure. Rather, opportunistic forecasting entails the use of various data sets and a number of different techniques. It is an eclectic method which deemphasizes rigid adherence to narrow procedural norms and stresses the need for tackling problems of economic prediction from multiple perspectives. In macroeconomic work, opportunistic forecasting typically involves a series of forecasts of the various components of aggregate demand that are part of most standard Keynesian models. The approach is iterative. The forecaster normally starts with factors which lend themselves readily to prediction (such as government expenditures) and then proceeds down the list, leaving the more difficult factors to the end. The process continues until all the individual forecasts are integrated and a total picture emerges.[6]

The third major attempt to survey and classify forecasting techniques has been that by Chambers, Mullick, and Smith.[7] These three authors have proposed the following classification scheme: (1) qualitative methods, (2) time series and projection, and (3) causal models. The first category utilizes qualitative data as a basis for prediction. The second constitutes a form of naive forecasting and has been discussed previously. The third relies on highly refined and specific information about relationships between economic variables and encompasses powerful tools such as barometric techniques, econometric methods, input-output analysis, intentions-to-buy surveys, and regression analysis.

Of the preceding approaches, forecasters formerly tended to focus almost exclusively on time-series work projection and causal modelling. In recent years, however, they have shown a growing interest in qualitative procedures. While acknowledging that some of these have considerable limitations, Chambers, Mullick, and Smith nonetheless welcome this gradual shift in emphasis and outline a number of possible techniques for generating qualitative data.[8] Their list includes visionary forecasts, historical analogy, market research, panel consensus, Delphi method, and cross-impact analysis.

Although the title employed to describe this procedure is impressive, the visionary forecast consists largely of subjective guesswork and is as a rule lacking in scientific character. Facts are not necessarily discarded by those who engage in such an informal exploration of the future, but the visionary forecast is above all the product of personal insights and judgements. For this reason, it is legitimate to equate it with prophecy, a rather loosely structured mode of prediction highlighted in the preceding chapter. Visionary forecasts are not known for their accuracy, yet if sufficient effort and skill are exerted, the values of the outcome may be substantially enhanced.

The quest for historical[9] analogies is deemed to be a somewhat more rigorous forecasting technique than the development of visionary forecasts. Here an attempt is made to identify similarities between some evolving environmental patterns and circumstances which prevailed in the past and to generalize from the latter to the former. In certain contexts, this may entail the quantification of the degrees of similarity and dissimilarity. To the extent that the situations subject to comparison exhibit significant differences, it is also common to endeavour to determine how such differences are likely to influence future trends.

Market research—which Chambers, Mullick, and Smith classify as a qualitative method in spite of the fact that it is assuming an increasingly quantitative form—constitutes a variant of sales forecasting. Some writers draw a distinction between market research and intentions-to-buy surveys because the former lacks the strong causal orientation of the latter, at least in the behavioural sense of the term. Chambers, Mullick, and Smith have adopted a similar approach and have placed these two types of consumer research in different categories. However, because sales forecasting as such cannot shed much light on the economic future of Hong Kong, neither technique merits further consideration in the present chapter. (The same applies to other methods of sales forecasting such as product life-cycle analysis).[10]

The panel consensus procedure is also a vehicle for opinion polling. In fact, executive polling, referred to earlier, is often conducted by means of the panel consensus technique, although its use extends far beyond the narrow confines of marketing. The meeting of experts (or a series of such meetings) is the principal mechanism for obtaining a panel consensus. The experts exchange information and engage in mutual learning which culminates in the production of a forecast. The rules governing expert interaction in face-to-face meetings have been refined considerably in recent years with a view to minimizing unproductive behaviour.[11] Yet such behaviour cannot be eliminated altogether, and hence presumably the need for the Delphi method.

Unlike panel consensus, the Delphi method excludes any form of interpersonal interaction. Knowledgeable persons or individuals who have attained a high level of expertise in their professional domain also serve here as the chief source of information about the future, but they are not required to meet face-to-face. Rather, expert opinion is channelled through a set of carefully designed sequential questionnaires which generate data that are analyzed and fed back to the participants until a broad consensus is reached. As indicated in the preceding chapter, Delphi exercises may be geared towards either prediction (technological or social system Delphis) or prescription (value Delphi).

The Delphi technique is thought to have two characteristics which distinguish it from other methods of information gathering: anonymity and iteration with feedback. The first allows those experts whose views are solicited to remain unknown to one another and not to meet in a group discussion. As a result, no social pressure whatever is exerted on the participants, and they are provided with the opportunity to change their opinions without any loss of face. The second characteristic—iteration with feedback—stems from the fact that information is gathered in a sequence of rounds, with the results of previous rounds provided to participants at the start of each new round of questioning. Thus, although no interpersonal interaction takes place, there is ample scope for exchange of information and mutual learning.

The Delphi technique doubtless has a clear advantage over other methods of soliciting expert views when differences of opinion are so substantial that face-to-face encounters are likely to lead to unproductive arguments. However, it may also prove useful when inputs are needed from a much larger number of individuals than can effectively be accommodated in a face-to-face meeting, when the participants are separated by great distances, or when face-to-face discussions might entail excessive expenditures of money and time. Such circumstances, not uncommon, are yet another factor accounting for the considerable popularity of the Delphi technique.[12]

Cross-impact analysis is a growing feature of Delphi exercises oriented towards prediction. The participants in such exercises are normally asked to employ subjective judgement in forecasting either the probability of a certain event occurring at a given future date or the date of the event with a stated level of probability. The function of cross-impact analysis in this context is to enable the explicit and systematic consideration of the mutual influence of future events, particularly those perceived as being closely interrelated. (Prior to the introduction of cross-impact analysis, no information was sought directly from Delphi panelists about the bearing that individual forecasts might have on each other.)

Table 3.4 Illustration of Cross-Impact Analysis Between Four Events

If this event occurs as stated	Then what is the impact on the probability of the other forecast events?			
	E_1	E_2	E_3	E_4
E_1	—	–1	–2	–7
E_2	–3	—	–8	–4
E_3	–1	0	—	–2
E_4	0	–7	–5	—

Source: H. Jones and B.C. Twiss, *Forecasting Technology for Planning Decisions* (London: Macmillan, 1978), p. 245.

The possible interactions between events are examined by means of a matrix (Table 3.4) bearing some resemblance to an input-output table. The vertical and horizontal primary lines that make up the matrix describe the same series of events. The occurrence of the first event, as forecast, is studied by intuitive subjective judgement in relation to each of the other forecast events; then the second in relation to the others; and so forth. The assessment of each cross-impact is entered into the corresponding cross box—first in terms of the direction of the effect (positive, neutral, or negative, as the case may be) and second on a weighting scale, which usually ranges from 0 to 10, in order to indicate the magnitude of the effect (low, medium, or high).

In the simplest cases, the events may be considered simply in chronological order, and revisions of the data in the original forecasts can be made according to the direction and degree of impact. Normally it is the probability for a given date which is the subject of the revision, but there is no reason why the time should not be revised for a stated probability. In the more complex cases, the events may be cascaded—that is, a revised probability can be brought forward so that the effect of revisions works through the set of events. Whether the case is deemed simple or complex, formulas are available for revising probabilities in the light of the expected cross-impacts.[13]

Like market research, the Delphi method and cross-impact analysis entail a considerable degree of quantification. It is a moot point, therefore, whether they should be placed in the qualitative category. Indeed, in another well-known systematic survey of forecasting techniques, Gross and Peterson[14] have opted to jettison the term "qualitative" altogether (they make no reference to "naive" modes of prediction either) and employ more "neutral" expressions. Approaches which utilize the subjective judgements of experts and others have thus been classified by them as "judgemental methods." All types of survey research (market or otherwise), on the other hand, are grouped in a separate category described as "surveys and test markets."

The scheme proposed by Gross and Peterson consists of six additional classes: trend analysis; time-series analysis; regression and correlation; models based on learned behaviour; model building and simulation; and indirect methods. Three of these have been discussed previously. Time-series analysis—of which trend analysis is a simple variant—features prominently in the review by Spencer, Clark, and Hoguet of naive forecasting. They, as well as the other authors referred to in this chapter, also pay considerable attention to regression/correlation analysis, a statistical technique relied upon in estimating the functional relationships between variables. Indirect methods embrace procedures which are instrumental in projections of national, regional, or industrial economic activity (e.g., leading series and input-output analysis); these also have been highlighted earlier.

The category of models based on learned behaviour encompasses techniques employed in studying consumer choice with respect to products which are subject to market transactions. (Consumption is a form of learned behaviour.) Gross and Peterson have identified three such techniques: static market share forecasts (which are developed by more or less mechanically projecting market share into a future period); dynamic market share forecasts or Markov chains (which take account of buyer brand loyalty and switching behaviour in determining market share); and product life-cycle analysis (which focuses on the relationship between the product's life cycle—i.e., "introduction," "growth," "maturity," or "decline"—and sales). As stated previously, these types of methods cannot be tangibly applied to a study of Hong Kong's economic future and so will not be discussed further here.

Model building and simulation, on the other hand, have a much wider scope. Simulation—which may be characterized as a "computer-age technique for analyzing systems"[15]—entails the construction of a mathematical model representing a real-world system (hence "model building and simulation"), which is subsequently analyzed by manipulating its variables. Simulation bears considerable similarity to the testing of physical—or iconic[16]—models. For instance, it is customary to build a model aeroplane and examine its performance in a wind tunnel before building the first real aeroplane. Inferences about the actual product are drawn on the basis of the wind tunnel tests. Social systems in general, and economic systems in particular, may also be simulated in such a manner—except that here mathematical relationships rather than physical performance are investigated.

Simulation is a useful vehicle for prediction, a fact reflected in the central place it occupies in Hirschhorn's typology of scenarios. Nonetheless, most writers tend to perceive it as part of a larger category (e.g., "quantitative techniques") rather than as a separate class. Indeed, in the most recent and comprehensive survey of forecasting methods,[17] Armstrong[18] refers quite often to simulation, but without suggesting that it should be regarded as a cluster of interrelated procedures. (He actually treats it as an adjunct to a number of sophisticated quantitative tools and not as a forecasting device in the conventional sense of the term.)

Armstrong's scheme revolves around the following distinctions: subjective versus objective techniques, naive versus causal techniques, and linear versus classification techniques. The subjective category pertains to those methods in which the processes utilized to analyze the data "have not been well specified. These methods are also called implicit, informal, clinical, experience-based, intuitive methods, guesstimates, WAGs (wild-assed guesses), or gut feelings. They may be simple or complex processes; they may use objective or subjective data; they may be supported by much formal analysis or by none; but the critical thing is that the inputs are translated into forecasts in the researcher's head.[19]

By contrast, objective techniques employ well-specified processes to analyze the data. Ideally, they should be specified so well that other researchers might replicate them and obtain the same forecasts. Objective techniques "have also been called explicit, statistical, or formal methods. They may be simple or complex; they may use objective data or subjective data; they may be supported by much formal analysis or none; but the critical thing is that the inputs are translated into forecasts using a process that can be exactly replicated by other researchers. Furthermore, the process could be done by computer.[20]

The distinction between naive and causal techniques stems from the fact that a continuum of causality underlies forecasting models: At the naive end, no statements are made about causality ("e.g., we can forecast how many people will die on the highways this Labor Day by using the number who died last Labor Day").[21] In the middle, some models take account of some of the causality ("e.g., we can predict Labor Day deaths on the basis of the number who died the previous Labor Day and also the weather forecast").[22] Finally, the model may incorporate a large number of causal variables ("e.g., Labor Day deaths can be forecast using information on weather, speed limits, the price of gasoline, the use of safety belts, the proportion of young drivers, the use of flexible time schedules for people who work in companies, and the number of miles in the interstate highway system").[23] The selection of a model from along this continuum is normally determined by situational factors.

Figure 3.1 Naive Versus Causal Methods

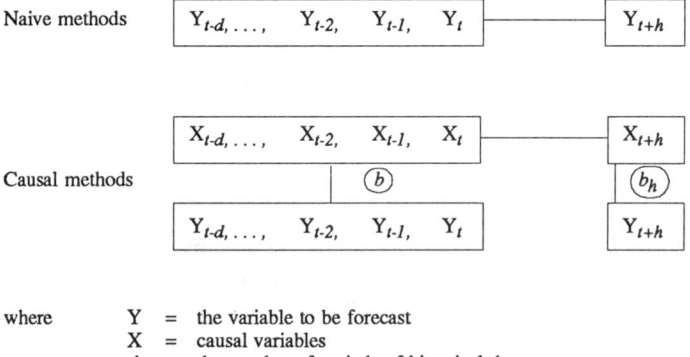

Naive methods $\boxed{Y_{t-d}, \ldots, Y_{t-2}, Y_{t-1}, Y_t}$ ———— $\boxed{Y_{t+h}}$

Causal methods

$\boxed{X_{t-d}, \ldots, X_{t-2}, X_{t-1}, X_t}$ ———— $\boxed{X_{t+h}}$

(b) (b_h)

$\boxed{Y_{t-d}, \ldots, Y_{t-2}, Y_{t-1}, Y_t}$ ———— $\boxed{Y_{t+h}}$

where
- Y = the variable to be forecast
- X = causal variables
- d = the number of periods of historical data
- h = the number of periods in the forecast horizon
- t = the year
- b = the causal relationships in the historical data
- b_h = the causal relationships over the forecast horizon

Source: Adapted from Armstrong, *Long-Range Forecasting*

The end points of the naive-causal continuum may be illustrated by graphic means (Figure 3.1). The naive techniques utilize data which are confined to the variable of interest and assume the form of projections of historical patterns into the future. Causal techniques, on the other hand, go beyond the variable of interest to ask "why." Estimates of causal relationships are obtained first (b). The problem then becomes one of forecasting the causal variables (the X's). Next, the estimates of the causal relationships are adjusted so that they are relevant for the period of the forecast (b_h). Last, the forecast (Y_{t+h}) is derived from the forecasts of the forecasted relationships and causal variables.

The term "causal" has been employed here in its common-sense meaning. A causal variable, X, is one that is necessary or sufficient for the occurrence of an event, Y. X must also precede Y in time. This interpretation appears useful notwithstanding the controversy it has engendered (which has led a good many researchers to prefer terms such as "functionally related," "structural estimate," "stimulus-response," "dependent upon," or "determinant of"). Causality is doubtless an attribute which may substantially enhance the quality of a forecasting model, but those engaged in prediction often find it necessary or expedient to resort to naive methods. Indeed, these can be quite sophisticated (e.g., Markov chains, exponential smoothing, the Box-Jenkins technique, and regression analysis)[24] and reasonably reliable.

Procedures that are objective and seek to establish causality have been classified by Armstrong into two further categories: linear and classification approaches. The former reflect the way we normally think about causality: "If X goes up, this will cause Y to go up by so much."[25] Specifically, an attempt is made to find linear relationships between X and Y. Linear relationships are the focus of attention because it is convenient to work with models in which the terms can be combined by using simple arithmetic operations. In particular, models of the following type are preferred:

$$Y = a + b_1 X_1 + b_2 X_2 + \ldots$$

where Y is the variable to be forecast, the X's are the causal variables, a is a constant, and the b's represent the relationships. This approach is "linear in the parameters." One might consider more complex forms of relationships (i.e., opt for approaches "nonlinear in the parameters"), but there is little advantage in so doing. As Armstrong has concluded, nonlinear models "are harder to understand . . . have not been shown to improve our ability to forecast . . . are more expensive . . . and, although not hopeless, . . . offer little promise for the future."[26]

Classification methods afford an alternative set of procedures for tackling the problem of causality. Here the analytical effort is directed at identifying behavioural units that respond in the same manner to the causal variables in grouping these units together. The objective of the exercise is to minimize the differences within the groups and maximize the differences between them. Prediction, then, becomes a matter of simply determining the category into which the unit falls. Armstrong illustrates the logic of classification thus:

> Assume that the task is to predict who will win the popular vote in the US Presidential election in 1984. Assume that the leading candidates are Brown, for the Democrats, and White, for the Republicans. The voters can be grouped into homogeneous categories, and the previous voting records of each group in a similar situation can be used to obtain a prediction for each category. For example:

Group Description	Probability of Voting for Brown
Urban, college educated, live in Northeast, age 35–50	.82
Rural, grade school, live in South, age 65 and up	.25

Such a procedure would be used to classify each voter, and votes from each category would be summed to obtain a forecast. Also, changes in the positions of the candidates can be evaluated by examining the groups that would be affected and revising the predictions for them.[27]

Figure 3.2 The Forecasting Methodology Tree

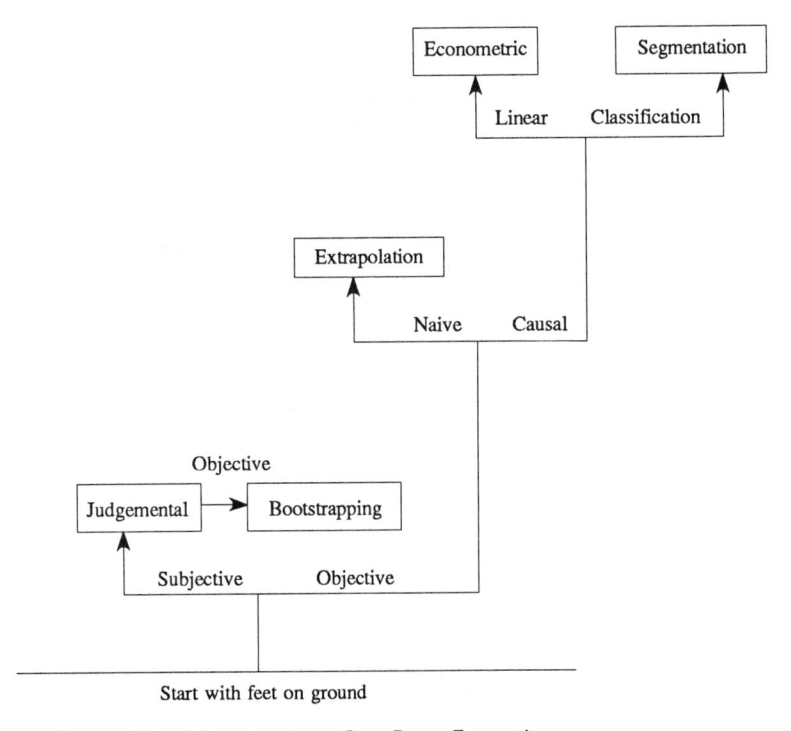

```
                                    ┌─────────────┐   ┌──────────────┐
                                    │ Econometric │   │ Segmentation │
                                    └─────────────┘   └──────────────┘
                                           ↑                 ↑
                                         Linear        Classification

                        ┌───────────────┐
                        │ Extrapolation │
                        └───────────────┘
                               ↑
                             Naive      Causal

                 Objective
      ┌─────────────┐      ┌───────────────┐
      │ Judgemental │ ───▶ │ Bootstrapping │
      └─────────────┘      └───────────────┘
             ↑
         Subjective      Objective

      ─────────────────────────────────────
              Start with feet on ground
```

Source: Adapted from Armstrong, *Long-Range Forecasting*

The distinctions between subjective and objective techniques, naive and causal ones, and linear and classification approaches underpin the forecasting methodology tree constructed by Armstrong (Figure 3.2). He considers the subjective-objective dichotomy the most fundamental and labels subjective techniques "judgemental." The objective category is then subdivided into naive and causal methods and the objective-naive type is equated with extrapolation. Finally, Armstrong differentiates between the linear and classification variants of the causal approach and describes objective-causal-linear techniques as "econometric" (in deference to the field that has contributed to their development) and objective-causal-classification ones as "segmentation."

An interesting feature of Armstrong's typology is the proposition that subjective/judgemental techniques can be converted into objective ones by means of "bootstrapping," which hinges on the assumption that the decision processes employed by those exercising subjective judgement may be rendered explicit. Bootstrapping can assume either a deductive or an inductive form. The first case involves a direct translation of judges' rules into a model, normally by asking them what rules they are using. (For instance: "Sometimes judges are not aware of how they make decisions. In such cases, one might ask the judges to think aloud as they make predictions. The researcher records this thinking and translates it into specific rules. Often the rules are stated as questions that can be answered by 'yes' or 'no.' . . . This procedure was used successfully in replicating decisions by a professional investor.")[28]

Inductive bootstrapping, on the other hand, starts with the judges' forecasts and works backwards to infer what rules the judges employ to make these forecasts. Here the prevailing approach is to construct a quantitative model which entails prediction of the judges' forecasts themselves by means of an equation. Put another way, the model uses the judges' forecasts as the dependent variable; the variables they relied upon serve as the causal variables. To date, the principal vehicle for constructing such models has been regression analysis. Armstrong provides the following example in the context of graduate school admissions:

> Dawes examined the admissions decisions for the Ph.D. program in psychology at the University of Oregon. There were six categories for rating applicants: (1) reject now; (2) defer rejection but looks weak; (3) defer; (4) defer acceptance but looks strong; (5) accept now; (6) offer fellowship. The committee used traditional measures in making its judgements, such as scores on Graduate Record Examination (GRE), quality of school where undergraduate degree was received (QI), grade point average (GPA), letters of recommendation, and record of work experience. A simple bootstrapping model (a regression of admissions committee decisions vs. GRE, QI, and GPA) reproduced the committee's decisions. . . . Faculty evaluations after the first year were used as a measure of student success in the program. The bootstrapping model provided a more accurate ranking of student success than that provided by the admissions committee.[29]

Although Armstrong's survey and classification of forecasting methods is characterized by greater sophistication than those of other writers, his approach complements rather than supersedes earlier work on the subject. The fact remains that the best way to gain an appreciation of the range of techniques available is still to examine most of the significant scholarly contributions in this field. Armstrong pays little attention to rudimentary judgemental procedures such as factor listing, visionary forecasts, historical analogy, and panel consensus, and the usefulness of his categories depends on one's purposes. (For example, in a nonmarketing context, a term such as "opinion polling" may be preferable to "segmentation.") A more complete picture thus emerges if wider sampling is utilized.

In addition to seeking exposure to the most authors possible, a would-be forecaster ought also to rely, when feasible, on more than one method. Practically all the scholars whose work has been discussed in this chapter are in agreement on this point. Perhaps the most concrete expression of the view that the study of the future calls for the harnessing of several techniques is Chisholm's and Whitaker's advocacy of opportunistic forecasting. The need for eclecticism is equally stressed by Armstrong, who maintains that the ideal approach to a given forecasting problem lies in searching for an effective "combination of methods."[30]

If opportunistic strategy is desirable in conventional economic prediction, it is even more so in any effort to grapple with a complex problem such as the long-term future of Hong Kong. In this particular case, it would doubtless be preferable to generate relevant data by means of several techniques rather than confine oneself to a single procedure. For instance, econometric model-building might prove useful in exploring certain dimensions of the problem, while sophisticated forms of extrapolation might be of assistance in investigating other dimensions. Moreover, survey research (e.g., to ascertain the intentions of business and professional elites in the territory with respect to investment and migration) and judgemental approaches could shed further light on the course that the Hong Kong economy is likely to follow in the next decade or two.

Nonetheless, it might be premature to resort to most of these methods at the present juncture. Econometric techniques, extrapolation, and survey research would probably furnish a solid basis for medium-term economic prediction in the territory in the early and mid-1990s, but it would be somewhat hazardous to employ them as a vehicle for the kind of crystal-ball gazing envisaged here. The desirability of a multimethod approach notwithstanding, there really is no alternative, given the time horizon involved, but to rely almost exclusively on judgemental procedures (in the hope, perhaps, of combining them subsequently with other and more objective techniques).

One such procedure which appears especially promising is the Delphi method. Unlike factor listing, visionary forecasts, and historical analogy, it seeks to integrate the views of several judges and is far more rigorous than panel consensus with respect to both data collection and data analysis. Delphi exercises are not in themselves a form of bootstrapping, nor do they constitute a mechanism for converting subjective data into objective information. Yet the results they produce justifiably inspire greater confidence than those generated by less structured modes of judgemental inquiry.

The Delphi technique, however, is not without its limitations. It may well be more reliable than other subjective procedures, but there are problems for which it is simply inappropriate. Thus, although futurologists have employed this method extensively as an instrument for obtaining specific forecasts (Chapter 2's example of experts' predictions of when 50 percent of all households will own an electrically powered automobile would be typical in this respect), they have seldom utilized it to explore in detail highly complex future configurations. The study of such configurations presumably calls for less formal approaches.

Given the limitations of the Delphi technique as a tool for investigating multifaceted problems, a more flexible method of collecting judgemental data should preferably be adopted to help construct long-term economic scenarios for Hong Kong. Like the Delphi technique and panel consensus, this method ought to aim at incorporating the opinions of a large number of judges in order to maximize the flow of relevant information and increase the "consensual validity"[31] of the findings. Unlike the Delphi technique, however, it should rely on personal interviews with the judges rather than mail questionnaires, and the interviews ought to be of the "nonschedule-structured' rather than "schedule-structured" variety. (In the latter case, the questions, their wording, and their sequence are fixed and identical for every interviewee; in the former case, although the encounter between the interviewer and the interviewee is structured and the key aspects of the study are explicated, interviewees are allowed considerable latitude in expressing their views.)[32]

The difficulty, of course, is that none of the data collection procedures employed in economic forecasting fully satisfies the criteria outlined here. Even panel consensus, which has greater built-in flexibility than the Delphi method, falls short of what is required because an issue such as the response of the Hong Kong economy to environmental turbulence can hardly be approached by a group of experts expected to forge an agreement in just a few relatively short sessions. Furthermore, an economic panel might not be easy to convene, and it would in all likelihood reach an impasse because of the kind of unproductive arguments the Delphi technique purports to eliminate. Thus the quest for an appropriate data collection procedure needs to be extended beyond the realm of the forecasting literature.

One potentially useful approach not featured in prediction exercises involves use of key informants.[33] This method entails identifying, selecting, and interviewing experts or some knowledgeable persons with a view to gaining insight into community characteristics, structure, processes, culture, and problems. The key informants are selected strategically (i.e., because they occupy strategic positions in the community and/or are well informed about it) rather than by means of random sampling, and they are interviewed intensively over an extended period of time in order to enable social researchers to construct a community portrait.

The key informants are normally easy to identify because they often enjoy a high profile by virtue of acting as community leaders or serving it in some significant professional capacity (e.g., as doctors, nurses, social workers, teachers, police officers, local civil servants, technical experts, or journalists). In situations in which only a small number of possible informants can be identified in advance, it is common to resort to a form of sampling referred to as "snowballing." Whenever this is the case, each informant is asked at the end of the interview to provide the names of one or two persons who are also knowledgeable about the community. During subsequent interviews with these people, they too are invited to suggest the names of additional informants. The process continues until a coherent picture of the community begins to emerge.

The interview format relied upon in studies in which key informants are utilized as a source of information tends to be on the flexible side. The researchers almost invariably construct a data guide (i.e., a list of questions to which each interviewee is asked to respond) prior to the interview phase. However, the questions are seldom couched in highly specific terms, and there is considerable scope for mutual adjustment between the interviewer and interviewee with respect to wording (of answers as well as questions) and sequencing. In fact, rigidity of format is eschewed to such an extent that additional questions frequently crop up in the course of the interview, which leads the pattern of information gathering to deviate substantially from the original plan.

The intensive nature of the interviews and the flexible manner in which they are conducted render the key informant approach particularly suitable in situations characterized by a high degree of complexity. The relative lack of structure, of course, may also be perceived as a drawback—the results are not likely to be as reliable as those generated by means of the Delphi technique. After all, flexibility of format constitutes a potential source of bias because it allows the interviewer considerable latitude in interpreting key informant responses (both in the course of the interview and subsequent data analysis). In a study such as the present one, however, reliability is a less critical concern than is the richness of information produced.

Another reservation which might possibly be expressed is that the key informant method is essentially a vehicle for exploring small communities, whether from a theoretical or an applied perspective. Put another way, there is no concrete evidence to suggest that it could be productively employed in researching the future, particularly outside the community context. Again, however, this limitation need not detract from the technique's potential value. The key informant method bears close similarity to well-established judgemental procedures—in fact, it may be legitimately viewed as a watered-down version of the Delphi method or a sophisticated type of panel consensus—and there is no reason to assume that it would serve futurologists less effectively. Indeed, the preceding examination of the merits and demerits of the available alternatives leads to the conclusion that interviews with key informants—experts on the Hong Kong economy and its political environment—are at the present juncture the most satisfactory way of investigating long-term economic trends in the territory.

The Choice for Hong Kong

To this point, the aim of this book has been to lay the conceptual and methodological groundwork for exploring economic developments in the territory against the backdrop of the transition from British to Chinese rule and other potentially significant environmental changes that loom on the horizon. The conceptual and methodological surveys described have culminated in the conclusion that the most sensible way of approaching the subject would be by constructing descriptive-anticipatory scenarios and relying on key informants for this purpose. In the three chapters that follow, views of individuals who are in a position to make informed judgements about the future course of the Hong Kong economy (i.e., key informants) are reported and evaluated within a descriptive-anticipatory framework.

Forty-one such individuals were interviewed by me personally (Table 3.5). Several of those interviewed are actively involved in economic management—whether in manufacturing, financial services, or government—and others enjoy considerable reputation as academic researchers, economic journalists, professional economists, and political commentators. As a cross-section of Hong Kong observers, they constitute a valuable source of information with regard to the dynamics of the local economy, prospects of its key sectors, and the political environment in which it is embedded. They also form a highly heterogeneous group, combining different types of experience and representing a wide range of politico-economic outlooks.

A small core of the interviewees were known to me through previous personal contact or by reputation. The bulk of them, however, were identified by means of the snowballing technique: Those I knew were asked during the

Table 3.5 List of Key Informants

1. David Bonavia, Specialist Writer (China), *Far Eastern Economic Review*, Hong Kong.
2. Philip Bowring, Deputy Editor, *Far Eastern Economic Review*, Hong Kong.
3. Francis K.M. Chan, Senior Economist, Citibank, Hong Kong.
4. Edward K.Y. Chen, Director, Centre of Asian Studies, University of Hong Kong, Hong Kong.
5. Joseph Y.S. Cheng, Senior Lecturer, Department of Government and Public Administration, Chinese University of Hong Kong, Hong Kong.
6. T.P. Cheng, Manager, Hang Seng Bank, Hong Kong.
7. Vincent H.C. Cheng, Manager, Economic Research Department, The Hong Kong and Shanghai Banking Corporation, Hong Kong.
8. Stephen K.C. Cheong, Managing Director, Lee Wah Weaving Factory and Member of the Legislative Council, Hong Kong.
9. Steven N.S. Cheung, Professor and Head, Department of Economics, University of Hong Kong, Hong Kong.
10. Frank Ching, Journalist (former Peking correspondent of the *Asian Wall Street Journal*) and Writer, Hong Kong.
11. Derek Davies, Editor, *Far Eastern Economic Review*, Hong Kong.
12. Robert Delfs, Correspondent (China Economy), *Far Eastern Economic Review*, Hong Kong.
13. Louise do Rosario, Editor, China Trade Report, *Far Eastern Economic Review*, Hong Kong.
14. Marc Faber, First Vice-President, Drexel Burnham Lambert, Hong Kong.
15. Leo P. Goodstadt, Honorary Research Fellow, Centre of Asian Studies, University of Hong Kong, Hong Kong.
16. John Greenwood, Director and Chief Economist, G.T. Management (Asia), Hong Kong.
17. George L. Hicks, Businessman and Economist, Hong Kong.
18. Ho Sai-chu, Company Director and Manager, Vice Chairman of the Chinese General Chamber of Commerce, Member of the Legislative Council, Hong Kong.
19. Y.C. Jao, Reader, Department of Economics, University of Hong Kong, Hong Kong.
20. Yasushi Kajiwara, General Manager, Industrial Bank of Japan, Hong Kong.
21. Emily Lau, Specialist Writer (Hong Kong), Far Eastern Economic Review, Hong Kong.
22. Alan P.F. Lee, President, AVA International, Managing Director and Chief Executive, MICA-AVA (Far East) Industrial Ltd., Member of the Executive and Legislative Councils, Hong Kong.
23. James K. Lee, Economist, Standard Chartered Bank, Hong Kong.
24. Kenneth C.H. Leung, Associate Economist, Bank of America, Hong Kong.
25. David K.P. Li, Chief Manager, Bank of East Asia and Member of the Legislative Council, Hong Kong.
26. Tzong-biau Lin, Professor and Chairman, Department of Economics, Chinese University of Hong Kong, Hong Kong.
27. Richard Margolis, General Manager, Upfin A.G., Hong Kong (formerly Deputy Political Adviser, Hong Kong Government).
28. W. Gage McAffee, Partner, Coudert Brothes, Hong Kong (formerly President of the American Chamber of Commerce in the territory).
29. James D. McGregor, Director, Hong Kong General Chamber of Commerce, Hong Kong.
30. Alan A. McLean, Deputy Secretary for Economic Services, Hong Kong Government, Hong Kong.
31. Lawrence Mills, Director General, Federation of Hong Kong Industries, Hong Kong.
32. Victor Mok, Senior Lecturer, Department of Economics, Chinese University of Hong Kong, Hong Kong.
33. Leonard Rayner, Honorary Regional Advisor, Confederation of British Industries, Hong Kong.
34. Gordon S.G. Redding, Professor and Head, Department of Management Studies, University of Hong Kong, Hong Kong.
35. Anthony Rowley, Business Editor, *Far Eastern Economic Review*, Hong Kong.
36. Willard D. Sharpe, Vice President and Area Economist, Chase Manhattan Bank, Hong Kong.
37. Victor F.S. Sit, Senior Lecturer, Department of Geography, University of Hong Kong, Hong Kong.
38. Thomas C. Thompson, Manager, Research Department, Wardley Investment Services, Hong Kong.
39. T.L. Tsim, Director, Chinese University Press, Chinese University of Hong Kong, Hong Kong.
40. Fumio Umemoto, Director and General Manager, Bank of Tokyo, Hong Kong.
41. Bryon S.J. Weng, Reader and Chairman, Department of Government and Public Administration, Chinese University of Hong Kong, Hong Kong.

first phase of the study to suggest others who might be able to shed light on likely long-term economic developments in Hong Kong. The persons recommended were subsequently interviewed, and their advice was also sought as to possible additional key informants. The process continued until I was satisfied that the size of the sample and diversity of opinion were adequate. It is interesting to note that despite the territory's reputation as a place where social researchers face formidable barriers in seeking access to sources of information, all of those approached were willing to cooperate, although one person was reluctant to submit to a formal interview and have his answers recorded.

Each key informant was presented with a set of three questions. (The interview schedule included a fourth question, the responses to which are discussed in Chapter 7.) Two of the questions were intended to produce answers that would enable me to construct descriptive-anticipatory scenarios in that they focused, first on economic effects of changes in the Hong Kong environment and then on their causes. The purpose of the third question was to add a process dimension to what were primarily envisaged as state scenarios by generating information that might indicate how the effects could unfold over time.

The first question addressed to the key informants was "How do you see the general Hong Kong economy in ten years time and beyond and particularly key sectors such as manufacturing and finance?" This question was followed by one directed at the causes of the anticipated effects: "For what reasons have you made these judgements?" The question pertaining to likely future economic conditions, or effects, preceded the one related to causes, in accordance with descriptive-anticipatory logic. If the object of the exercise had been to construct descriptive-exploratory scenarios, the approach would of course have been to establish causes first and then pinpoint effects (Table 3.6).

Table 3.6 Questions Addressed to Key Informants

1. How do you see the general Hong Kong economy in ten years time and beyond and in particular key sectors such as manufacturing and finance? (Effects.)

2. For what reasons have you made these judgements? (Causes.)

3. What events, and at what times, do you think will occur to bring about your predictions? (Process.)

The third question to which the key informants were asked to respond was "What events, and at what times, do you think will occur to bring about your predictions?" This question, which centred on the process aspects of possible long-term economic developments in Hong Kong, was included in the interview schedule on the assumption that a purely static analysis of

Table 3.7 Chronology of Significant Hong Kong Events

1842: China cedes Hong Kong Island to Britain "in perpetuity" in the Treaty of Nanking.

1860: Kowloon Peninsula and Stonecutters Island ceded to Britain "forever" in the First Convention of Peking.

1898: The New Territories are leased to Britain for ninety-nine years in the Second Convention of Peking.

1941–1945: Hong Kong comes under Japanese occupation during the Second World War.

1945: Britain resumes control of the colony.

January 1982: With the expiration of the lease on the New Territories only fifteen years away, the traditional Hong Kong practice of granting fifteen-year leases precipitates uncertainty about the territory's political and economic future.

August 1982: Stock market and property prices plunge prior to a visit by British Prime Minister Margaret Thatcher to Beijing in September, in which the Hong Kong issue is expected to figure prominently.

September 1982: The UK and the PRC begin negotiations on the future of Hong Kong following a meeting between British Prime Minister Thatcher and Chinese leader Deng Xiaoping in Beijing. Periodic rounds of negotiations to continue on a regular basis.

February 1983: The Bank of China announces that it will offer cut-rate loans with 50-year maturities to Hong Kong manufacturers, marking the first time Beijing's foreign-exchange bank has stepped in with such aid for the British colony.

September 1983: The fourth round of talks begins with a spate of anti-British statements from China, perceived as an attempt to pressure Britain to accept termination of its rule in 1997. The pressure ceases a day later as the Hong Kong dollar hits an all-time low.

October 1983: Measures are taken to bolster the local currency. The government announces that just-issued Hong Kong dollar notes will be pegged at HK$7.80 : US$1 and removes a 10 percent withholding tax on bank deposits in Hong Kong dollars.

November 1983: The PRC warns that it will announce a unilateral solution for the future of Hong Kong by September 1984 if no agreement is reached with the UK before that time.

January 1984: Promises emerge from Beijing that Hong Kong will remain capitalist for at least fifty years after 1997.

January 1984: Hong Kong taxi drivers strike over a government decision to raise taxi licence fees. The protest leads to the worst rioting in nearly seventeen years. New China News Agency (NCNA) officials, the PRC's *de facto* representatives in the territory, express sympathy for the drivers' demands, but claim that this incident is Hong Kong's affair. The government rescinds the increase.

March 14, 1984: Hong Kong's Legislative Council (LEGCO), the locally appointed lawmaking body, demands that the acceptability of the outcome of negotiations between the PRC and UK be debated in the Council. This is the first attempt by the local government to pierce the shroud of secrecy surrounding the talks.

March 28, 1984: Jardine Matheson sets up a holding office in the British Dependent Territory of Bermuda. The move by the giant trading house, whose presence in Hong Kong dates back to 1841, shocks many in the territory.

April 20, 1984: British Foreign Secretary Sir Geoffrey Howe announces that Britain will no long administer Hong Kong when the lease ends in 1997.

May 1984: A delegation of unofficial members of the Executive and Legislative Councils (UMELCO) led by Sir S.Y. Chung goes to London to advocate an autonomous Hong Kong administration and seek clarification with respect to the status of British passport holders whose right of abode is limited to the territory. The delegation's visit coincides with the House of Commons debate on Hong Kong.

May 25, 1984: Chinese leader Deng Xiaoping announces that China will station troops in Hong Kong. The announcement reverses earlier assurances that no troops would be sent to the territory by Beijing in 1997. The Hang Seng index plunges 30 points.

June 1984: UMELCO members S.Y. Chung, Lydia Dunn, and Q.W. Lee go to Beijing to express the anxieties and wishes of the Hong Kong people. They are sharply rebuked by Chinese leader Deng Xiaoping when they try to persuade him that the territory is gripped by a crisis of confidence.

August 1, 1984: The PRC and the UK announce plans to sign a draft agreement in September outlining the terms under which Hong Kong will be turned over to the former in 1997. The announcement signals a breakthrough in the negotiations.

September 1, 1984: An assessment office is established under the authority of the Governor of Hong Kong, separate from the ordinary machinery of the local government, to provide the British Government and Parliament with analysis and assessment of opinion in Hong Kong on the draft agreement between the PRC and the UK on the future of the territory.

September 19, 1984: The PRC and the UK announce that they have concluded negotiations on the draft agreement.

September 20, 1984: The British Cabinet approves the draft of the Sino-British Joint Declaration on Hong Kong, clearing the way for initialling the document the following week.

September 26, 1984: Text of the draft agreement is initialled by Chinese and British negotiators at a ceremony in the Great Hall of the People in Beijing. The signing, which follows two years and twenty-two rounds of formal negotiations, freezes the 42-page text of the agreement so that it can be submitted to the legislatures of both countries for approval.

October 16, 1984: The Hong Kong Legislative Council endorses the draft agreement and commends it to the people of the territory.

November 1984: The Hong Kong government publishes its White Paper endorsing modest steps towards more representative government in the territory, as part of the attempt to build more representative institutions before 1997.

November 14, 1984: China's National People's Congress endorses the Sino-British Joint Declaration on Hong Kong.

November 24, 1984: The Assessment Office presents its report to the Governor of Hong Kong with the conclusion that most of the people of the territory find the draft agreement acceptable.

December 6, 1984: The British House of Commons unanimously approves the Sino-British Joint Declaration on Hong Kong. Only about fifty MPs, out of 635, are present to vote on the issue.

December 19, 1984: British Prime Minister Margaret Thatcher and Chinese Premier Zhao Ziyang formally sign the Sino-British Joint Declaration returning the crown colony to Chinese sovereignty in 1997. Mrs. Thatcher hails the Chinese leaders for their "one country, two systems" policy that will allow Hong Kong to preserve its current economic, political, and social systems for fifty years.

March 1985: The British Parliament gives final approval to the joint declaration.

April 10, 1985: The Third Session of the Sixth National People's Congress of the PRC ratifies the joint declaration.

May 27, 1985: The Sino-British Joint Declaration on Hong Kong is formally ratified as both sides exchange signed documents.

June 1, 1985: The PRC and the UK register the joint declaration with the United Nations.

July 1985: Implementation of the agreement begins as the Sino-British Liaison Group starts full-time work exchanging information on matters pertaining to the joint declaration. The group will function until January 1, 2000. Committees also begin to be formed to draft the Basic Law of Hong Kong.

September 1985: Indirect elections to the Legislative Council are held; regarded as a possible first step towards representative government in Hong Kong.

1987: Review of the Hong Kong political system, which might conceivably result in modest reforms.

July 1, 1988: The Sino-British Joint Liaison Group moves its base of operations to Hong Kong.

April 1988: Release of the first draft of the Basic Law of Hong Kong.

February 1989: Release of the second draft of the Basic Law of Hong Kong.

1990: Target date for completion of the Basic Law of Hong Kong.

July 1, 1997: Hong Kong to become a "special administrative region" (SAR) under the sovereignty of the PRC.

Source: H. Harding, "The Future of Hong Kong," *China Business Review* 12 (September-October 1985): 32–33.

effects, even if coupled with an examination of underlying causes, would prove methodologically insufficient and be perceived as rather unilluminating. Events are a useful conceptual tool for tackling historical and future-oriented research problems in the territory (Table 3.7) and should arguably be considered here in conjunction with effects and their causes.

The interviews tended to revolve around the specific questions I prepared in advance, and the sequence was adhered to insofar as possible, but the key informants were encouraged to raise and answer other potentially relevant questions. Thus, although the interviews were conducted within a structured framework, it would be more appropriate to describe them as "semistandardized" rather than "standardized" in nature. In fact, the interview format was characterized by such a high degree of flexibility in some cases that it approximated the "nonstandardized" type of personal interview.[34] The extent to which the key informants were inclined to operate within the framework imposed by me largely determined the length of the interview: Those who confined themselves to the specific questions asked normally required thirty to forty-five minutes, whereas interviews with those preferring a somewhat more informal mode of interaction usually lasted about twice as long.

Given the element of built-in flexibility, key informant responses, whether more or less formal, proved difficult to analyze. The questions produced answers which often differed markedly in both form and substance and which could not, therefore, be easily integrated into a number of mutually exclusive and internally consistent clusters. The key informant technique is based on the premise that capturing complexity is a more important research objective than achieving reliability in the narrow sense of the term, and it offers no elegant formula for converting loosely structured responses into structured ones. Rather, the researcher is compelled to rely mostly on subjective judgement in seeking to aggregate the data in a meaningful fashion. The present study is no exception in this respect—the fragmented pieces of information provided by the interviewees were combined into broad scenarios by resorting, in the absence of any satisfactory alternatives, to the crude device of subjective judgement.

Three scenarios emerged from the analysis (and reanalysis) of the views of the key informants: optimistic, pessimistic, and trend. The optimistic and pessimistic configurations obviously represent the extremes of the economic spectrum if the status quo (or some variant thereof) is regarded as an ideal. The trend scenario falls somewhere between these two contrasting patterns, although on balance it appears to be closer to the optimistic end of the continuum. The majority of the interviewees tended to picture the Hong Kong economy a decade or two hence along the lines of the trend scenario, but a significant minority shared a sanguine outlook and a fair number offered unmistakably gloomy predictions.

The three scenarios are described in considerable detail in the following three chapters. However, the discussion is not confined to a descriptive account of effects, causes, and process. The assumptions underlying each scenario are subjected to evaluation with a view to determining to what extent they are tenable. Furthermore, greater attention is accorded to causes than to effects and process because of the realization that in the final analysis the contribution of futures research in Hong Kong lies in identifying and explaining environmental forces which shape local events rather than in predicting and describing the outcomes of the interplay of those forces.

Notes

1. M.H. Spencer, C.G. Clark, and P.W. Hoguet, *Business and Economic Forecasting* (Homewood, Ill.: Irwin, 1961).

2. Ibid., p. 3.

3. See also G.A. Lancaster and R.A. Lomas, *Forecasting for Sales and Materials Management* (London: Macmillan, 1985).

4. R.K. Chisholm and G.R. Whitaker, *Forecasting Methods* (Homewood, Ill.: Irwin, 1971).

5. F.A. Lindsay, *New Techniques for Management Decision Making* (New York: McGraw-Hill, 1958), p. 43.

6. See, for example, J.P. Lewis and R.C. Turner, *Business Conditions Analysis* (New York: McGraw-Hill, 1967).

7. J.C. Chambers, S.K. Mullick, and D.D. Smith, *An Executive's Guide to Forecasting* (New York: Wiley, 1974). See also W.G. Sullivan and W.W. Claycombe, *Fundamentals of Forecasting* (Reston, Va.: Reston, 1977).

8. See also: H. Jones and B.C. Twiss, *Forecasting Technology for Planning Decisions* (London: Macmillan, 1978); M. Firth, *Forecasting Methods in Business and Management* (London: Arnold, 1977); M.J. Piore, "Qualitative Research Techniques in Economics," in *Qualitative Methodology*, ed. J. Van Maanen (Beverly Hills, Calif.: Sage, 1983), pp. 71–85.

9. Analogies need not necessarily be historical in nature. See in this connection Jones and Twiss, *Forecasting Technology for Planning Decisions*; J.W. Dickey and T.M. Watts, *Analytic Techniques in Urban and Regional Planning* (New York, McGraw-Hill, 1978).

10. See Chambers, Mullick, and Smith, *An Executive's Guide to Forecasting*. See also Lancaster and Lomas, *Forecasting for Sales and Materials Management*.

11. See, for example, A.L. Delbecq, A.H. Van de Ven, and D.H. Gustafson, *Group Techniques for Program Planning* (Dallas, Tex.: Scott, Foresman, 1975); F.L. Ulschak, L. Nathanson, and P.G. Gillan, *Small Group Problem Solving* (Reading, Mass.: Addison-Wesley, 1981).

12. See for further discussion G. Welty, "The Necessity, Sufficiency and Desirability of Experts as Value Forecasters," in *Developments in the Methodology of Social Sciences*, ed. W. Leinfellner and E. Kohler (Dordrecht, The Netherlands: Reidel, 1974), pp. 363–379; H.A. Linstone and M. Turoff, *Delphi Method* (Reading,

Mass.: Addison-Wesley, 1975); H. Sackman, *Delphi Critique* (Lexington, Mass.: Heath, 1975).

13. See, for example, T.J. Gordon and H. Hayward, "Initial Experiments with the Cross-Impact Method of Forecasting," *Futures* 1 (December 1968): 100-116.

14. C.W. Gross and R.T. Peterson, *Business Forecasting* (Boston: Houghton Mifflin, 1976).

15. See ibid., p. 205.

16. See P.H. Rigby, *Models in Business Analysis* (Columbus, Ohio: Merrill, 1969). See also M. Greenberger, M.A. Crenson, and B.L. Crissey, *Models in the Policy Process* (New York: Russell Sage Foundation, 1976).

17. However, see also W. Ascher, *Forecasting* (Baltimore, Md.: Johns Hopkins University Press, 1978); R. Fildes and D. Wood, eds., *Forecasting and Planning* (Westmead: Saxon House, 1978); C.W. Granger, *Forecasting in Business and Economics* (New York: Academic Press, 1980); S.C. Wheelwright and S. Makridakis, *Forecasting Methods for Management* (New York: Wiley, 1980); J. Chandler and P. Cockle, *Techniques of Scenario Planning* (London: McGraw-Hill, 1982); W. Ascher and W.H. Overholt, *Strategic Planning and Forecasting* (New York: Wiley, 1983); S. Makridakis, S.C. Wheelwright, and V.E. McGee, *Forecasting* (New York: Wiley, 1983); H. Levenbach and J.P. Cleary, *The Modern Forecaster* (Belmont, Calif.: Wadsworth, 1984).

18. J.S. Armstrong, *Long-Range Forecasting* (New York: Wiley, 1978).

19. Ibid., p. 67.

20. Ibid.

21. Ibid., p. 68.

22. Ibid.

23. Ibid.

24. See ibid., pp. 138–170.

25. See ibid., p. 70.

26. Ibid.

27. Ibid.

28. See ibid., p. 253.

29. Ibid., pp. 257–258.

30. Ibid., p. 248.

31. Consensual validity hinges on the consensus of experts or some knowledgeable persons. See in this connection H.C. Sullivan, *Conceptions of Modern Psychiatry* (Washington, D.C.: Williams Alanson White Psychiatric Foundation, 1940); L. Festinger, "Informal Social Communication," *Psychological Review* 57 (September 1950): 271–282; P. Kelvin, *The Bases of Social Behaviour* (London: Holt, Rinehart and Winston, 1970).

32. See, for example, C. Nachmias and D. Nachmias, *Research Methods in the Social Sciences* (New York: St. Martin's Press, 1981).

33. See, for example, S.F. Nadel, *The Foundations of Social Anthropology* (London: Cohen and West, 1951); J.H. Madge, *The Tools of Social Sciences* (London: Longman, 1953): W.F. Whyte, "Interviewing for Organizational Research," *Human Organization* 12 (Summer 1953): 15–22; H.S. Becker, "Field Methods and Techniques," *Human Organization* 12 (Winter 1954): 31–32; D.T. Campbell, "The Informant in Quantitative Research," *American Journal of Sociology* 60 (January

1955): 339–342; K.W. Back, "Field Methods and Techniques," *Human Organization* 14 (Winter 1956): 30–33; J.P. Dean and W.F. Whyte, "How Do You Know If the Informant Is Telling the Truth," *Human Organization* 17 (Summer 1959); 34–38; F.W. Young and R.C. Young, "Key Informant Reliability in Rural Mexican Villages," *Human Organization* 20 (Fall 1961): 141–148; P.D. Killworth and H.R. Bernard, "Informant Accuracy in Social Network Data," *Human Organization* 35 (Fall 1976): 269–286; K.W. Eckhardt and M.D. Ermann, *Social Research Methods* (New York: Random House, 1977); L.M. Siegel, C.C. Attkisson, and L.G. Carson, "Need Identification and Program Planning in the Community Context," in *Evaluation of Human Service Programs*, ed. C.C. Attkisson et al. (New York: Academic Press, 1978), pp. 215–252; P.J. Pelto and G.J. Pelto, *Anthropological Research* (Cambridge: Cambridge University Press, 1978): A.L. Epstein, *The Craft of Social Anthropology* (Oxford: Pergamon, 1979); M. Quinn Patton, *Qualitative Evaluation Methods* (Beverly Hills, Calif.: Sage, 1980); P.H. Rossi and H.E. Freeman, *Evaluation* (Beverly Hills, Calif.: Sage, 1982); M.A. Tremblay, "The Key Informant Technique," in *Field Research*, ed. R.G. Burgess (London: Allen and Unwin, 1982), pp. 98–104; R.G. Burgess, *In the Field* (London: Allen and Unwin, 1984); D.L. Stufflebeam et al., *Conducting Educational Needs Assessment* (Boston: Kluwer-Nijhoff, 1985); B.R. Witkin, *Assessing Needs in Educational and Social Programs* (Beverly Hills, Calif.: Sage, 1985).

34. Standardized, semistandardized, and nonstandardized interviews are discussed in Nachmias and Nachmias, *Research Methods in the Social Sciences*.

FOUR

The Optimistic Scenario for the Hong Kong Economy

Effects

Key informants inclined towards optimism expect the Hong Kong economy in a decade or two to possess overall characteristics similar to those it possesses at present and generally conform in its mode of operation to the provisions of the Sino-British Joint Declaration. That is, they envisage an entity largely free of external and internal barriers to the mobility of factors of production and the flow of goods and services (as well as other macro- and microeconomic controls), combining maximum external openness with a very high degree of internal flexibility. Optimists assume that in the absence of elaborate regulatory mechanisms, the market will continue to exert the dominant influence in resource allocation decisions.

Those who subscribe to this view also do not foresee any significant departures from the status quo in the realm of public finance. Specifically, they postulate that taxation will remain low in both absolute and relative terms, neither imposing an undue burden on households and businesses nor interfering with the efficient working of the economy by creating disincentives and distortions. This is coupled with the belief that excessive public spending will be avoided and that government expenditures will seldom be allowed to exceed revenues. In fact, the expectation is that budget surpluses, rather than merely balanced budgets, will be a common feature of fiscal policymaking in the Hong Kong SAR.

Fiscal conservatism is likely, according to optimists, to manifest itself in official attitudes towards welfare provision as well. They are confident that the tax system will not be restructured along more progressive lines and that the scope of social programming will not be widened. Put another way, the authorities will, as in the past, accord priority to wealth creation over its redistribution and seek to alleviate poverty through vigorous growth. In such a politico-economic climate, no substantial resources will be channelled to satisfy environmental needs either, and labour interests will not become a more potent societal force.

Optimists even detect a trend towards a "smaller" and economically more "rational" public sector. Noting that the hiving off of government departments or parts thereof has been proceeding at a reasonable pace, they anticipate further privatization schemes to be implemented in the future. Another development they regard as inevitable is the commercialization of a wide range of public services—that is, their financing by means of user charges rather than taxation—and the adoption of quasi-market mechanisms such as vouchers in lieu of direct allocation of funds to service providers. This presumably will enhance the efficiency of the economy and facilitate growth.

Two noteworthy deviations from the principle of laissez-faire are, however, envisaged by optimists. Thus, they acknowledge that the authorities are likely to persist in their efforts to render the financial sector less vulnerable to abuses and shocks (without necessarily modifying its modus operandi in any fundamental way) and that consequently this sector will be regulated more closely than it is at present. In addition, they foresee somewhat greater willingness on the part of the government to take steps to stabilize the economy in the face of cyclical fluctuations; no suggestion is made that Keynesian policies will be relied upon to supplant market forces, but it is thought that sociopolitical circumstances will compel policymakers to act to ensure smoother macroeconomic adjustment, particularly in case of a severe recession.

There is less consensus among optimists with respect to the future of the link between the HK dollar and its US counterpart, perhaps the most glaring departure from laissez-faire philosophy. Many of them insist that the link will be jettisoned as soon as the remaining political uncertainty evaporates and that the value of the local currency will then be determined again through the interplay between the forces of demand and supply. Others, however, are convinced that it will be retained in some form well beyond 1997 in order to maximize political stability and deter economic speculation. This viewpoint also holds that in the absence of a central bank, the link serves a useful monetary control function and will not be abandoned on this ground as well.

Notwithstanding their divergent views on the issue of currency linkage in the future, optimists agree that the local dollar will not lose its separate status (i.e., will not be replaced by the renminbi or some other externally controlled medium of exchange), certainly not within the period covered by the study. They are equally confident that the territory will preserve its high degree of autonomy, at least in the economic sphere, and that its relationship with the PRC will be characterized by mutual accommodation and tolerance based on appreciation of legitimate differences between the capitalist enclave and the mainland. The implication is that the "one country, two systems" formula will scrupulously be adhered to both in theory and practice and that Hong Kong will enjoy considerable freedom to pursue its economic interests in the international as well as the domestic arena.

Indeed, optimists believe that the territory will continue to exhibit a strong international orientation and will not turn inwards to become merely a "Chinese" city. Furthermore, its external role will not be confined to a narrow range of economic activities and a limited geographical area; rather, it will develop into an even more sophisticated international manufacturing, commercial, and communications centre and will remain Asia's de facto economic capital despite the competitive challenge posed by cash-rich and gradually deregulated Tokyo (and—to a lesser extent—Singapore, Sydney, Seoul, Taipei, and eventually Shanghai). Nor is it just a matter of the primacy of external economic linkages over ties with China; Hong Kong's Western-type administrative infrastructure, legal system, and lifestyle will not be affected by Britain's exit.

Optimists, of course, do not deny that the local economy will become more closely integrated with that of the PRC and that business organizations from the mainland will grow in number, size, and influence. The realization that this is the direction in which the territory is heading manifests itself most clearly in the common assertion that the Bank of China will be allowed, in conjunction with the Hong Kong Bank and the Standard Chartered Bank, to issue notes and will in all likelihood eclipse the Hong Kong Bank as the leading local financial institution. (It is also suggested that the two note-issuing banks will assume an increasingly "local" character.) Optimists nonetheless maintain that the territory will be propelled primarily by international economic forces and the PRC-related business activities, although highly significant, will be deemed less important both quantitatively and qualitatively. Moreover, they argue that PRC-controlled organizations in Hong Kong will, like other players, abide by the rules of the free market and will not undermine them by seeking unfair advantages.

The assumption that the territory's position as an international manufacturing centre is not threatened reflects the belief that Hong Kong will not succumb to protectionist pressures and intense competition from low-cost producers (mainly in Asia, including China, but also elsewhere) and will not undergo a rapid process of deindustrialization, as some fear. Although optimists do not anticipate dramatic change in the present pattern of product concentration, given the fact that it is unrealistic to expect the local manufacturing sector to specialize in anything but a fairly limited range of popular consumer products, they foresee a somewhat more diversified industrial output and have no doubts that the unhealthy dependence on a small number of markets (market concentration) will give way to a less troublesome geographical distribution of domestic exports. Above all, however, they emphasize that manufactures will adapt by moving up-market in areas in which they have encountered success in the past and by capitalizing on opportunities in China. Thus, although industry may continue to decline in relative terms, it will remain the principal source of employment and, in several respects, the backbone of the economy.

The strength of manufacturing will, according to optimists, be coupled with a robust service sector. They predict a particularly bright future for financial services, import and export (including re-export) trade, transport services, the communications industry, business services, and tourism. Some of them even suggest that Hong Kong will emerge as an important cultural centre and that its scientific (including medical) institutions will acquire considerable reputation, both generally and in specific fields. Again, the role of the service sector will not be confined to Hong Kong and China, but will extend to the rest of Asia and other key regions such as Europe, the Middle East, North America, and Latin America. The strength of the manufacturing and service sectors will ensure balanced development, with the two sectors reinforcing each other and forming a finely tuned economic whole which is more than the sum of its parts.

It is interesting to note that although they tend to embrace economic liberalism passionately, optimists are more ambivalent towards the notion of a "free political market." For one thing, they concede that the PRC will not allow the development of a highly representative government and strongly competitive politics; in fact, they intimate that the territory will probably have a less benign and more authoritarian government (in substance, if not in form) than at present. Optimists, however, do not think that the absence of full-fledged liberal democratic institutions will hamper economic progress. They contend that Japan, Singapore, South Korea, and Taiwan, for instance, have opted for a more oppressive variant of capitalism than is practiced in the West (referred to by Johnson[1] as the "capitalist developmental state"), one in which "better socio-economic performance is traded for "less political participation," without suffering any adverse consequences on the business front. On the contrary, these countries have enjoyed impressive rates of economic growth. The corollary is that the viability of the local economy does not hinge on progressive democratization of the political decision-making structure.

Given their expectations of a propitious business and political climate, optimists are unabashedly bullish about the long-term prospects of the Hong Kong economy. Some predict truly spectacular performance, surpassing even previous records. Most, however, are more cautious in their forecasts, envisaging a highly respectable but by no means extraordinary rate of growth of about 6–9 percent a year in real terms. This, they argue, may be short of the double-digit figures that appeared to be a realistic goal only a few years ago—and the lower end of this range in particular is perhaps not likely to be viewed with great enthusiasm in light of the historical record—yet such growth, if sustained, would constitute a considerable achievement for an increasingly mature economy with a nearly stationary population susceptible to external shocks.

Causes

An important reason for the confidence displayed by optimists is to be found in their perception of the status of the Sino-British Joint Declaration and their evaluation of its content.[2] They do not dismiss the Joint Declaration as a document whose significance lies primarily in the symbolic realm or as a sophisticated tactical device to ensure prosperity and stability during the transition from British to Chinese rule but to be jettisoned later; nor do they regard it as merely a policy statement which, although reflecting the strategic intentions of the parties, does not impose any formal constraints on future behaviour. Rather, they see the Sino-British declaration as a legally binding international agreement whose existence precludes erosion of prevailing rules of the economic game in the territory.

Optimists are aware that Chinese policymakers do not have a reputation for consistency and that wide swings in strategy may have been the rule rather than the exception in the PRC. However, they draw a distinction between the domestic arena and foreign affairs, arguing that whereas domestic policies have been characterized by a high degree of volatility, the conduct of foreign relations has been marked by greater continuity of ends and means. In fact, according to them, the Chinese have an impeccable record of respecting international agreements and practices both in letter and in spirit, particularly those which are not the product of "coercion." The PRC is even known not to undermine international legal instruments which it perceives as flawed, such as the three "unequal" treaties sustaining British rule in Hong Kong. The corollary is that the Chinese are not likely to deviate from the provisions of the Joint Declaration.[3]

Nor is it just a matter of observing treaties qua treaties, whether equal or unequal. Optimists maintain that the care and detail with which the Joint Declaration was negotiated reflect the PRC's determination to abide by it. The wide publicity China has given to the agreement, internationally as well as domestically, is also said to be indicative of its desire to signal firm commitment to the principles embodied in the Joint Declaration and their implementation. Furthermore, having "internationalized" the issue, the PRC is under enormous pressure to adhere to the legal agreement it has signed and promoted; any attempt to dilute the Joint Declaration would severely damage the country's national reputation.[4]

Some optimists go beyond merely underscoring the dichotomy between domestic and foreign policy behaviour and insisting that it would be completely out of character for the Chinese to discard their international treaty obligations. They also contend that it is no longer appropriate to portray the domestic scene in the PRC as volatile because since 1978 strategic shifts have largely taken the form of fluctuations around the trend rather than fundamental reorientation. China is seeking stability both in its external and internal environments and is doggedly pursuing the same goals while occasionally experimenting with different tactics. Moreover, the PRC places a growing emphasis on "socialist legality" and is consequently bound to respect the formal agreement with the UK concerning Hong Kong.

As indicated, optimists express a high degree of satisfaction with the content of the Joint Declaration as well as its status. They stress in particular that the territory will remain a free port and a separate customs territory; that it will retain its identity as an international financial centre and that its markets for foreign exchange, gold, securities, and futures will continue to operate; that there will be a free flow of capital and that the local dollar will remain a separate and freely convertible currency; that the Hong Kong SAR will have its own independent finances and that the Chinese government will not levy taxes there; and that the territory will be able to maintain its own economic and cultural relations with other countries and issue its own travel documents. Optimists believe that these and other guarantees encompass virtually all those critical elements that have contributed to Hong Kong's phenomenal success for the past three decades, except for the British link.

That is not to say that optimists do not perceive any ambiguities and gaps in the Joint Declaration. They expect, however, most of the remaining legal uncertainty to dissipate with the promulgation of the Basic Law, which in their opinion will give concrete expression to the principles enshrined in the declaration and will thus reinforce the institutional foundations which account for the territory's economic dynamism. The Basic Law will obviously constitute a domestic rather than an international legal document, but optimists have no doubt that it will be observed scrupulously because of the close link with the Joint Declaration. Again, some of them go further and argue that this link should not be overemphasized because the PRC is rapidly developing into a political system in which the rule of law is accorded considerable importance.[5]

Neither the Joint Declaration nor the apparent concern with socialist legality in China is, however, the principal factor fuelling the optimists' expectations with respect to the future of the Hong Kong economy. Their sanguine outlook is primarily rooted in the conviction that the PRC will preserve the economic status quo in the territory because it is in its best interest to do so.[6] The point is that China derives substantial benefits from Hong Kong and is, therefore, unlikely to take any steps which might undermine the territory's capitalist economy. Should the "one country, two systems" formula prove unworkable, the PRC would incur massive losses and deny itself significant potential gains, political as well as economic.

Thus, rather than tamper will the local system, China will doubtless be guided by a strong desire to maintain its present features.

Optimists perceive Hong Kong as a source of many tangible benefits for the PRC, but they place particular emphasis on the crucial role that it plays in satisfying the mainland's need for convertible foreign exchange. They point out that the territory provides China with more than 30 percent of its hard foreign currency income and state that the PRC is to all intents and purposes using its trade surplus with Hong Kong to finance its deficits with other countries. Thus, although foreign trade constitutes only a fraction of China's national product and the enormous size of the mainland economy cushions it against external shocks, the foreign exchange earnings generated in the territory are of vital importance.

The importance of these earnings, according to optimists, is growing rather than diminishing, mainly because of the ambitious modernization programme the PRC has embarked upon and the rapidly rising expectations of its population which have resulted in much greater demand for imports. These factors have coincided with difficulties in China's export trade stemming from the poor quality of its products, intensification of protectionist pressures, and relative decline in world trade. The PRC has also experienced serious setbacks in the energy sector, both in terms of disappointing exploration efforts and falling oil prices, and its export performance has consequently suffered. None of these problems is regarded as temporary in nature and hence the decisive importance of foreign currency income originating in Hong Kong.

Part of that income is earned through direct sales in the territory. Although Hong Kong is a relatively small market, its geographical proximity and the loyalty of the local population to traditional Chinese products have made it a profitable outlet for mainland exports which cannot be sold in large quantities in other parts of the world. Optimists postulate that the PRC will achieve somewhat greater market diversification in the future, but they do not envisage a significant lessening of the dependence on the territory as a major and reliable trading partner. The corollary is that the Chinese will strive to ensure the continuing prosperity of Hong Kong, for otherwise the capitalist enclave will not be able to absorb a growing volume of goods and services from the mainland.

The PRC also uses the territory to boost its foreign currency income by channelling through it exports to third countries. The Chinese traditional proclivity to trade directly with other nations notwithstanding, the mainland has been compelled to rely heavily on Hong Kong as an entrepôt because of the PRC's long isolation, lack of commercial experience, and poor infrastructure. Goods from the PRC are thus shipped to the territory where they are further processed, assembled, or repackaged and then sold abroad by local businesses attuned to conditions in foreign markets and possessing advertising and sales skills in short supply on the mainland. Optimists assume that China's ability—both physical and institutional—to engage in direct trade will improve considerably in a decade or two, but they believe that Hong Kong will continue to serve as an important economic bridge between the developing mainland and the outside world. It follows that the PRC will endeavour to capitalize on rather than discourage the openness and flexibility of the local economy.

Some of the countries to which China directs its exports through the territory do not have official ties with the PRC. Hong Kong also performs a similar function with respect to goods imported by China from those countries. Given the PRC's increasing diplomatic pragmatism and its emergence as a status quo–oriented power, optimists acknowledge that the mainland will be able to engage in direct commercial transactions with most members of the international community well before 1997. Yet they are of the opinion that lack of formal diplomatic relations and direct channels of communication will continue to hamper trade with a number of external actors, most notably Taiwan. Therefore, the need for a conveniently located semi-autonomous free port, a role for which Hong Kong is ideally suited, will diminish only marginally.

In addition to exporting to the territory on a large scale and relying upon it heavily as a transshipment centre, the PRC has invested extensively in Hong Kong, and the resulting profits further bolster its foreign exchange earnings. China now has a substantial stake in virtually every sector of the territory's economy, including manufacturing, and its Hong Kong portfolio is growing rapidly in both size and diversity. Optimists maintain that this growth is bound to accelerate in the future and that the PRC will refrain from pursuing policies which might undermine its massive investments. The implication is that it will seek to sustain the territory's capitalist climate.

Optimists also contend that China's investments in the territory clearly indicate that it intends to honour the obligations assumed under the Sino-British Joint Declaration. After all, were this not the case, would the PRC be energetically buying tangible assets in Hong Kong at prevailing market prices? Rather, it might have been more expedient to defer investment decisions until prices declined drastically in the wake of a deteriorating political atmosphere or simply to take possession by nonmarket (i.e., coercive) means after the British departure. The Chinese are reputed to be very careful in the use of investment funds, and they would have not been channelling scarce resources to the territory unless they expected the economic status quo to remain intact.

Another aspect of PRC investment in Hong Kong to which optimists draw attention is the advantage the mainland derives from operating locally incorporated companies; these companies are not subject to the kind of political constraints which hinder direct Chinese business expansion in parts of Southeast Asia. Because the desire to minimize direct contacts with the PRC is abating in the region, optimists posit that this factor will carry less significance in the future. Nonetheless, they argue that residual fears of Chinese nationalism will exert some influence on foreign policy decisions in Southeast Asia for a long time to come and that it would be easier to promote PRC business interests in the region from the free port of Hong Kong.

Optimists also emphasize the importance of the territory to China as a source of credit. The PRC's sales to Hong Kong, whether for final use or with a view to re-export, and the profits generated from local investments do not produce enough foreign currency income to satisfy China's growing developmental needs. Consequently, the PRC has been compelled to resort to external borrowing in order to pay for a wide range of imported goods and services. The territory has played an important role in providing bank loans and other forms of credit to the PRC. Optimists see the relentless drive by mainland financial institutions in Hong Kong to increase their market share as a sign that China has targeted the territory as an even more crucial reservoir of external finance. They reason, therefore, that it will do nothing to reduce the local capacity and incentive to save and will allow sufficient freedom to financial intermediaries in Hong Kong to perform their numerous functions and maintain their competitive edge.

Financial flows from the territory to the PRC are not in the form of credit alone. Thus, parallel to the substantial influx of Chinese capital into Hong Kong, local investors have poured considerable funds into the mainland. In fact, despite its small size, the territory has supplied more than 50 percent of the total foreign capital invested in the PRC and nearly all the foreign capital invested in the special economic zones (SEZs), which the mainland has established in the hope that the capital attracted might facilitate economic rejuvenation. Hong Kong's role as a source of investment funds assumes even greater importance if one takes into account projects in which local business intermediaries have played an active part. The inference optimists draw from this is that China will cultivate the territory's entrepreneurs and will not transform the environment in which they operate.

Nor can the PRC, optimists insist, overlook substantial financial flows from Hong Kong in the shape of travel and tourist expenditure and remittances (some of which are in kind rather than in money) and unrequited transfers. Tourism is a particularly important source of foreign exchange income for China—it has a salutary effect on employment as well—and local residents account for over 60 percent of "visitors" to the mainland. The PRC also earns considerable sums from foreign tourists who proceed there after enjoying a holiday in Hong Kong. Affluence results in more travel and greater remittances and unrequited transfers; capitalist prosperity also serves as a magnet to foreign tourists. It stands to reason, then, that China will try to make sure that the territory remains "open" and that the economic boom does not taper off.

There is another point. Unless Southeast Asian countries perceive Hong Kong as a genuinely separate entity after 1997, they may restrict their nationals from travelling there and curtail visits from the SAR. This, in addition to the adverse impact on the local economy, would not be conducive to the PRC's modernization and reunification efforts. At present, many ethnic Chinese from Southeast Asia are able to slip unobtrusively into China through Hong Kong to visit relatives and friends. If this channel is blocked, the PRC may find itself deprived of easy access to a community which is expected to assist in the process of economic restructuring and national reconciliation. Optimists think that this will prompt China to grant Hong Kong a high degree of autonomy.

The benefits the PRC derives from the territory are not confined to foreign exchange income. Because it is deemed undesirable to allow foreigners to live on the mainland in large numbers or for extended periods because of possible political repercussions and poor facilities—and yet a high premium is placed on controlled contact with foreigners—Hong Kong serves a crucial function as a conveniently located place where foreigners can operate comfortably and where Chinese-Western interaction proceeds generally uninhibited. In time, the constraints which prevent foreigners from using the PRC, particularly Beijing and the major coastal cities, as a permanent base may be removed, but optimists do not envisage fundamental changes in this respect within the next decade or two. Accordingly, they posit that China will foster the image of the territory as a separate entity and will not be inclined to modify those features of the local lifestyle which are attractive to foreigners with business or professional backgrounds.

The PRC's interest in maintaining a large-scale foreign presence in Hong Kong stems from the fact that it creates opportunities for export and is conducive to investment in the mainland. (Foreign investment is highly valued in China because it normally entails the transfer of technology.) The territory, however, is more than just a "foreign ghetto." It is an economically sophisticated city in which the PRC gathers commercial intelligence and gains insight into capitalist management techniques and institutional practices. Optimists assert that Hong Kong's indispensable role as China's business laboratory cannot be overemphasized and that the mainland will be eager to facilitate performance of this role by encouraging strong links between the territory and the Western world and adhering to the colonial government's policy of respecting private market forces.

Large-scale foreign presence in Hong Kong and the strong links between the local economy and those of the major Western powers are perceived by optimists as advantageous to the PRC from a political, as well as business, perspective. For one thing, the combination of these two factors renders China's southern flanks more secure, particularly from a possible Soviet threat. Given the international character of the territory, it is less likely than other parts of the PRC to serve as a target for would-be aggressors. The stake that the Western world has in Hong Kong, though circumscribing somewhat China's freedom of political action, may also enable the PRC to exert subtle pressure on Western countries as a means of promoting its strategic objectives. Benevolent PRC policies in the territory will call for a quid pro quo, and the fear that it could prove unaccommodating in the local context will compel Western nations to offer tangible concessions in bilateral and multilateral contexts. This analysis leads optimists to the conclusion that China will be favourably disposed towards the idea of Hong Kong as an international city which is an integral part of the Western capitalist system.

Another political advantage that accrues to the PRC from the status quo in the territory relates to the domestic arena. Specifically, Hong Kong has traditionally functioned as an outlet for dissatisfied elements from the mainland, particularly overseas Chinese who returned there in the early 1950s, and has thus helped to regulate the level of internal dissent. Although optimists expect the need for such an outlet to diminish in the wake of gradual political liberalization in the PRC, they nevertheless feel the territory could continue to perform the same role on a smaller scale by absorbing individuals who desire to live in China, even contribute to its development, without having to pay the price of abiding by the stricter rules of the economic and political game prevailing there. This, in turn, will strengthen the PRC's commitment to a successful implementation of the "one country, two systems" formula.

Optimists also contend that if China jettisoned this formula, it would precipitate a serious crisis in Hong Kong and threaten political stability on the mainland, particularly in Guandong Province. The territory's population is largely made up of dedicated capitalists who might deeply resent any attempt to interfere with their lifestyle. These people speak Cantonese rather than Mandarin, distrust their northern brethren, and reject communist ideology and form of political organization. (After all, many of them fled the PRC for political, as well as economic, reasons.) Their "reeducation" could pose massive problems, and their resentment might prove difficult to control both locally and, in view of likely spillover effects, in the South China context. Optimists note that Shanghai remained a source of political difficulties for nearly three decades after its takeover and that Hong Kong's integration into the Chinese body politic, unless undertaken in accordance with the spirit of the "one country, two systems" formula, would be far more painful. Now, because the PRC leadership sees a positive correlation between the degree of domestic stability and the rate of modernization, it will take pains not to violate that spirit.

Optimists employ a similar logic in analyzing the international implications of China's policy towards the territory. A benevolent policy, they observe, would generate political goodwill, whereas a rigid one would provoke negative responses on the diplomatic front, particularly in Asia where the handling of the Hong Kong question is regarded as a litmus test of the mainland's broader intentions. The PRC, they amplify, needs a stable international as well as domestic environment in order to pursue its strategic objectives, and it will thus be anxious to avoid confrontation with the major Western powers and its Asian neighbours. This caution presumably is another political factor which cannot be overlooked in seeking probable explanations for future economic developments in the territory.

However, by far the most important political factor to take into account, according to optimists, is the linkage between China's policy towards Hong Kong and the Taiwan issue. In short, Hong Kong may be viewed as a "bait to lure the Taiwan fish" because if the PRC scrupulously adheres to the provisions of the Sino-British Joint Declaration and the territory continues to prosper after 1997, Taiwan might show willingness to come to terms with the mainland. On the other hand, denial of genuine autonomy to capitalist Hong Kong would heighten Taiwan's distrust of the Chinese Communist Party (CCP) and foreclose the option of promoting constructive dialogue between the two sides with a view to peaceful reunification. The desire to make substantial headway in the relationship with Taiwan in the foreseeable future is believed to be so strong in the upper echelons of the CCP that the Chinese leadership will go to great lengths to demonstrate the feasibility of the "one country, two systems" formula.

To abandon this formula, given the enormous economic and political benefits it promises, would indeed be unthinkable, optimists reiterate. After all, without the foreign exchange earnings the territory generates and the access it provides to valuable information and technology, the PRC might plunge even more deeply into debt to foreign bankers and not be able to lift itself out of the backwardness and poverty that characterized the Mao Zedong era. It would remain a divided nation, plagued by domestic instability and alienated from key segments of the international community. The twin objectives of the economic modernization and national reunification, which have provided a sense of direction to the country in the period following the chaos of the Cultural Revolution, would thus prove unattainable.

Optimists moreover emphasize that failure on China's part to honour the Sino-British agreement would precipitate a severe crisis in the territory itself—a crisis that would turn Hong Kong from a great asset into a heavy liability for the mainland. Capital outflow, brain drain, and loss of international export quotas would cripple the local economy, and the PRC would be compelled to assume the burden of feeding about 6 million disaffected people. Optimists argue that it would be inconceivable for China to pursue policies that are bound to turn one of its principal stepping-stones into a stumbling-block. On the contrary, it will act decisively to make certain that the capitalist enclave continues to serve its interests as efficiently and effectively as in the past.

Optimists go further than merely postulating that it is to the PRC's advantage to implement the "one country, two systems" formula. They insist that the Chinese leadership is fully cognizant of the benefits that the mainland derives from Hong Kong and the costs involved in transforming its socioeconomic character. The reassurances offered in this respect extend beyond the realm of armchair speculation: Optimists point to concrete evidence in the form of actual PRC conduct towards the territory over a period spanning nearly four decades. Their view is that the PRC displayed remarkable restraint in the post-1949 period in the face of what might have been construed as considerable provocation. That the United States made extensive use of the territory when Washington and Beijing were at loggerheads is a case in point. For example, while enjoying virtually free access to Hong Kong, the US strongly opposed the admission of the PRC to the United Nations, placed an embargo on Chinese goods, and allied itself closely with Chiang Kai-shek's Kuomintang (KMT) government in Taiwan. The principal instrument of this pro-Taiwan/anti-PRC policy was the US Seventh Fleet, which was interposed between the two Chinas in the Taiwan straits in 1950 and employed to break the blockade of Quemoy in 1958—those two instances being in addition to its general deterrent role. Yet ships of the Seventh Fleet were victualled in Hong Kong—this presumably included food supplies from the mainland—and crews used the territory for rest and recreation.

Even when the PRC and the US were at war in all but name, first in Korea and again when the People's Liberation Army (PLA) deployed support troops in Vietnam, the territory continued to offer facilities—economic, military, and political—to the Americans. Nor was there anything surreptitious about US presence and activities there. As one observer has noted: "Anyone crossing the Star Ferry from central Hong Kong to Tsim Sha Tsui (one of the busiest ferry routes in the world) passed within a few hundred yards of American naval vessels lying on moorings that were in practice reserved for their exclusive use. If more colourful evidence of the American presence was sought it could always be found in the girlie-bars of Wanchai.[7]

Not only US activities in the territory but also those of the PRC's erstwhile allies, the Chinese Nationalists and supporters of the KMT, must have been a standing provocation. Because the Communists themselves had used Hong Kong (in the years before 1949 when the KMT was still in power in Canton) as a link between their forces in the north and guerrillas and supporters in the south, they were aware that Taipei could derive strategic advantages from its presence in the territory. Yet Beijing has allowed Hong Kong to remain the sole place in China other than Taiwan where supporters of Chiang Kai-shek and his successors have been free to display their political loyalties. Thus

> On October 10 ("the double tenth") each year blue and red flags of the Chinese Republic are flown in clear defiance of the red regime some fifteen miles away. Some areas—Rennies Mill for example—were virtually KMT enclaves where Chiang Kai-shek's supporters substituted pictures of the Generalissimo for those of the Great Helmsman. The Royal Hong Kong Police keep a watchful eye on the situation and discourage—or if need be forbid—more active demonstrations by KMT supporters; but there can be little doubt that the People's Republic has enjoined restraint on its much more numerous supports. The Taiwan flag carrier, China Airlines, flies frequently in and out of Hong Kong and Taiwan maintains a travel agency there which to those unversed in the minutiae of protocol appears very much like a consulate.[8]

Quite apart from the use made of the territory by the Americans and the freedom of action enjoyed by the Nationalists there, the mere fact of the British presence in Hong Kong must doubtless be regarded as an irritant to the PRC. The UK, it is true, avoids as far as it can any deliberate steps which might antagonize Beijing or be interpreted as anti-Chinese. However, given its status as a medium power with international commitments and the obligations that stem from its colonial role, Britain cannot adopt an overly passive posture in the territory. Some of the activities it undertakes there, such as the monitoring of mainland communications, may legitimately be viewed as hostile to the PRC. Moreover, the

> Outward trappings of imperialism are . . . still exhibited and play an undefined but important role in symbolizing British rule. British regiments beat the retreat; Ghurkas and British soldiers mount military parades and tattoos; the Royal Hong Kong Police Band—complete with bagpipes and a (Chinese) pipe-major—entertains the populace; Her Majesty the Queen visits her colony and is greeted with a fireworks display when the local population are forbidden traditional Chinese crackers; local Chinese dignitaries are created Knights of the British Empire—the list could be extended indefinitely. Above all capitalism flourishes with a colourful gaiety and panache that make the socialist achievements of nearby Canton dull and drab in comparison.[9]

Indeed, many people north of the border make this comparison and opt for the territory. The flow of refugees from the PRC has posed a serious social problem for Hong Kong, but it has also served as a continuing rebuke to the mainland. Voting with one's feet is a common phenomenon in the developing world, yet nowhere over such a long period have so many faced such hardships to escape difficult living conditions and an oppressive regime.

Unlike the recent exodus from Vietnam, the flight from the PRC to the territory has no taint of ethnic persecution. Rather, Chinese flee other Chinese from one Chinese environment to another, which can only be interpreted as an affront to the policies and practices on the mainland.

Optimists maintain that the PRC has consciously chosen to turn a blind eye to the stream of provocations emanating from the territory because of the realization that it is a price worth paying for the benefits obtained. They dismiss the suggestion that the reason China has not acted to gain control of the capitalist enclave is that it lacked the capability to engineer a takeover. After all, the PLA is a force to be reckoned with, commanding the largest army in the world and certainly a match for the local garrison. As one commentator has put it: "What the local forces, beefed up to 30,000 after the 1967 riots, could have done to stop them is uncertain."[10] And as he has further elaborated:

> Besides Hong Kong has neither natural resources nor land to speak of. It needs Chinese food, Chinese raw materials, even Chinese water in order to survive. A boycott, let alone a siege, could have brought the Colony to its knees in short order. Merely by making threatening noises, Peking could have frightened off foreign investors, undermined the work will of the local population and severely crippled the economy. More intriguing is the idea of a "peaceful invasion" mooted by Richard Hughes, in which unarmed civilians would simply march into Hong Kong in vast numbers and could hardly be turned back or shot down by the border guards. We have seen what problems arise when thousands of refugees sneak in on their own. What would happen if hundreds were ordered by Peking?[11]

Nor has there ever been any indication, optimists add, that the UK would fight for the colony.

> The Crown has already given away much larger territories as soon as there was a demand for self-government and it would be very easy for China to incite such demands and arouse a considerable show of popular support for them. Moreover, one of Hong Kong's main uses is as a listening post and back door to China, and in many ways its real purpose is to consolidate the good relations with the People's Republic of China. If Peking wished to get Britain out, it could probably negotiate a reversion without too much difficulty or arm twisting. If Britain stays, it is largely ... because China has not asked it to leave.[12]

Another suggestion dismissed by optimists is that the PRC has refrained from assuming control over the territory because this would have constituted a departure from its policy of conflict avoidance and risk minimization. They claim that, arguments to the contrary notwithstanding, the Communists have shown themselves quite prepared to employ the PLA on several occasions for pursuing political objectives by other means. For instance, in Korea in 1950, on the Indian-Tibetan frontier in 1962, and in Vietnam in 1979, the PLA has been committed to fight even though each encounter brought with it a very real danger of the conflict escalating into an all-out war. By contrast, Hong Kong could have been overrun in hours rather than days at any time—and with no more risk than an expression of mild indignation in Western media. As indicated, even this limited military action would have been unnecessary had China relied on diplomatic demarches instead.

Optimists also reject the suggestion that the PRC has not absorbed the territory, whether by coercive or more subtle means, because a convenient opportunity to do so has simply not presented itself. On the contrary, they assert that an excellent opportunity to reintegrate Hong Kong into the Chinese body politic existed in 1967, yet the mainland opted not to challenge the political status quo on that occasion. In fact, the PRC took no steps to aggravate the tension which engulfed the territory at the height of the Cultural Revolution and provided no encouragement to local elements which sought to undermine the colonial system through direct confrontation. Moreover, when the Portuguese signalled at the time their willingness to return Macao to China, the PRC did not respond positively, in part out of desire not to cause panic in Hong Kong. The Chinese approach has been summarized as follows:

> [T]he People's Republic of China has exercised remarkable restraint over Hong Kong since 1949 when events within and outside China and the Colony could have precipitated a Chinese takeover. Rational decision making has prevailed in Peking on this question when opportunity, capability and provocation for the precipitate action were all present and even at a time when hierarchical control within the CCP had broken down. That rationality on Hong Kong was maintained in these circumstances argues for its continuance in all but extreme conditions, and this is an assurance that Hong Kong's position will continue to depend on Peking's careful assessment that the status *quo* is in Chinese interests. There is no reason to believe the assessment will change in the near future and certainly no justification for the belief that it will be affected by the shadow of 1997.[13]

Optimists do not confine their observations to the fact that the PRC has chosen not to challenge the political status quo in the territory. Additionally, they point out that China has treated the colonial authorities with respect, bolstering their legitimacy rather than detracting from it, and has lent them support, whether directly or indirectly, to the extent that the mainland is increasingly seen as a partner, albeit a silent one, in running Hong Kong. The PRC has pursued a policy of accommodation towards the territory, optimists contend, because it is fully aware of the benefits this policy brings and the costs of embracing a less supportive strategy. Furthermore, with the signing of the Sino-British Joint Declaration, Hong Kong has largely ceased to be a thorn in China's side, and the cooperation between the mainland and the capitalist enclave is no longer the source of embarrassment it might have been when colonial rule was entrenched. Therefore, the policy of accommodation towards the territory is likely to be subject to fewer political constraints, and its underlying logic may be brought into sharper focus.

Optimists also believe that there is growing realization in Hong Kong itself that it is in the PRC's interest not to tamper with the workings of the local economic system and that the mainland more than appreciates the rewards to be reaped from noninterference and the dangers of excessive intervention. Given the element of risk involved and the "refugee mentality"[14] which influences business and personal decisions in the territory, Hong Kong people will continue to seek security through "precautionary diversification" of their assets and acquisition of foreign passports. However, upon achieving a better balance between local and overseas assets and obtaining a right of residence abroad, these individuals will redirect their energies towards entrepreneurial and professional pursuits in the territory—the place which affords them the best opportunities for maximizing material gains and which they perceive as the most attractive social environment.

It is interesting to note that optimists do not consider the quest for asset diversification and foreign passports as a threat but as a factor which ultimately works to Hong Kong's advantage. For one thing, the outflow of capital and people has coincided with a substantial inflow of investment funds, and there has been no dearth of entrepreneurs and professionals willing to come to the territory and practice their skills in Asia's most dynamic city. The injection of foreign capital and increase in foreign personnel, particularly insofar as they reflect growing American and Japanese involvement in the local economy, may help transform Hong Kong into an even more sophisticated manufacturing and service centre and enhance its cosmopolitan character. Nor is this all. Asset diversification and exposure to other business cultures in the process of fulfilling residence requirements in leading developed countries are likely to improve local people's understanding of the international economic environment and make them better equipped to capitalize on global opportunities when they return to the territory. Their temporary departure, therefore, can be seen as a form of investment rather than divestment.

Another development perceived by optimists not as a threat but as an opportunity is the lowering of the barriers between Hong Kong and China and the high degree of interdependence characterizing the relationship between the two systems. They point out that local companies are increasingly exploiting the mainland's attractive labour costs by setting up manufacturing operations across the border and that this helps to keep their products competitive in saturated markets. In addition, optimists are confident that the PRC will continue its inexorable march towards a market-driven, mixed, and open economy and that it will enjoy rapid economic growth over the next few decades. Given China's enormous size, its efforts to liberalize and modernize the economy present excellent opportunities for Hong Kong businesses both in manufacturing and in services.

Optimists believe the emergence of the PRC as a viable market for local products will lessen the territory's economic dependence on the US and Western Europe. The spectacular performance of the South Korean and Taiwanese economies is also a relevant factor because it will facilitate intra-Asian, particularly intra–East Asian, investment and trade flows and will thus enable the territory to diversify its markets. An even stronger impetus for an upsurge in economic activity in Asia will come from the acute need to shift manufacturing operations from Japan to low-cost production centres in order to counter the effects of the dramatic appreciation of the yen and the Asian giant's desire to boost effective demand throughout the continent with a view to lessening its own dependence on the American and West European markets. The Japanese will undertake massive investments in Asia and substantially increase their assistance to countries in the region—initiatives from which Hong Kong will greatly benefit.

In assessing the territory's long-term economic prospects, optimists lay considerable emphasis on the fact that, unlike the US and Western Europe, it is located in the heart of an area which has "new frontiers" beckoning for rapid expansion over the next few decades. The US does not have a natural new frontier—it has Canada to its north and the depressed parts of Central and South America to its south. Nor does the Middle East (because of declining oil prices, cultural impediments, and political instability) offer Western Europe significant expansion opportunities. By contrast, Hong Kong lies close to a number of new frontiers. Given its enormous potential and determination to pursue an open-door policy, China is doubtless the most important of these, but India too may be said to qualify because its young leaders appear firmly committed to reinvigorating the economy through market-oriented strategies.

The third possible new frontier, optimists believe, is provided by Australia and New Zealand, which are also engaged in a process of economic liberalization (ironically under nominally socialist governments). Their resolve to shed rigid controls over the economy and its component parts may have in the long run far-reaching domestic and regional repercussions. Both countries have a small population, but optimists expect them, particularly Australia, to increase their level of immigration from Asia in the next few decades. The new arrivals will have solid professional qualifications and/or substantial capital and will act as agents of socioeconomic change because of their work ethic and propensity to accumulate. Moreover, although optimists concede that Australia and New Zealand will remain relatively small markets even if their governments adopt more forward-looking immigration policies, they argue that these two countries enjoy a reasonably high standard of living and hence revitalization of the Australian and New Zealand economies will produce spillover effects throughout Asia by manifesting itself in stronger effective demand.

The fourth new frontier regarded by optimists as a potential source of future regional dynamism is Siberia. In view of the emergence of a more pragmatic leadership in the Soviet Union, the possibility that Japan and the USSR might solve their territorial disputes—or at least find a way to manage them in a less damaging fashion—cannot be ruled out. The Japanese have long been interested in resource-rich Siberia, and their interest could be translated into large-scale investment when political circumstances are propitious. Such a development would scarcely be as significant from the perspective of Hong Kong as the deradicalization of the PRC, yet the territory might benefit considerably in the process because of the strategic role it plays in the economy of Asia and the Pacific region.

Optimists are aware of the argument that China could flood the world with cheap products and undermine Hong Kong's manufacturing industry in the process, but they discount this threat for at least two reasons. First, strong pent-up demand in the PRC will compel the mainland to divert the bulk of its resources towards satisfying domestic needs. Second, the Hong Kong manufacturing sector will undergo a structural transformation and become geared almost exclusively to production emphasizing high technology and craftsmanship. Rather than having to contend with a competitive threat from China, local industrialists will, as indicated, benefit by moving labour-intensive operations to the mainland and concentrating on skill-intensive ones, and by establishing vertically integrated businesses with land-intensive and resource-intensive processes in the PRC and management-intensive and technology-intensive ones in the territory. (The factor endowments of China and Hong Kong are said to be largely complementary: China has abundant land, natural resources, raw materials, unskilled labour, a large industrial system and heavy industries, and relatively advanced basic research in electronics. Hong Kong excels in management—particularly marketing—and product design and is blessed with an educated and disciplined work force, flexible economic environment, and an efficient physical and institutional infrastructure.)

Optimists are somewhat more concerned about the competitive threat from South Korea and Taiwan, two countries in a better position than the PRC to challenge local manufacturers in world markets. Unlike the territory, South Korea and Taiwan have a fairly large population and a reasonably broad industrial base; unlike the PRC, they are capable of producing high-quality goods and services. Nonetheless, optimists doubt that South Korean and Taiwanese exporters will drive their Hong Kong counterparts from key markets. According to them, the world economy will grow at a sufficient pace to allow continuing expansion throughout East Asia (and, for that matter, Southeast Asia). Furthermore, Hong Kong's greater flexibility and the synergy to be achieved through integration between the local industry and manufacturing activities in China will help the territory to assume its previous role as the region's most dynamic exporter.

Nor is there a danger, optimists assert, of the territory being overshadowed as a service centre by other large cities in China. It is true that Hong Kong's preeminence partly hinges on the failure of the urban system in the PRC to perform sophisticated economic functions and that Chinese policymakers accord the problem a high priority. Yet the mainland will need several decades to restore Shanghai to its rightful place as the country's economic capital, and the territory will continue to enjoy a virtual monopoly in supplying high-quality urban services to the PRC for a long time to come. It is also unrealistic to assume that Hong Kong will lapse into a state of decay in the wake of the development experienced by other Chinese cities. On the contrary, urban reform in the PRC will be a source of new opportunities and will stimulate rather than retard the growth of the territory's service sector.

Optimists acknowledge that the emergence of Tokyo as an international financial centre poses a greater threat to Hong Kong in this respect. They dismiss, however, the notion that international finance is a "zero-sum game" in which the gains achieved by one player inevitably result in losses to the other participants. Asia, it is argued, can accommodate at least four major financial centres: Hong Kong, Singapore, Sydney, and Tokyo. Moreover, the expansion and deregulation of the Tokyo market might actually benefit all four cities by substantially increasing the volume of transactions in the region. If Tokyo thrives, then Hong Kong, Singapore, and Sydney are likely to prosper by becoming to it what Frankfurt, Paris, and Zurich are to London. Indeed, thus far the rapid development of the Tokyo market has not attracted business from financial centres located in different time zones (e.g., London and New York) and those adjacent to it. Tokyo's growth, after all, has primarily taken the form of mobilizing Japan's capital surplus for the rest of the world. As one key informant has suggested: "What we are creating in Tokyo is something that did not exist in the past. It does not involve taking away things from other people."

Even the opening of an offshore banking market in Tokyo is not viewed by optimists as a cause for alarm. In discussing the regional implications of this step, they invoke again their thesis that "the greater the number of players, the greater the volume of business." The thesis is buttressed by empirical evidence of an indirect nature, particularly the fact that the New York offshore banking unit, which commenced operation in 1981, has had no adverse effect on existing offshore centres and has favourably influenced the development of the Euromarkets. As elaborated later in this chapter, there is no reason why the impact of the Tokyo offshore market should diverge from this pattern.

It ought to be emphasized that optimists do not expect Hong Kong's financial institutions to become mere adjuncts to their Tokyo counterparts but rather to maintain the leading regional role they have enjoyed since the 1970s. The assumption is that Japan—given the large foreign trade surpluses it generates, the high propensity to save of its population, the traditionally low interest rates prevailing there, and the strength of the yen—will continue to serve as the world's principal exporter of capital without, however, seriously challenging Hong Kong's position as the place best equipped to package financial products suitable to the needs of Asian borrowers. (The territory's ability in this respect, optimists assert, has never been backed by a locally held pool of foreign funds.) This assumption, in turn, is rooted in the belief that because Hong Kong provides a far more attractive business environment, it cannot be eclipsed by Tokyo.

Specifically, the territory is thought to have the following advantages: a liberal regulatory climate, low taxation, British legal system (which also governs Euromarket transactions), central location, cosmopolitan orientation, ample supply of English-speaking professionals and paraprofessionals, and a moderate cost of living. Tokyo, on the other hand, is subject to rigid controls, imposes heavy taxes on corporate entities (as well as high-income earners), operates within an unfamiliar and perhaps even obscure legal framework, is located on the region's periphery, tends to be inward-looking, suffers from an inadequate supply of English-speaking personnel, and is prohibitively expensive.

Japan could, of course, relax its financial regulations and lower tax rates and thus enhance the attraction of Tokyo as a centre of international finance. Optimists, however, are of the opinion that the process of financial liberalization in Japan is going to be painfully slow. They contend that the restrictive nature of the Tokyo offshore market, which opened in 1986, is a case in point. (The term "offshore market" does not refer to a physical entity but to accounts kept separate from those pertaining to domestic business, so to fit the concept of an out-out market.) Offshore banking markets are normally exempt from many regulations and taxes that apply to domestic banking. They offer a place for depositors—in Japan for corporate nonresidents only—to park surplus cash on favourable terms and for banks to lend the funds with relative freedom. The problem with the Tokyo offshore market, though, particularly as foreign bankers see it, is that few inducements have been furnished to transfer trading from other offshore centres in the region. Although entities are exempt from the 20 percent withholding tax, interest regulations, reserve requirements, and deposit insurance schemes, operators in the market are liable for corporate and local taxes as well as stamp duties. Consequently, the tax burden on offshore business may be as high as 62.5 percent, compared with 10 percent in Singapore and zero in Hong Kong. Furthermore, the Ministry of Finance has set strict rules insulating the domestic market from the offshore market, which is being confined to deposits and loans. Securities transactions, an increasingly important aspect of international finance, are forbidden.

The corollary, optimists conclude, is that banks are not likely to transfer assets to Tokyo from either Hong Kong or Singapore. What will be transferred to the new market, according to them, are foreign loans and other assets, totalling an estimated US $80 billion to US $130 billion, presently booked by Japanese and foreign banks in Tokyo. Optimists note that a similar accounting exercise took place when New York opened its international banking facilities (IBF). The IBF, upon which the somewhat more rigidly regulated Tokyo market is modelled, aimed at drawing business from Caribbean banking centres as well as London. However, as one key informant has vividly recalled: "It was the biggest nothing of the twentieth century. Those assets that were transferred were all in New York in the first place. It will probably be the same in Tokyo."

Hence, although the opening of the Tokyo offshore market is a step forward in the process of economic liberalization in Japan, optimists scarcely see it as a formidable challenge to Hong Kong's buoyant financial sector. The new facility will doubtless stimulate the growing world Euroyen market and might help the small Japanese banks enter the world stage. However, unless Japan offers more substantial regulatory and tax concessions, booking of offshore business in Asia will continue to take place predominantly in Hong Kong and Singapore. Indeed, given the prevalence of regulatory and tax disincentives, it is reasonable to assume that the loans likely to end up in the Tokyo offshore market will be yen-denominated, raised from the vast pool of yen funds in Japan and provided to corporations and governments throughout the world, thereby contributing to the growing use of the yen as an international currency but in no way detracting from the role of Hong Kong and Singapore as intermediaries for dollar-denominated financing.

Optimists, however, are less interested in outlining the restrictive features of the Tokyo offshore market and analyzing their consequences than in dissecting the official attitudes which account for the slow pace of liberalization. They perceive Japanese bureaucrats as excessively cautious and resistant to change. Their deep-rooted conservatism—of which the half-hearted attempt to develop offshore banking facilities is presumably symptomatic—will remain a stumbling block to the emergence of Tokyo as a financial centre of a genuinely international character. Nor is it just a matter of bureaucratic culture and inertia. Optimists doubt the willingness of Japanese officials to allow Tokyo to assume a dominant position in international finance. They argue that Tokyo's progress will be less spectacular than that of Hong Kong because of government policies that emphasize Japan's role as a manufacturing and exporting nation rather than as a financial centre. (The same possibly applies to the US and West Germany, which may explain why New York and Frankfurt lag behind London as centres of international finance.)

Optimists lay particular stress on the fact that Japanese bureaucrats are decidedly uneasy about the inevitable internationalization of the yen. They do not want the yen exposed to the kind of pressures that previously afflicted the pound sterling and presently plague the dollar, and thus they intend to facilitate the process only to the extent necessary to minimize American discontent. Both Japanese officials and financiers draw parallels between Hong Kong and London as highly deregulated and multicurrency financial centres and insist that restrictive climate and reliance on the home currency detract from the attraction of New York and Tokyo. They, as well as others, claim that Hong Kong essentially serves as an "offshore Tokyo" (though both centres are in the same time zone) and that Japan's policy is to preserve the status quo in this respect for as long as possible. In fact, some of the key informants I interviewed held such strong convictions with regard to Japan's strategic posture vis-à-vis the territory that they were prepared to argue that the uncharacteristic measure of support received by Hong Kong from the Japanese during the Sino-British negotiations stemmed from a desire to safeguard a working arrangement that dovetails with their economic plans.

Optimists concede that Tokyo's development as an international financial centre might be more dramatic than they envisage or than the bureaucratic-industrial establishment in Japan wants it to be. Even under such circumstances, however, the territory need not suffer. Specifically, the China market should offset any loss to Hong Kong caused by Tokyo's emergence. In the absence of any major policy reversal there, the PRC will continue to be among the world's fastest-growing countries. Although foreign bankers often complain that conducting business in China is slow and frustrating, the opportunities are considerable. One of my key informants, for instance, has estimated that between 1986 and 1995 the PRC will have to introduce foreign capital amounting to about US $70 billion. As in the past, China will doubtless aim to obtain cheap funds from foreign governments and multinational organizations such as the World Bank and the Asian Development Bank. This concessionary funding will probably account for 70 to 80 percent of its total borrowings. A significant portion, however, will need to be financed from commercial sources through loans and securities. (Although it is relatively easy for established PRC entities to raise funds by issuing bonds, less prominent organizations have to resort to loans; this is why syndication is not expected to become obsolete on the mainland.)

Optimists postulate that Hong Kong–based banks will be the institutions to which China will turn for commercial borrowing and that the territory will consequently become the principal lender to the PRC, albeit not to the exclusion of other places. Hong Kong's attraction for China lies in its proximity to the mainland, its sophisticated and flexible financial infrastructure, the fact that it is populated by people who are not complete strangers and with whose ways visitors from the PRC are reasonably familiar, and the role it plays in facilitating investment in China and supporting the mainland's external trade. Optimists contend that to bypass the territory and borrow directly in, say, Tokyo would not constitute a sensible strategy. They predict that the PRC will step up its fund-raising activities in Hong Kong by issuing more bonds there—and in the process help the territory develop its capital market and strengthen its edge over Tokyo as an international financial centre. Optimists also take the view that the territory is seen as a gateway to China by foreign banks hoping to provide retail services there. Hence, should Tokyo experience rapid expansion, its rise would in all probability prove more costly for Singapore, which cannot count on the PRC factor to cushion the effects of regional economic transformation, than for Hong Kong.

Indeed, optimists believe that Singapore too will not be able to mount a serious challenge to the territory in the domain of international finance. The island republic already trails Hong Kong in several important financial areas, including domestic capital market activities, fund management, and loan syndication. Its relative strengths—foreign exchange trading, interbank lending, and offshore deposit-taking—have made Singapore an Asian leader in external assets, but it cannot rely on such basic services to sustain itself as a major financial centre. In addition, unlike the territory, which serves as a base to numerous institutions engaged in finance, Singapore has not established an imposing reputation in the financial sector, and given that its population is considerably smaller than Hong Kong's, foreign banks find less scope for undertaking retail operations there. Finally, Singapore does not have the advantage of the territory's central location, and it suffers from the proximity to the potentially vulnerable economies of two commodity producers, Indonesia and Malaysia. By contrast, Hong Kong is part of a dynamic East Asian subregion consisting of itself, China, South Korea, and Taiwan.

Singapore obviously has some potential as a centre of international finance because of its political stability, legal system (which is based on the common law), English-speaking population, and excellent physical and social infrastructure. More significantly, the country's leadership appears determined to loosen its tight grip on the economy and lower business costs. Optimists, however, argue that the attempts to foster a better corporate climate are not sufficiently far-reaching and that the turnaround in government policy has come so late that it may not fully restore foreign confidence for a long period of time. Actors in the international financial arena will continue to operate in the Singapore market—where, like in Tokyo, the distinction between domestic and offshore business is strictly adhered to—but they will be more inclined to establish presence and seek opportunities in Hong Kong.

Another potentially damaging development optimists do not view with trepidation is the upsurge in protectionism. They maintain that the gains from free trade outweigh by far the costs and that the clamour for protectionist legislation in the West, particularly in the US, will prove to be a temporary phenomenon. The trend is towards lowering barriers to free trade rather than raising them, and the present imbalances in the international economic system and the tough posturing they have engendered will sooner or later lead to market-opening initiatives that will be of wide geographical scope and more than cosmetic in nature. Equally important, optimists suggest, is the fact that the "new political culture" is not conducive to protectionism. As one key informant has observed:

> The post–Second World War baby boomers tend to be conservative and materialistic. They are not about to part with their Audis or their Panasonic stereos. The ageing population is known to have a strong fear of inflation. It will want low-cost imports. Minorities—especially the rapidly expanding Hispanic and Asian populations—will have a greater cultural affinity for foreign goods. More and more interest groups will become less protectionist. The US has a growing services sector which seeks access to foreign markets. Service industries will not wish to jeopardize their chances with a protectionist stance at home and the retaliation that it might provoke. US farmers are also preoccupied with exports. They will fight protectionism vehemently. There are some industries like cars where the import penetration is so great that neither consumers nor all the businesses that have grown up around the imports will tolerate major new protectionist measures. Finally, there is a new internationalist movement at the state and local level. Governors and mayors have established offices all over the world to promote trade and foreign investment. Congress may occasionally get carried away with protectionist rhetoric. But below the federal level most politicians are not listening.

Reasonably easy access to foreign markets will help sustain the dynamism of the Hong Kong economy, optimists assert. They further elaborate that the territory will benefit perhaps even more than will other trading entities from the dismantling of barriers which hinder international business transactions because of the "maturing of the computer age." Specifically, the advent of sophisticated means of data management, coupled with rapid product obsolescence, will prove advantageous to economic systems which are able to cope with constant shifts in demand. Hong Kong is the epitome of such a system and should, therefore, enjoy a high degree of prosperity.

Process

Optimists contend that the uncertainty surrounding the future of the territory has largely evaporated in the wake of the signing of the Sino-British Joint Declaration and now that it has become apparent that the reform process in the PRC has reached a point of no return. The residue of uncertainty which remains is perceived as tolerable by most economic actors who have a stake in Hong Kong and is expected to be reduced to an absolute minimum (e.g., the level which prevailed before the 1997 issue surfaced in the early 1980s) sometime after 2000. Optimists anticipate that the remaining uncertainty will be reduced in three stages.

The first stage will culminate in the promulgation in 1990 of the territory's Basic Law, which will render the grey areas in the Joint Declaration less grey, will be liberal in spirit, and will embody institutional arrangements designed to promote prosperity and stability. The promulgation of the Basic Law will coincide with the realization of the objectives of the current five-year plan in China and the implementation of further financial and industrial reforms there. (For example, by 1990 the PRC should lease the operation of small-scale enterprises to individuals and collective entities.) Another landmark event during the first stage will be the smooth transfer of power from China's present leaders to their younger and even more reform-minded successors.

The second stage will last from 1991 to 2000. During this period Hong Kong will function within the framework provided by the Basic Law (optimists think most of the post-1997 institutions will emerge in the early 1990s), under Sino-British guidance but gradually moving towards de facto self-government. Internal progress in the territory will, again, be matched by external progress in the PRC. Specifically, the privatization programme there will gather momentum and be extended to medium- and large-scale enterprises. Put another way, the operations of business entities will no longer be subject to official interference, and the government will exercise control by manipulating indirect macro- and microeconomic policy instruments. China will also become a more open society based on the "rule of law" rather than the "rule of man," the CCP will disengage itself from state activities, and the rigid "top-down" system of societal steering which has prevailed since the revolution will give way to one entailing a measure of public accountability.

Optimists foresee less uncertainty in the second stage of Hong Kong's evolution from a British colony into a Chinese SAR than in the first one. However, they emphasize that local confidence may not return to the high level witnessed before the PRC signalled its intention to assume the exercise of sovereignty over the territory until the year 2000 or shortly thereafter. Given China's unhappy record of broken promises and gross mismanagement, local residents will be fully reassured only after Hong Kong has enjoyed about three successful years as a self-governing entity administered in accordance with the spirit and the letter of the Sino-British Joint Declaration. Yet because there is little doubt that the necessary "demonstration effect" will be achieved, the territory may expect to enter around the year 2000 a long period devoid of any significant uncertainty and characterized by impressive growth. This period constitutes the third stage in the optimists' developmental model.

Evaluation

Criticism of the optimistic scenario is implicit in its pessimistic and trend counterparts—and, of course, vice versa. Therefore, the critical assessment offered in the present section focuses on those aspects of the scenario whose problematic nature cannot be readily inferred, whether directly or indirectly, from the more gloomy constructs. Moreover, rather than dissecting each of the assumptions underlying the optimists' vision of the Hong Kong future, I instead attempt to examine key assumptions which merit particular attention. A similar approach will be adopted in evaluating the pessimistic and trend scenarios.

Thus, one fairly serious criticism which may possibly be levelled at optimists is that they tend to engage in a form of analysis referred to as "economism" (or, alternatively, "economic determinism").[15] This involves (1) the overestimation of the political influence of economic variables, which are deemed exogenous and hence independent of political variables, and (2) the underestimation of the influence of political variables in the determination of political outcomes. In other words, variation in political variables is explained predominantly in terms of economic variables whose values are determined independently of political factors.

For instance, optimists portray Chinese policymakers as being propelled almost exclusively by economic considerations, an orientation which manifests itself both internally and externally. In the internal context, the PRC leadership is said to be preoccupied with the material benefits that would accrue from reforming the economy; in the external context, the leaders stress the economic advantages that China derives from the status quo in Hong Kong and the costs that would be incurred if the capitalist enclave were prevented from practicing its particular brand of laissez-faire. Optimists are not oblivious to the influence of other factors, such as the desire to bring about national unification, but they accord to net material benefits far greater significance and perhaps distort reality somewhat in the process.

Even when they incorporate noneconomic variables into their explanatory models, optimists appear to postulate that policymakers in the PRC are concerned primarily with promoting the "national interest."[16] The possibility that the Chinese leadership may also seek to further more parochial interests—e.g., those of the party (or factions within it), of the state apparatus, of particular regions, of different generations, of specific individuals—or that it may still be driven by ideology is scarcely given any attention. Top decisionmakers in the PRC may indeed be imbued with a strong sense of "national mission." To the extent that they are, Hong Kong is likely to benefit, but it is unrealistic to assume that they refrain from pursuing narrow interests[17] and that the mainland is witnessing the "end of ideology."[18]

In addition, optimists seem to attribute to Chinese leaders greater "rationality" than they may in fact possess. To be more explicit, policymakers in the PRC are depicted as having a set of carefully formulated and well-integrated objectives with respect to Hong Kong (i.e., a "utility function").[19] These objectives and the relationships among them are virtually immune to change, and the multiple actors who make and execute policy affecting the territory display such a consensus that they may be thought of as a single decisionmaker (hence the phrase "Beijing wishes"). Another remarkable quality ascribed to the actors in question is their ability to be intimately familiar with conditions in Hong Kong and devise strategies which dovetail with these conditions and serve best the objectives of prosperity and stability that are shared by China and the territory.

Nor are the PRC leaders' formidable talents, as viewed by optimists, confined to the rigorous specification of objectives, consistent expression of preferences, conflict management, acquisition of perfect information, and design of optimal policies. The PRC is apparently capable of ensuring that the rational strategies it has proposed as a solution to the "Hong Kong problem" are implemented according to plan, but this too is an assumption which ought perhaps to be challenged. Policy implementation poses considerable difficulties under most circumstances. In the particular case of steering the territory towards long-term prosperity and stability, the conversion of what may well constitute good intentions into workable arrangements could arguably prove to be a far more daunting task than optimists envisage.

Indeed, there is ample evidence to suggest that policymakers, even those operating in a relatively sophisticated institutional milieu, often act contrary to the assumptions underlying the optimistic scenario. For one thing, public decisions are shaped by political as well as economic forces[20]—certainly, the kind of narrow economic cost-benefit calculus employed by optimists seldom serves as the sole criterion in formulating national strategies.[21] By the same token, policymakers do not seem to be motivated by the noble desire to advance the national interest alone; in fact, a good many social scientists see public officials as "political entrepreneurs" engaged in a quest for personal gains rather than collective benefits.[22] The prevalence of political entrepreneurship, however, has by no means spelt the end of ideology, and ideologically inspired behaviour is not uncommon in the public arena.[23] Policymaking also does not really qualify as a purely rational activity: Public officials "muddle through,"[24] "satisfice,"[25] "adapt,"[26] pursue a mixture of rational and superficial strategies referred to as "mixed scanning,"[27] and are part of complex organizational bureaucratic dynamics[28]—that is, their performance falls short of translating in a consensual fashion a stable utility function into an optimal policy. Finally, sensible strategies do not meet expectations because of implementation failures.[29]

Nor do studies of Chinese politics lend unequivocal support to the assumptions relied upon by optimists. There is no dearth of scholars who believe that the PRC leadership is involved in a quasi-rational search for ways to promote modernization objectives,[30] but the academic literature abounds with alternative models of the policy process on the mainland.[31] One salient feature of these models is the emphasis on the lack of consensus among members of the Chinese political elite. Even those researchers who, to paraphrase Downs, [32] regard top cadres in the PRC as "advocates" or "statesman," guided principally by their perception of the national interest, deem them markedly divided on questions of policy.

Thus, Oksenberg and Goldestein[33] have divided Chinese leaders into four opinion clusters: militant fundamentalists, radical conservatives, eclectic modernizers, and Westernized Chinese. Similarly, Ahn[34] has differentiated between those inclined towards transformation and those favouring consolidation. Another writer who has highlighted elite conflict in the PRC is Chang,[35] whose work explores the policy implications of the schism between radicals and conservatives. The typologies produced by these authors largely reflect the turmoil of the Cultural Revolution and possibly no longer accurately mirror Chinese political realities. The theme of a divided leadership, however, continues to loom large in post-1978 analyses of policymaking in the PRC.

Moody,[36] for instance, places considerable emphasis on the differences between reformers and restorationists. (According to him, leftists are no longer a significant force in Chinese politics.) Restorationists display less liberal attitudes than reformers and are particularly inclined to favour centralized/command forms of economic management. They are referred to as "restorationists" because of their belief that the PRC economy can be revitalized by restoring the policies pursued before the Great Leap Forward. Reformers, on the other hand, contend that mistakes have occurred throughout the period since 1949.

A somewhat more elaborate classification has been suggested by

Table 4.1 Three Positions on Economic Policy in the PRC

	Speed	Investment in light industry versus heavy	Central planning	Timing of decentralization	Deficits/ inflation	Foreign trade	Administrative versus economic regulation of the economy
Reformers	Slow[a]	Pro-light[a]	Anti	Sooner	Less concerned[a]	Pro	Economic primary
Adjusters	Slow[a]	Pro-light[a]	Pro[a]	Later[a]	Concerned	Have reservations[a]	Administrative primary[a]
Conservers	High	Pro-heavy	Usually pro[a]	Usually later[a]	Some in this group do not pay attention to this issue;[a] others do	Have reservations[a]	Usually favour administrative[a]

Source: D.J. Solinger, "The Fifth National People's Congress and the Process of Policy Making," *Asian Survey* 22 (December 1982), p. 1244.
[a]Indicates agreement between two stances on a given issue.

Harding,[37] who maintains that top Chinese cadres can be characterized as utopians, developmentalists, and liberals. Perhaps the most influential typology constructed in recent years, however, has been that of Solinger.[38] She has come to the conclusion that the political elite in the PRC is fragmented along the following lines: reformers, adjusters, and conservers. The issues on which their views appear to diverge are shown in Table 4.1. As Solinger has explained:

> Adjusters and Reformers agree on slowing down growth and on putting more investment into light industry, but differ on the importance of central planning and on the timing of decentralization. Reformers favour carrying it out sooner, and Adjusters later. Adjusters are more concerned about deficits and inflation than Reformers are, and the Conservers generally pay less attention to this issue than Adjusters do. Conservers, like Adjusters, usually are more oriented towards planning and centralization than Reformers are, although this is not always the case with the Conservers, and the two disagree on the questions of speed and on whether or not to invest more in heavy industry. Finally, Reformers are the most prone to advocate foreign trade, with Adjusters worrying about its effect on the budget and Conservers uneasy about the possibility of importing machinery that could be made by the factories in China itself.[39]

Nor is it just a matter of genuine policy differences. Some students of Chines politics[40] do not subscribe to theories of leadership behaviour which rest on the assumption that top cadres on the mainland are driven by the desire to promote their vision of the national interest. Rather, these observers regard the leaders, to paraphrase Downs[41] again, as "zealots" whose actions reflect the parochial interests of segments of the party and state bureaucracies. Other but broadly similar models of the Chinese policy process portray decisionmaking in the PRC as a competition among the different generations which enjoy elite status[42] or as an interaction of the various socioeconomic groups discernible in the political arena.[43] Needless to say, the national interest motive does not feature in such models either.

Possibly an even greater challenge to the premises upon which the optimistic scenario is based is posed by the work of scholars who reduce the complexities of Chinese politics to factional conflicts dominated by self-interested players. A recent study by Pye[44] is a case in point. He sets out by acknowledging that the "Chinese, whether Confucianists or Communists, have persistently believed that government should be guided only by ethical imperatives and ideological prescriptions, never by the dynamics of political contention. Indeed, one of the most distinct characteristics of the Chinese has been their uncompromising denial of legitimacy to the clash of power and values, of men and opinions, which nearly all other people accept as the normal basis for public life."⁴⁵ However, having stated that Chinese culture accords great importance to consensus, Pye then proceeds to develop the thesis that policymaking in the PRC largely revolves around the formation and maintenance of personal factions:

> The prime bases of factions are power constellations of clusters of officials who for some reason or other feel comfortable with each other, who believe that they can share mutual trust and loyalties, and who may recognize common foes. More often than not, the real motivation is that of career security and enhancement, whether it be at the lowest county or provincial committee level or among those on the Politburo and the State Council jockeying for greater influence. The glue that holds factions together can thus be either mutual career self-interest or the highly particularistic sentiments associated with personal ties in Chinese culture, that is, the spirit of *guanxi*. . . . Chinese factions are *not* formed primarily in response to policy issues, bureaucratic interests, generational differences, or geographical bases, although these considerations do play a part, and policy is indeed affected by the outcome of factional tensions. Neither are ideological considerations of prime importance, although in their differing collective orientations, the current political factions in the PRC do have certain policy biases. The prime basis for factions among cadres is the search for career security and the protection of power. The extraordinary force that holds together the networks of officials is the intense attraction of mutual dependency in Chinese culture between superiors and subordinates, each of whom needs the other for his own protection and each of whom is vulnerable to the other, which means that both must be loyal to each other. Thus, the strength of Chinese factions is the personal relationships of individuals who, operating in a hierarchical context, create linkage networks that extend upward in support of particular leaders who are, in turn, looking for followers to ensure their power.⁴⁶

Equally problematic from the optimistic perspective are studies⁴⁷ which lend support to the argument that policymaking in the PRC is not characterized by a high degree of continuity. Rather, strategic commitments are made and discarded with considerable frequency, and the ensuing change is often drastic both in form and substance. As Nathan has observed: "That Chinese policy since 1949 has been characterized by a pattern of left-right oscillations is one of the most widespread . . . assumptions among analysts of Chinese politics. In the popular press, we often read of a 'return to a moderate phase' or a 'resurgence of radicalism,' while in academic writing, we frequently find contemporary Chinese history set in periods according to the alternate ascendancy of 'bureaucratic' or 'mobilizational' models or of 'realist' and 'visionary' groups of leaders."⁴⁸

There is also ample evidence[49] to suggest that policies in the PRC are not implemented in accordance with the plans of those who formulate them. This partly reflects the fact that the political elite is fragmented and that the factions which make it up are determined to ensure that policy implementation dovetails with their particular vision of China and is conducive to their special interests. The problem is compounded by the loose control exercised by policymakers over policy implementers, who tend to respond to initiatives emanating from the political centre with tactics designed to minimize the threat to the values they uphold and the advantages they (and those associated with them) derive from the status quo.

The corollary of this conclusion presumably is that one cannot take it for granted, as optimists are inclined to do, that Chinese policymakers will endeavour to adhere faithfully to the spirit of the Sino-British Joint Declaration out of fear that any departures from it might prove prohibitively costly in the economic sense of the term—political considerations could prompt them to adopt a mix of strategies that might sap the vitality of the Hong Kong economy. Moreover, the assumption that the PRC leadership will strive to guarantee the success of the "one country, two systems" formula on grounds that it serves the nation's interest is not entirely valid: Top cadres on the mainland subscribe to different conceptions of the national interest and are, in any event, often propelled by motives which do not concern the well-being of the nation. Finally, and irrespective of whether the intentions of key segments of the Chinese political elite are honourable or not, one cannot rule out the possibility that the blueprint produced by PRC and British negotiators will fail to materialize because of implementation difficulties.

There is another point. Optimists are convinced that politico-economic evolution in China is proceeding in a manner consistent with what students of social change[50] describe as "unilinear theories of social progress." That is, they see uninterrupted movement towards market socialism (and possibly beyond), "regularization" (i.e., substituting state institutions that abide by the rule book in place of arbitrary decision and action),[51] and "spiritual materialism" (i.e., substantial relaxation of ideological controls).[52] The inevitable transformation of the PRC along such lines is, of course, regarded by them as highly reassuring from Hong Kong's standpoint because it will bring about a partial convergence between two systems not presently compatible. However, a good many scholars[53] doubt that China will undergo in the foreseeable future, if at all, the kind of metamorphosis optimists envisage, and they question that the development path it will follow will be free of twists and turns. Most of the notes of caution these observers have sounded have been supported by careful analysis; thus, the foundation upon which the optimistic scenario rests may well be less solid than those who believe it to represent an accurate picture of the future tend to assume.

Notes

1. C.A. Johnson, *MITI and the Japanese Miracle* (Stanford, Calif.: Stanford University Press, 1982); C.A. Johnson, "Political Institutions and Economic Performance," in *Asian Economic Development—Present and Future*, ed. R.A. Scalapino, S.S. Sato, and J.Wanandi (Berkeley: Institute of East Asian Studies, University of California, 1985), pp. 63–89. See also L.W. Pye and M.W. Pye, *Asian Power and Politics* (Cambridge, Mass.: Belknap Press, 1985).

2. For a detailed analysis of the Joint Declaration, see C.D. Day, "The Recovery of Hong Kong by the People's Republic of China—A Fifty-Year Experiment," *Syracuse Journal of International Law and Commerce* 11 (Winter 1984): 625–649; E.M. Amberg, "Self-Determination in Hong Kong," *San Diego Law Review* 22 (July/August 1985): 839–858; D. Bonavia, *Hong Kong and 1997* (Hong Kong: South China Morning Post, 1985); L.A. Castle, "The Reversion of Hong Kong to China," *Wilamette Law Review* 21 (Spring 1985): 327–348; F. Ching, *Hong Kong and China* (New York: The China Council of the Asia Society and Foreign Policy Association, 1985); H. Chiu, "The 1984 Sino-British Implications on China's Unification," *Issues and Studies* 21 (April 1985): 13–22; S.L. Karamanian, "The Legal Future of Hong Kong," *Texas International Law Journal* 20 (Winter 1985): 167–188; T.S. Macintyre, "Impact of the Sino-British Agreement on Hong Kong's Future," *Journal of Comparative Business and Capital Market Law* 7 (June 1985): 197–216; J.Y.S. Cheng, "Hong Kong," *Asia Pacific Community* 31 (Winter 1986): 19–44; R. Mushkat, "The Transition from British to Chinese Rule in Hong Kong," *Denver Journal of International Law and Policy* 14 (Winter/Spring 1986): 171–206; P. Wesley-Smith, "Settlement of the Question of Hong Kong," *California Western International Law Journal* 17 (Winter 1987): 116–132.

3. As Deng Xiaoping has asserted: "Since the Korean War, China has won a good reputation internationally. Even in the years of turmoil [the Cultural Revolution] the Chinese people meant what they said in international affairs. Acting in good faith is a tradition of our nation and also its strong point. This really indicates that ours is a great, proud and ancient country. A big nation should have its own dignity and its own principles to follow." See Ching, *Hong Kong and China*, p. 61.

4. The national reputation factor is also accorded considerable weight by the senior unofficial member of the Hong Kong Legislative Council (LEGCO):

> I believe there are a number of reasons why the terms of the Agreement will be implemented faithfully. In the first place, it is a formal, legally binding international agreement freely negotiated, against a background of friendship, between two sovereign states. The agreement may not be legally enforceable but, with the Joint Declaration now signed, both governments have formally agreed to implement the terms of the Joint Declaration and its Annexes. The honour and reputation of both governments is thus committed internationally. The world at large will be watching during the next twelve years or so for any signs that the terms of the Agreement will be disregarded. . . . [T]he Chinese leadership has stated with conviction and apparent sincerity in explicit terms that the Agreement will be implemented.

The Chinese leaders have therefore publicly staked their personal prestige and reputation in the eyes of the world.

See L. Dunn, "Hong Kong After the Sino-British Declaration," *International Affairs* 61 (Spring 1985): 197–204.

5. For a discussion of the Basic Law, see Bonavia, *Hong Kong and 1997*; Ching, *Hong Kong and China*; Cheng, "Hong Kong"; N.J. Miners, *The Government and Politics of Hong Kong* (Hong Kong: Oxford University Press, 1986). See also A.P. Blaustein, "Drafting a New Constitution for the Hong Kong Special Administration Region," in *Hong Kong and 1997*, ed. Y.C. Jao et al. (Hong Kong: Centre of Asian Studies, University of Hong Kong, 1985), pp. 201–212; W.S. Clarke, "The Constitution of Hong Kong 1997," in *Hong Kong and 1997*, ed. Jao et al., pp. 215–233; A.H.Y. Chen, "Hong Kong's Legal System," in *Hong Kong and 1997*, ed. Jao et al, pp. 235–261.

6. See also J. Woronoff, *Hong Kong* (Hong Kong: Heinemann Asia, 1980); Bonavia, *Hong Kong and 1997*; Ching, *Hong Kong and China*; Miners, *The Government and Politics of Hong Kong*; P.B. Harris, "The International Future of Hong Kong," *International Affairs* 48 (January 1972): 60–71; D. Wilson, "New Thoughts on the Future of Hong Kong," *Pacific Community* 8 (July 1977): 588–599; P.B. Harris, *Hong Kong* (Hong Kong: Heinemann Asia, 1978); N.J. Miners, "Can the Colony of Hong Kong Survive 1997?" *Asia Pacific Community* 6 (Fall 1979): 100–104; A. Rabushka, *Hong Kong* (Chicago: University of Chicago Press, 1979); G. Lawrie, "Hong Kong and the People's Republic of China," *International Affairs* 56 (Spring 1980): 280–295; J.Y.S. Cheng, "The Future of Hong Kong," *International Affairs* 58 (Summer 1982): 476–488; G. Newsham, "Rethinking Hong Kong," *UCLA Pacific Basin Law Journal* 1 (Fall 1982): 247–264; A.J. Youngson, *Hong Kong* (Hong Kong: Oxford University Press, 1982); J. Greenfield, "The Hong Kong Solution," *Australian Outlook* 37 (April 1983): 29–33; A.J. Youngson, ed., *China and Hong Kong* (Hong Kong: Oxford University Press, 1983); H.T.K. Au, *Possible Futures of Hong Kong* (Manoa: University of Hawaii, 1984); C.A. Johnson, "The Mouse-Trapping of Hong Kong," *Asian Survey* 24 (September 1984): 887–909; W.H. Overholt, "Hong Kong and the Crisis of Sovereignty," *Asian Survey* 24 (April 1984): 471–484; C.E. Beckett, "Hong Kong's China Market," *China Business Review* 12 (September-October 1985): 41–43; B.B. de Mesquita, D. Newman, and A. Rabushka, *Forecasting Political Events* (New Haven, Conn.: Yale University Press, 1985); H. Harding, "The Future of Hong Kong," *China Business Review* 12 (September-October 1985): 30–37; Y.C. Jao, "The Monetary System and the Future of Hong Kong," in *Hong Kong and 1997*, ed. Jao et al., pp. 361–395; Y.C. Jao, "Hong Kong's Future as a Financial Centre," *Three Banks Review* 145 (March 1985): 33–53; A.G. Kuhn, "Hong Kong and Its Future in Asia," *Aussen Politik* 36 (April 1985): 444–456; V. Menezes, "Hong Kong—Financial Centre for the Future?" in *Hong Kong and 1997*, ed. Jao et al., pp. 351–357; V. Mok, "Hong Kong's External Trade Relations at the Crossroads," in *Hong Kong and 1997*, ed. Jao et al., pp. 279–288; W.H. Overholt, "Hong Kong and China," *Current History* 84 (September 1985): 256–259, 274; D.K. Patel, "One Country, Two Systems—Prospects for Hong Kong's Economy Under Chinese Sovereignty," in *Hong Kong and 1997*, ed. Jao et al., pp. 325–344; V.F.S. Sit, "Hong Kong Industries," in *Hong Kong and 1997*, ed. Jao et al., pp. 271–277; Y.W. Sung, "The Role of the Government in the Future Industrial Development of Hong Kong,"

in *Hong Kong and 1997*, ed. Jao et al., pp. 405–440; J.F. Williams, "The Economies of Hong Kong and Taiwan and Their Future Relationships with the PRC," *Journal of Northeast Studies* 4 (Spring 1985): 58–80; J. Domes, "The Impact of the Hong Kong Problem and the Hong Kong Agreement on PRC Domestic Politics," *Issues and Studies* 22 (June 1986); 13–30; P.B. Harris, "Hong Kong Confronts 1997," *Pacific Affairs* 59 (Spring 1986): 45–68; P. Jacobs, "Hong Kong and the Modernization of China," *Journal of International Affairs* 39 (Winter 1986): 63–75; Y.C. Jao, "Hong Kong's Future as a Free Market Economy," *Issues and Studies* 22 (June 1986): 111–143; G.E. Johnson, "1997 and After," *Pacific Affairs* 59 (Summer 1986): 237–254; I. Kelly, *Hong Kong* (London: Macmillan, 1986); A.Y.C. King, "The Hong Kong Talks and Hong Kong Politics," *Issues and Studies* 22 (June 1986): 52–75; S.K. Lau and H.C. Kuan, "Hong Kong After the Sino-British Agreement," *Pacific Affairs* 59 (Summer 1986): 214–236; J.S. Prybyla, "The Hong Kong Agreement and Its Impact on the World Economy," *Issues and Studies* 22 (June 1986): 92–110; H. Chiu, Y.C. Jao, and Y.L. Wu, eds., *The Future of Hong Kong* (New York: Quorum Books, 1987).

7. See Lawrie, "Hong Kong and the People's Republic of China," p. 286.
8. Ibid., p. 287.
9. Ibid., pp. 287–288.
10. See Woronoff, *Hong Kong* pp. 232–233.
11. Ibid., p. 233.
12. Ibid.
13. See Lawrie, "Hong Kong and the People's Republic of China," p. 294.
14. See G. Benton, *The Hong Kong Crisis* (London: Pluto Press, 1983).
15. See R.K. Ashley, "Three Modes of Economism," *International Studies Quarterly* 27 (December 1983): 463–496
16. See J. Frankel, *National Interest* (London: Pall Mall Press, 1970).
17. See, for example, A. Downs, *Inside Bureaucracy* (Boston: Little, Brown, 1967); W.A. Niskanen, *Bureaucracy and Representative Government* (Chicago: Aldine-Atherton, 1971); J.M. Buchanan and R.E. Wagner, *Democracy in Deficit* (New York: Academic Press, 1977).
18. See D. Bell, *The End of Ideology* (Glencoe, Ill.: Free Press, 1960).
19. See H.A. Simon, *Reason in Human Affairs* (Oxford: Blackwell, 1983).
20. See, for example, E.R. Tufte, *Political Control of the Economy* (Princeton, N.J.: Princeton University Press, 1978); J.E. Alt and K.A. Chrystal, *Political Economics* (Brighton: Wheatsheaf Books, 1983); T.R. Dye, *Understanding Public Policy* (Englewood Cliffs, N.J.: Prentice-Hall, 1984).
21. See, for example: C.E. Lindblom, "The Science of Muddling Through," *Public Administration Review* 19 (Spring 1959): 79–88; C.E. Lindblom, *The Intelligence of Democracy* (New York: Free Press, 1965); D. Braybrooke and C.E. Lindblom, *A Strategy of Decision* (New York: Free Press, 1970); C.E. Lindblom, "Still Muddling, Not Yet Through," *Public Administration Review* 39 (November/December 1979): 517–526; A. Wildavsky, *Speaking Truth to Power* (Englewood Cliffs, N.J.: Prentice-Hall, 1980); A. Wildavsky, *The Politics of the Budgetary Process* (Boston: Little, Brown, 1984).
22. See, for example, Downs, *Inside Bureaucracy*; Niskanen, *Bureaucracy and Representative Government*; Buchanan and Wagner, *Democracy in Deficit*.

23. See R.E. Goodin, "Rational Politicians and Rational Bureaucrats in Washington and Whitehall," *Public Administration* 60 (Spring 1982): 23–41; S. Kelman, "'Public Choice' and Public Spirit" *Public Interest* 87 (Spring 1987): 80–94.

24. See Lindblom, "The Science of Muddling Through"; Lindblom, *The Intelligence of Democracy*; Braybrooke and Lindblom, *A Strategy of Decision*; Lindblom, "Still Muddling, Not Yet Through"; Wildavsky, *Speaking Truth to Power*; C.E. Lindblom, *The Policy Making Process* (Englewood Cliffs, N.J.: Prentice-Hall, 1980); Wildavsky, *The Politics of the Budgetary Process*.

25. See Simon, *Reason in Human Affairs*; H.A. Simon, *Models of Man* (New York: Wiley, 1957); H.A. Simon, *Administrative Behavior* (New York: Free Press, 1976).

26. See J.G. March and H.A. Simon, *Organizations* (New York: Wiley, 1958); J.D. Steinbruner, *The Cybernetic Theory of Decision* (Princeton, N.J.: Princeton University Press, 1974).

27. See A. Etzioni, "Mixed Scanning," *Public Administration Review* 17 (November-December 1967): 385–392; J.I. Gershuny, "Policymaking Rationality," *Policy Sciences* 9 (June 1978): 295–316; A. Etzioni, "Mixed Scanning Revisited," *Public Administration Review* 47 (January-February 1986): 8–14.

28. See G.T. Allison, "Conceptual Models and the Cuban Missile Crisis," *American Political Science Review* 63 (September 1969): 689–718; G.T. Allison, *Essence of Decision* (Boston: Little, Brown, 1971).

29. See J.I. Pressman and A. Wildavsky, *Implementation* (Berkeley: University of California Press, 1973).

30. See D.S. Zagoria, "China's Quiet Revolution," *Foreign Affairs* 62 (Spring 1984): 879–904.

31. See J.B. Starr, "From the Tenth Party Congress to the Premiership of Hua Kuo-feng," *China Quarterly* 67 (September 1976): 98–114; H. Harding, "Competing Models of the Chinese Communist Policy Process," *Issues and Studies* 20 (February 1984): 13–36.

32. Downs classifies public officials as follows (emphasis added):

Purely self-interested officials are motivated almost entirely by goals that benefit themselves rather than their bureaus or society as a whole. There are two types of such officials:

Climbers consider power, income and prestige as nearly all-important in their value structures.

Conservers consider convenience and security as nearly all-important. In contrast to climbers, conservers seek merely to retain the amount of power, income and prestige they already have, rather than to maximize them.

Mixed-motive officials have goals that combine self-interest and altruistic loyalty to larger values. The main difference among the three types of mixed-motive officials is the breadth of the larger values to which they are loyal:

Zealots are loyal to relatively narrow policies or concepts, such as the development of nuclear submarines. They seek power both for its own sake and to effect the policies to which they are loyal. We shall call these their *sacred policies.*

Advocates are loyal to a broader set of functions or to a broader organization than zealots. They also seek power because they want to have a significant influence upon policies and actions concerning those functions or organizations.

Statesmen are loyal to society as a whole, and they desire to obtain the power necessary to have a significant influence upon national policies and actions. They are altruistic to an important degree because their loyalty is to the "general welfare" as they see it.

See Downs, *Inside Bureaucracy,* p. 88.

33. M. Oksenberg and S. Goldstein, "The Chinese Political Spectrum," *Problems of Communism* 23 (March-April 1974): 1–13.

34. B.J. Ahn, *Chinese Politics and the Cultural Revolution* (Seattle: University of Washington Press, 1976).

35. P.H. Chang, *Power and Policy in China* (University Park: Pennsylvania State University Press, 1978).

36. P.R. Moody, *Chinese Politics After Mao* (New York: Praeger, 1983).

37. Harding, "Competing Models of the Chinese Communist Policy Process."

38. See in particular D.J. Solinger, "The Fifth National People's Congress and the Process of Policy Making," *Asian Survey* 22 (December 1982): 1238–1275; D.J. Solinger, *Chinese Business Under Socialism* (Berkeley: University of California Press, 1984). See also C.L. Hamrin, "Competing Policy Packages in Post-Mao China," *Asian Survey* 24 (May 1984): 487–518.

39. Solinger, "The Fifth National People's Congress and the Process of Policy Making," p. 1244.

40. See F.C. Teiwes, "Provincial Politics in China," in *China,* ed. J.M.H. Lindbeck (Seattle: University of Washington Press, 1971), pp. 116–118; W.W. Whitson, "Organizational Perspectives and Decision-Making in the Chinese Communist High Command," in *Elites in the People's Republic of China,* ed. R.A. Scalapino (Seattle: University of Washington Press, 1972), pp. 381–415.

41. Downs, *Inside Bureaucracy.*

42. See W.W. Whitson, "The Concept of Military Generation," *Asian Survey* 8 (November 1968): 921–947; M. Yahuda, "Political Generations in China," *China Quarterly* 80 (December 1979): 793–805.

43. See M. Oksenberg, "Occupational Groups in Chinese Society and the Cultural Revolution," in *The Cultural Revolution,* ed. M. Oksenberg et al. (Ann Arbor: Center for Chinese Studies, University of Michigan, 1968), pp. 1–44; A.P.L. Liu, *Political Culture and Group Conflict in Communist China* (Santa Barbara: ABC-Clio, 1976); P.R. Moody, *Opposition and Dissent in Communist China* (Stanford: Hoover Institution Press, 1977).

44. Pye, *The Dynamics of Chinese Politics.* See also, A. Nathan, "A Factional Model for Chinese Politics," *China Quarterly* 53 (January-March 1973): 34–66.

45. Pye, *The Dynamics of Chinese Politics,* p. 1.

46. Ibid., pp. 6–8.

47. See Winckler, "Policy Oscillations in the People's Republic of China;"

Skinner and Winckler, "Growth and Decline Processes in Organizations;" F. Schurmann, *Ideology and Organization in Communist China* (Berkeley: University of California Press, 1966); A. Eckstein, "Economic Fluctuations in Communist China's Domestic Development," in *China in Crisis*, ed. P.T. Ho and T. Tsou (Chicago: University of Chicago Press, 1968), pp. 691–752; P.J. Hiniker and R.V. Farace, "Approaches to National Development in China, 1949–1958," *Economic Development and Cultural Change* 18 (October 1969): 51–72; S. Eto, "Communist China," in *Modern East Asia*, ed. J.B. Crowley (New York: Harcourt, Brace/World, 1970), pp. 337–373; R. Lowenthal, "Development vs. Utopia in Communist Policy," in *Change in Communist Systems*, ed. C.A. Johnson (Stanford: Stanford University Press, 1970), pp. 33–116; L.W. Pye, *China* (Boston: Little, Brown, 1972); B.J. Ahn, "The Cultural Revolution and China's Search for Political Order," *China Quarterly* 58 (April/June 1974): 249–285; J.R. Townsend, *Politics in China* (Boston: Little, Brown, 1974); P.Y. Hiniker and J.J. Perlstein, "Alternation of Charismatic and Bureaucratic Styles of Leadership in Postrevolutionary China," *Comparative Political Studies* 10 (January 1978): 529–554; R.L. Petrick, "Policy Cycles and Policy Learning in the People's Republic of China," *Comparative Political Studies* 14 (April 1981): 101–122.

48. Nathan, "Policy Oscillations in the People's Republic of China," p. 720.

49. See Lampton, ed., *Policy Implementation in the Post-Mao Era*; R.A. Morse, ed., *The Limits of Reform in China* (Boulder: Westview Press, 1983); D. Zweig, "Strategies of Policy Implementation," *World Politics* 37 (January 1985): 267–293.

50. See J.A. Ponsioen, *The Analysis of Social Change Reconsidered* (The Hague: Mouton, 1969); R.A. Applebaum, *Theories of Social Change* (Chicago: Markham, 1970); K.E. Boulding, *A Primer on Social Dynamics* (New York: Free Press, 1970); R.A. Nisbet, ed., *Social Change* (Oxford: Oxford University Press, 1972); R.H. Laufer, *Perspectives on Social Change* (Boston: Allyn and Bacon, 1973); W.E. Moore, *Social Change* (Englewood Cliffs: Prentice-Hall, 1974); R.S. Edari, *Social Change* (Dubuque: Brown, 1976); A.D. Smith, *Social Change* (London: Longman, 1976).

51. See D. Duncanson, "Is China Unbending," *World Today* (July-August 1983): 263–270.

52. See Ibid.

53. See R.F. Dernberger, ed., *China's Development Experience in Comparative Perspective* (Cambridge, Mass.; Harvard University Press, 1980); R.F. Dernberger, "Communist China's Industrial Policies," in *Mainland China's Modernization* (Berkeley: Institute of East Asian Studies and Institute of International Studies, University of California, 1981), pp. 122–161; J.S. Prybyla, *Readjustment and Reform in the Chinese Economy* (Baltimore: University of Maryland School of Law, 1981); J.S. Prybyla, *The Chinese Economy* (Columbia: University of South Carolina Press, 1981); R.F. Dernberger, "The Chinese Search for the Path of Self-Sustained Growth in the 1980s," in *China Under the Four Modernizations*, ed. Joint Economic Committee, US Congress (Washington, D.C.: US Government Printing Office, 1982), pp. 19–76; J.S. Prybyla, "Where is China's Economy Headed? A Systems Analysis," *Journal of Northeast Asian Studies* 1 (December 1982): 3–24; R.F. Dernberger, "The Domestic Economy and the Four Modernizations Program," in *China Policy for the Next Decade*, ed. A. Johnson et al., (Boston: Oelgeschlager, Gunn and Hain, 1984), pp.

139–179. C. Clark, "The Nature of Chinese Communism and the Prospects for Teng's Reforms," *Issues and Studies* 21 (January 1985): 12–37; R.F. Dernberger, "Mainland China's Economic System," *Issues and Studies* 21 (April 1985): 44–72; J.S. Prybyla, "The Chinese Economy," *Asian Survey* 25 (May 1985): 553–586; J.S. Prybyla, "China's Economic Experiment," *Problems of Communism* 35 (January-February 1986): 21–38; J.S. Prybyla, "Mainland China and Hungary," *Issues and Studies* 23 (January 1987): 43-83.

FIVE

The Pessimistic Scenario for the Hong Kong Economy

Effects

Key informants who display a high degree of pessimism expect the Hong Kong economy in a decade or two to become closely integrated with that of the PRC and lose many of its present characteristics. Some of them go so far as to argue that the territory's economic system will be virtually indistinguishable from that of China and that the expression "one country, one system" will provide a better description of the post-1997 reality than the phrase "one country, two systems." Most pessimists, however, are of the opinion that full convergence will not take place and that Hong Kong will serve as a "special" economic zone. Yet even these individuals insist that it will not markedly differ in its mode of operation from the other SEZs the PRC has established and that it will be a far less open and far more regulated city than it is today.

In fact, those pessimists who portray the territory as a special SEZ are careful to emphasize that its slightly different character will not be the result of policies intended to preserve its quintessentially capitalist institutions. On the contrary, they argue that China will seek uniformity rather than diversity and that the concept of SEZs as presently understood will fall into oblivion. According to them, however, some differences between the two societies will continue to manifest themselves well into the early part of the next century because of Hong Kong's long legacy of laissez-faire practices, more sophisticated infrastructure, and higher standard of living.

Pessimists also assert that the Hong Kong SEZ, while special in certain respects, will not enjoy genuine autonomy but be to all intents and purposes administered by officials employed by the central government and/or CCP. Specifically, although "patriotic" locals will occupy positions of authority, real power will lie in the hands of a small number of high-level representatives from the mainland (e.g., the director of the New China News Agency—NCNA—and the head of the Bank of China in the territory). Some pessimists even contend that the Hong Kong government will become an integral part of the central government and that appointees from the mainland will emerge as the dominant force within it (playing a role similar to that of senior expatriate, particularly British, civil servants in the current transitional situation).

In any event, it will be the CCP rather than the government that will, according to pessimists, shape policies in Hong Kong. They do not doubt that the party will grow in size, improve its organizational effectiveness, and surface as the official organ of PRC power in the territory. It is important to stress that pessimists are not predicting that the CCP will function merely as a "shadow" government, exercising considerable political control albeit indirectly. They envisage a formal takeover of government institutions and other key organizations by the party and active participation by CCP members, both local and from the mainland, in policy formulation and implementation.

Furthermore, the party will not countenance any power-sharing schemes which might allow non-CCP elements to influence strategic decisions. Of course, individuals with useful experience and skills will be co-opted into the politico-bureaucratic elite and will enjoy some latitude in performing their roles, but they will be encouraged to adopt a reactive rather than an initiatory posture. Pessimists point out that it will be in the interest of such individuals to join the party or one of the organizations affiliated with it, for without openly embracing the United Front cause they will not be able to operate effectively in policy councils other than perhaps on an ad hoc basis.

To all appearances, the inevitability of CCP rule would not be regarded as such a negative factor if the party were likely to modify its political outlook and organizational practices. Pessimists, however, rule out the possibility of significant departures from the status quo in this respect. They do not see the CCP jettisoning the Four Cardinal Principles of communist orthodoxy (adherence to socialism, dictatorship of the proletariat, leadership of the party, and subscribing to Marxist-Leninist-Maoist thought) or adopting a command structure inconsistent with the spirit of democratic centralism. The reluctance to compromise in matters of ideology and organization will, pessimists emphasize, manifest itself in Hong Kong as well as on the mainland.

The ascendancy of the CCP over other institutions and the reliance in the territory on concepts and practices rooted in the doctrines espoused by Chinese officialdom will probably have the greatest repercussions in the executive/bureaucratic and legislative spheres, which will become highly politicized. Another branch of the system which will be seriously affected is the judiciary. Pessimists assert that strict limits will be placed on judicial autonomy and that judges will not act as a buffer between the authorities and the individual but will serve to facilitate executive/bureaucratic control (and, in the final analysis, party control). This may not require any far-reaching changes in the law because it is common in the PRC to distinguish between *li* and *fa* (roughly translated as "customary norms of behaviour" and "enacted law," respectively), with *li* normally prevailing.[1]

In addition to a less favourable political climate, pessimists anticipate setbacks in the economic domain. They anticipate reform in the mainland grinding to a halt and China reverting to central planning as a principal means of steering the economy (at least its urban component). The implication is that no concrete steps will be taken to decontrol prices and privatize enterprises. Although there will be no return to the excesses of the Great Leap Forward and the Cultural Revolution, the PRC will abandon the quest for greater productivity through market incentives and resort to mass mobilizations (*yundong*) in order to achieve its economic objectives.[2] Put another way, Hong Kong will be part of a system run largely through an iron chain of command and by exhortation—an approach radically different from that which has evolved in response to the colonial government's policy of benign neglect.

Pessimists do not necessarily suggest that the local economy will resemble in every respect its mainland counterpart. Thus, they expect most small and medium-size companies to remain in private hands in the immediate post-1997 period and prices in some sectors of the economy to be determined primarily by the forces of demand and supply. On the other hand, they believe that large firms will be converted into state enterprises and that price controls will be imposed in a wide range of areas of economic activity. They also think that the labour market will be regulated (more tightly in some sectors, more loosely in others) and that foreign exchange controls will be instituted. Needless to say, Hong Kong will not have its own currency—the renminbi will become the medium of exchange—and the Bank of China will perform the functions of a central bank.

Another change pessimists envisage is in the rules of the economic game. Specifically, they argue that the market will cease to serve as perhaps the ultimate arbiter of value and that the interests of the PRC as a whole, as perceived by those with the power to interpret them, and mainland organizations operating in the territory will dictate economic outcomes. Mainland companies in particular will seek advantages not available to those without similar political influence (i.e., engage in forms of behaviour referred to by economists as "rent-seeking")[3] and in the process distort the working of market forces. This doubtless will detract from the efficiency of the system and its ability to adapt.

Pessimists foresee the emergence of equally questionable practices within organizations, particulary those in which the CCP will establish strong presence. They maintain that decisions concerning recruitment, selection, training, and promotion will be based increasingly on political criteria rather than merit. Furthermore, they argue that the allocation of resources other than personnel—for instance, finance—will also largely reflect political considerations and objectives. These concerns lead pessimists to the conclusion that notwithstanding the greater degree of political control, organizations will be ill-equipped to respond efficiently and effectively to external economic stimuli.

Pessimists dismiss the idea that the politicization of the economy might be superficial in nature, an idea grounded in the theory that utility-maximizing economic agents would continue to engage in mutually beneficial exchanges under the facade of communist rule. They insist that the restructuring of the polity and the economy will have far-reaching effects on individual behaviour. Specifically, the shift in the balance of power in favour of the CCP and the forces allied with it and the remodelling of political and economic institutions will induce a behavioural adjustment. The values prevailing during the heyday of capitalist rule will suffer erosion, and patterns of individual behaviour will come to resemble quite closely those to be found on the mainland. Value reorientation, pessimists contend, will also turn Hong Kong into a more inward-looking, less cosmopolitan city. Patriotism, not materialism and pragmatism, will be the main motivating factor, and the receptivity to foreign cultures, particularly of Western origin, will decline significantly. Insofar as the economy is concerned, pessimists place special emphasis on the face that the English language will not be accorded as much importance as previously and that it will not be so widely used. Restrictions on activities such as gambling and prostitution (in fact, most forms of nightlife) and the dearth of good cultural and recreational facilities (including restaurants) will not endear Hong Kong to business people, whether foreign or local, either.

Westerners may, in any event, shun the territory because of the more oppressive political climate. Even if they opt to remain, they are not likely to be encouraged to do so on a large scale. Pessimists assert that Hong Kong will be a Chinese city run by the Chinese for the benefit of the Chinese. Foreign involvement in local business will be the exception rather than the rule, and an attempt will be made to confine it within fairly narrow bounds. Direct foreign participation in strategic sectors of the economy (e.g., power generation) will certainly not be countenanced, and cooperation with foreigners will normally take the form of joint ventures extending over a limited period of time.

One of the major attractions of Hong Kong to business people, both foreign and local, lies in the policy of low public spending/low taxation. Pessimists, however, are convinced that this policy will be reversed. Taxes will rise across the board—and markedly—in order to support a higher level of state activity in the territory and generate funds for public consumption and investment in the mainland. Pessimists draw special attention to the second of these two points: It serves to illustrate that the post-1997 Hong

Kong economy will not function as a self-contained entity but will be managed in accordance with national objectives. They also argue that foreigners will bear a disproportionate burden of taxation and that their business costs will escalate quite dramatically, particularly because they will be subject to implicit taxes in addition to those of the explicit variety.

Disenchantment with the political and economic climate in the territory, pessimists believe, will spread beyond the confines of the foreign business community. Loss of political power, diminishing economic opportunities, and deterioration in the quality of life will prompt wealthy locals and local middle class professionals to pursue the exit option and seek new outlets for their entrepreneurial and professional talents. As a result, Hong Kong will be transformed into a working class and lower middle class city presided over by a handful of United Front officials. The social pyramid will consequently flatten, but the stock of human capital will shrink, and the absence of interclass mobility will act as a disincentive to would-be successful entrepreneurs and fast-track professionals.

The service industry cannot flourish when professional skills are in short supply. It also suffers in a highly regulated environment, particularly one in which information is not allowed to circulate freely. It is not surprising, therefore, that pessimists expect Hong Kong to decline as an international service centre. They see a future for entrepôt-related activities and certain traditional forms of banking (i.e., the type of activities normally associated with commercial, as distinct from merchant, banks). The wholesale and retail trade, transport services, and some personal services will continue to expand at a reasonable pace as well, but in none of these areas, not even entrepôt-related activities, will the present momentum be maintained.

Rather than consolidate its position as a leading international service centre, Hong Kong will develop into a primarily industrial city, according to pessimists. They think that the first decade of the next century will be similar to the 1960s, when the territory experienced rapid industrialization, but without the spectacular growth of that period. Its industries, though not necessarily as labour intensive as in the early phases of the industrial takeoff, will mainly be engaged in low-tech production. Furthermore, most of their output, largely in the form of consumer goods, will be directed to the mainland, which will lag behind the territory in light industry and will be reluctant—for economic and ideological reasons—to import sophisticated consumer goods from Japan, South Korea, Singapore, Taiwan, and the West.

Pessimists are generally unwilling to commit themselves on the issue of the likely rate of expansion of the Hong Kong economy in a decade or two from now. They assert that there will be years of negative growth, stagnation, moderate growth, and even respectable growth. On the other hand, the possibility of a sustained and vigorous expansion is ruled out categorically. Pessimists also stress that growth will proceed from a lower base or that the standard of living will be lower, in fact considerably lower, than at present. A reduced living standard is of greater significance to them than the fact that some expansion will take place, although sporadically.

The pessimistic scenario obviously paints a rather gloomy picture if looked at from a laissez-faire and pro-growth perspective. It is interesting to note, however, that few pessimists are of the opinion that Hong Kong will disintegrate to a point of becoming ungovernable by means other than sheer coercion. They anticipate serious crises and some lean years but not a near collapse of the social order of the kind experienced by a number of postcolonial societies. The adaptability, homogeneity, and inner strength of the community will prevent disintegration, yet these qualities will prove insufficient in themselves to ensure fast economic growth or even avoid an economic deceleration.

Causes

Pessimists offer a number of reasons to support their predictions.[4] Above all, they emphasize that the CCP is not concerned primarily with economic modernization. Rather, the party's principal objective is to restore its legitimacy after the setbacks it suffered during the Great Leap Forward and the Cultural Revolution and extend its control over pieces of Chinese territory such as Hong Kong and Taiwan. Better economic performance thus essentially serves as a means to an end (i.e., refurbishing the image of the CCP and its leaders) and is generally pursued within the constraints imposed by the goal of enhancing party dominance. The main issue at stake in Hong Kong, therefore, is CCP control and not prosperity and stability.

That is not to say, of course, that China does not wish the territory to remain as prosperous and stable as under British rule. The opposite is true. The point pessimists stress is that the objective of ensuring prosperity and stability in Hong Kong is far less important than that of safeguarding the monopoly of power enjoyed by the CCP and its leaders. Consequently, Chinese policies towards the territory, both during the transition period and after 1997, will reflect the need for a high degree of party control. The preoccupation with party control, in turn, will profoundly affect economic organization and performance in Hong Kong and make the territory less prosperous.

Pessimists maintain that the problem is compounded by the latent conflict between the North and the South in the PRC. According to them, relations between the two regions can scarcely be described as harmonious. With the South perceived by the North as a potentially rebellious area, control-minded officials in the North with responsibility for Hong Kong are likely to advocate a highly centralized power structure for the territory coupled with a rigid regulatory regime. Needless to say, such a posture is not conducive to capitalist prosperity.

Nor is it just a matter of party control and a lingering distrust of the South. Pessimists argue that the concept of "one country, two systems" is not viable for historical reasons as well. They observe that the idea of autonomous Hong Kong, with a socioeconomic system markedly different from that of the mainland, is simply inconsistent with Chinese political history. Specifically, the central government in China has traditionally been reluctant to grant meaningful autonomy to local units and is thus inherently incapable of grasping the notion of "one country, two systems"—let alone inclined to implement it in accordance with the putative spirit of the Sino-British Joint Declaration.

Pessimists attribute China's strong historical urge to curb centrifugal tendencies to the country's authoritarian political culture, which has spawned distinctly hierarchical forms of government and ideological uniformity. As Pye has noted:

> The tenacity with which Chinese politics has been able to resist modernizing influences stems in no small part from certain key structural characteristics, its hierarchical nature, and its heavy dependence upon formal ideologies. As though immutably decreed, Chinese politics after chaos and revolution has always returned to being elitist and hierarchical in organization, closed and monopolistic in spirit; and while the content and the goals have now been irrevocably changed, the Chinese system still steadfastly depends for integration upon an overweening sense of righteousness.[5]

And as he further elaborated:

> The entire structure of both imperial and Communist politics has rested upon self-cultivation as the ultimate rationale for legitimizing high office and the manipulations of political power. . . . Confucianism and communism in their different ways have sustained this unique Chinese belief in authority's right to arrogance. . . .
>
> Thus the first and most essential characteristic of the persisting structure of Chinese politics has been the degree to which it has been a self-contained system very little influenced by citizens or nongovernmental elites. . . .
>
> It has been this cardinal belief in the popular autonomy of government and in the need for officials to be responsive only to their ideals that has made Chinese politics so peculiarly insensitive to changes in the social and economic environment. The Chinese political class has focused its attention on intra-elite relations and has concerned itself with general development in the society only to the extent that these threatened the security of the class

or were the objects of governmental policies....

The traditional Chinese political order was remarkably monolithic, with all political action centred in a single bureaucracy headed by the Emperor. Although there was little sense of specialization, there was a strong appreciation that all officials shared a common ideological orientation based on the Confucian tradition and an informal understanding of life within officialdom....

The combination of bureaucratic hierarchy and ideological conformity governed nearly every dimension of the traditional Chinese political culture. As numerous observers have noted, the Communists have once again given the Chinese a political system that centers around a bureaucratic hierarchy, this time in the form of the Communist Party, and is again integrated by an all-pervasive ideology, that of Marxism and Maoism.

The Chinese have always felt profoundly uncomfortable, dissatisfied, and threatened whenever their politics has not been characterized by a dominant hierarchy and a single ideology. It is this sense of all-pervasive malaise, which they exhibit whenever they are without a one-party, one-ideology system, that proclaims the extent to which the Chinese, both in their collective national history and in their personal views, have tended to treat politics as a matter essentially of authority.[6]

The authoritarianism pervading Chinese political culture, pessimists contend, is a crucial factor which cannot be overlooked. It will unleash pressures for a complete absorption of Hong Kong into the Chinese body politic and will stifle expressions of autonomous spirit in the territory, however innocuous. It will also result in a spate of regulations and a propensity to impose punitive taxes. The business environment of Hong Kong will consequently be transformed, thus depriving the territory of its extraordinary vitality.

Pessimists believe that the experience in Weihaiwei,[7] a coastal district in the northern province of Shandong, lends substance to the cultural explanation because it parallels somewhat the Hong Kong situation. Britain returned Waihaiwei to China in 1930 after leasing it for thirty-two years. The district developed under British rule as a free port with a hands-off administration and low taxes, and when Britain decided to withdraw, it laboured to negotiate a settlement that would help preserve Weihaiwei's commercial status. But the negotiated agreement preserved little: When the British commissioner departed in 1930, the Chinese brought in outside officials, turning Waihaiwei into a special administrative zone directly under central government control. The local bureaucracy mushroomed to unmanageable proportions. Taxes were raised, leading to riots. And when China placed Weihaiwei within the national customs system, trade moved elsewhere. Pessimists assert that Hong Kong cannot escape a similar fate because of China's cultural penchant for highly centralized forms of government, rigid regulatory schemes, and heavy taxes.

The Weihaiwei experience also serves to illustrate that China does not deem itself constrained by international agreements, particularly those which purport to circumscribe its sovereign powers. For this reason, pessimists attach no importance to the Sino-British Joint Declaration as a possible determinant of events in Hong Kong. They claim that the Chinese have hedged many of their "legal" commitments and that they will proceed to interpret the Joint Declaration as they see fit. In fact, already PRC representatives and their local allies appear to be less closely guided by the provisions of the Sino-British agreement than by the dictates of Chinese realpolitik.

Pessimists are sceptical not only of the legal commitments the PRC has undertaken with respect to Hong Kong but its more informal promises as well. They maintain that commitments, whether formal or informal, carry little significance in Chinese politics and cannot act as a constraining factor when the political logic of the situation propels the relevant actors in a direction contrary to that implied at previous junctures. Developments in postrevolutionary Shanghai are a case in point, for promises given to its capitalists proved no more effective than the bilateral agreement reached with regard to Weihaiwei.[8] Pessimists again offer a cultural explanation in endeavouring to shed light on the use/misuse of political commitments in China:

> Politically, the Chinese feel freer than Westerners to profess their intentions, for statements of intentions do not commit one to much, and it is expected that intentions will change with circumstances and in response to the behaviour of the enemy. In Western politics, statements of goals tend to be moral imperatives, and leaders feel threatened by having to confess changes in their intentions. In contrast, Chinese tend to shroud their means in secrecy and not to publicize the day-to-day activities of those in power, for surprises and deception are assumed to be vital.
>
> In Chinese political culture, leaders proclaim their intentions, hoping to influence their enemies or their subjects, but if their ploy fails they can casually ignore what Westerners would assume to have been commitments critical to the continuing self-esteem and reputation of the leaders. For the Chinese, declarations of intentions thus become manoeuvres designed to probe or provoke the behaviour of others. Westerners often feel that it is important to make their intentions unambiguous, that they must ensure clarity of communications. Chinese tend to assume that efforts to "clarify intentions" must be a ruse or an act of simplemindedness, because the intentions of all actors must change with circumstances.[9]

There are those, of course, who expect the PRC to honour its commitments towards Hong Kong because the stakes in this case are so high that Britain, other Western powers, and Japan will exert pressure on the

Chinese to act in accordance with the spirit of the Sino-British Joint Declaration. Pessimists, however, dismiss this argument unceremoniously. They contend that both the Hong Kong and the UK governments will be responsive to Chinese demands because of the perception that they are powerless to influence the course of events and the need not to jeopardize Sino-British economic cooperation in particular. American, European, and Japanese passivity in the face of Chinese intransigence is also assured for essentially similar reasons.

Pessimists assert that nothing but British presence and administration beyond 1997 could guarantee capitalist prosperity in Hong Kong. Neither Chinese commitments nor external pressures are sufficient in themselves to ensure the preservation of the economic status quo. The territory has thrived because Britain has provided a physical and institutional buffer to insulate it from influences emanating from the mainland. After the British departure, and even in the period preceding it, such influences will prove the decisive factor; countervailing forces will fade into insignificance.

This perception also applies to countervailing forces within Hong Kong. Pessimists observe that a sense of powerlessness pervades the local community and that the level of political mobilization in the territory is too low to neutralize external influences. They perceive Hong Kong as a "bureaucratic polity" controlled by the civil service through its quasi-monopolistic powers and underpinned by a culture of "utilitarianistic familism" that results in an almost single-minded pursuit of the objective of maximizing the family's material welfare.[10] In such an environment, the active expression of community interests is neither encouraged nor accorded a high priority. Even if it were, the territory is so powerless vis-à-vis China that it could not stem the tide of mainland influence. The leftist press in Hong Kong has sought to dramatize this point by drawing attention to the fact that "while the People's Republic would take into account the wishes of the five million people in Hong Kong, the wishes of the one billion people of China must prevail."[11]

CCP control and Chinese cultural influences are not the only threat to the territory's capitalist prosperity, pessimists claim. According to them, the lack of understanding that prevails in the PRC with respect to Hong Kong and how it functions is another cause for concern. They argue that Chinese policymakers and bureaucrats have a distorted picture of the territory's socioeconomic system because of their ideological rigidity, excessive reliance on the leftist press in Hong Kong for relevant information, low educational level which inhibits learning (particularly when the learning process is directed at a city that is highly sophisticated in most respects), and the tendency of officials to report to their superiors in a manner which reinforces the latter's prejudices.

Thus, one potentially serious problem to which pessimists point is the widely held perception in the PRC that Hong Kong is not, at least insofar as political control in concerned, fundamentally different from the mainland. The assumption there is that the territory practices its own version of democratic centralism and that it is subject to an iron rule by a handful of civil servants and prominent business leaders. Pessimists see no evidence of a recognition that the local economy is a highly decentralized entity which derives much of its vitality from a multitude of small enterprises that respond to market signals. Nor do they see evidence of a recognition that Hong Kong's success is not the product of administrative guidance by a small and omnipotent bureaucratic elite and its business allies but instead is the result of noninterventionist policies which emphasize individual initiative, responsibility, and freedoms.

Pessimists are equally concerned about the Chinese tendency to overstate the vulnerability of Hong Kong and its dependence on the mainland. This tendency manifests itself in attempts to portray Hong Kong as a city which lacks natural resources and whose sole strength lies in capitalizing on market opportunities in developed countries by transforming cheap supplies from the mainland into competitively priced consumer goods. Unlike the PRC, Hong Kong does not even have a research and development capability—and is not particularly interested in acquiring one. It is completely exposed on the periphery of the capitalist system and highly susceptible to the shocks which periodically disrupt the operation of that system. The absorption into the resource-rich and self-sufficient mainland economy will provide the long-term stability which it has been denied as a British colony and will facilitate the building of a thoroughly modern society.

To pessimists, such views are indicative of the poor appreciation among Chinese cadres of the dynamics of Hong Kong society. They observe that the territory does not seek stability for stability's sake or modernization for modernization's sake. Rather, it is a profit-making machine whose outstanding performance is the result of a very flexible posture in the face of highly volatile economic conditions. The PRC's type of stability and modernization will bring greater predictability and will allow closer integration between Hong Kong and mainland industries, but it will stifle the territory's entrepreneurial spirit.

Another danger pessimists see lies in China's inability to come to grips with the fact that the Hong Kong economy is not a closed system which functions without any support from the sociocultural environment in which it is embedded. The point is that economic activity in the territory is sustained by a quintessentially capitalist lifestyle which PRC officials deem objectionable—and in the process of trying to moderate that lifestyle, they are bound to cause (not necessarily deliberately) damage to the economy. As Cross has commented in challenging the conventional interpretation which attributes Hong Kong's impressive economic record to a combination of Chinese business talents and British notions of law and order:

> I hope that I'm not too cynical, but much of Hong Kong's success comes not from being a decent place, a fair society, even though the British try to hold it in some bounds. It is well run only because so much is allowed: e.g., gambling at the race tracks pays for most of the social services; triads keep in line many immigrants. I don't see how a formula could be devised which would allow any 21st-century Chinese government to disavow responsibility for such an anachronistic society in China while claiming sovereignty. At the same time, I don't see Hong Kong being "reformed" in its social aspects without losing the incentives which drive Hong Kong's inhabitants.[12]

Of course, it would not be unreasonable to assume that although the Chinese do not fully understand how the territory operates and what accounts for its success, they have sufficient time to learn. However, pessimists contend that effective learning cannot take place in an environment in which information is distorted because it is relied upon to sustain existing beliefs (one might even say ideological dogma), is obtained from selective sources, and is relayed by subordinates and fellow travellers in Hong Kong who are overly eager to please (and, doubtless, reluctant to report the strength of anticommunist sentiments in the territory).

The problem is compounded, according to pessimists, by the fact that Hong Kong no longer receives the attention of top Chinese leaders. These officials have formulated a strategy for regaining control over the territory, have secured Britain's cooperation in producing an internationally acceptable blueprint which embodies that strategy, and are presently content to leave the task of implementing their grand design to lower-level officials. Insofar as the leaders are concerned, the issue has been settled on their terms; there is no pressing need to engage in learning with a view to gaining a better appreciation of the Hong Kong situation.

Pessimists maintain that ignorance, coupled with a reluctance to learn, normally breeds arrogance. The Chinese claim that the PRC is more than capable of administering the territory—after all, it has been highly successful in administering Shenzen and Shanghai. (As Pei Yiming, publisher of a pro-CCP newspaper in Hong Kong and member of the National People's Congress, has put it: "Did some people not say that the Chinese could not rule Shanghai well? Facts have shown that the Chinese are completely capable of ruling Shanghai well. Since they can rule Shanghai well, they can also rule Hong Kong well."[13] Pessimists are convinced that the arrogance underlying this claim will lead the Chinese to repeat in Hong Kong the kind of mistakes they have made in Shanghai, Shenzen, and elsewhere.

Arrogance, or perhaps overconfidence, also tends to find expression in attitudes prevailing in the PRC with respect to the country's development potential. The enormous problems likely to be encountered in the process of modernization are often overlooked, and there is a tendency to assume that

China will reach economic maturity by the end of this century. Pessimists concede that ambitious developmental goals may serve a useful purpose in providing inspiration to a nation emerging from a period characterized by backwardness and turmoil. Nonetheless, they think that excessive confidence in the mainland's ability to pursue successfully a high-growth strategy and transform its economy will result in a less accommodating posture vis-à-vis Hong Kong and will lessen the willingness to learn from the territory.

The belief that the PRC is capable of administering Hong Kong and that its wide-ranging modernization programme will be implemented smoothly and expeditiously is viewed by pessimists as problematic in yet another respect. Specifically, they assert that this belief reinforces the perception that China could assume direct control over the territory, substantially restructure its political and economic institutions, and at the same time continue to derive many of the benefits Hong Kong produces for the mainland by virtue of its semiautonomous status and laissez-faire policies. Given such a perception, there is obviously no strong incentive to preserve the institutions whose special nature is widely regarded as the principal factor accounting for the buoyancy of the territory's economy. As Pye has noted:

> Advocates of an optimistic view of Hong Kong's prospects have made much of the argument that China needs Hong Kong because the Crown Colony is her major source of foreign exchange, a consideration which they hold will grow in importance as China becomes more deeply committed to modernization. . . . There are several problems with the foreign exchange argument. First, the degree to which it is based on wishful speculation rather than fact is revealed by the awkward truth that there is no solid basis for the figures usually used in characterizing this supposed Chinese need. Even before negotiations began, the *Economist* (London) was arguing that Britain "starts out with one big advantage" in that "China earns about 40 percent of its foreign exchange in Hong Kong." Both Mrs. Margaret Thatcher and Hong Kong Governor Sir Edward Youde picked up this figure. Sensing that the argument might have been fanciful, the *Asian Wall Street Journal* assigned a team to discover what the figure was, and they produced statistics varying from 25 percent (given by an unnamed United States authority), to 33 percent (according to the Hong Kong and Shanghai Bank), to 35–40 percent (offered by the Colonial Financial Secretary). Gu Nianliang, head of the Canton-based Hong Kong–Macao Research Centre of the Chinese Academy of the Social Sciences, has estimated that 31 percent of Chinese foreign exchange is derived from Hong Kong trade. Regardless of what the actual figure should be, the significant fact is that the importance of foreign exchange is stressed by British and Hong Kong interested parties but not by the Chinese side. Aside from negotiating tactics, there may be sound economic reasoning behind the Chinese dismissal of the matter. The implicit conclusion that were China to take over

Hong Kong she would lose between 30 and 40 percent of her foreign exchange earnings is nonsense. It is true that China receives convertible foreign exchange by selling to Hong Kong such hinterland products as vegetables, fruits, chicken, meats and even water, but the reason why Hong Kong is able to pay in a convertible currency is that its people produce goods and services that meet an international demand, and presumably (especially in Chinese thinking) they would be able to continue to do this after sovereignty reverted to China. Thus, although China would no longer earn foreign exchange by providing agricultural produce for Hong Kong, it would, on the other hand, obtain all the foreign exchange that Hong Kong would still get from its international trade with others. Indeed, depending upon developments, it is conceivable (and the Chinese probably believe it likely) that they would end up with more foreign exchange.[14]

Significant economic gains are, of course, merely one of the reasons often advanced in support of the argument that the PRC will act decisively to preserve the status quo in the territory. Equally important is said to be the strong desire to bring about a rapprochement and, eventually, reunification with Taiwan. Indeed, pessimists are somewhat more favourably disposed towards explanations which stress the Taiwan factor than those premised on the assumption that China will opt for policy continuity in Hong Kong because of the economic advantages this strategy will bring. Yet they insist that even the need to signal to Taiwan that reunification will not necessarily spell loss of autonomy and the dismantling of capitalist institutions will fail to induce the PRC to take a flexible stance towards the territory.

As pointed out earlier, pessimists view the near obsession with control and domestic political manoeuvres as the key forces determining policy outcomes in China. If this were not the case, the PRC would have presumably granted far greater autonomy to Tibet and would have refrained from launching destabilizing campaigns against phenomena such as "spiritual pollution" and "bourgeois liberalization." After all, by exercising self-restraint in Tibet and the domestic arena, the Chinese would have been able to reassure the sceptical Hong Kong public and possibly even make some headway in winning the confidence of Taiwan. The fact that they have not followed such a course, pessimists deduce, indicates that the objective of reunification with Taiwan will be pursued without offers of any tangible concessions in Hong Kong. The PRC propaganda machine will provide some reasons for showering Taiwan with promises while denying Hong Kong the freedoms which underpin its prosperity.

Pessimists also contend that it is unrealistic to assume China is capable of managing in a sophisticated manner the Taiwan problem, which calls for a fine tuning of its Hong Kong policies, because it is poorly informed about Taiwanese realities. As Pye has observed, the PRC may acknowledge the remarkable economic achievements of Taiwan, but it claims that "political life under the Kuomintang . . . is highly centralized, authoritarian and probably highly repressive.[15] (Pye, on the other hand, asserts that for someone like himself, "who has been immersed in analyzing the conformist politics of the PRC, in which latent factional strife is only indirectly and subtly manifest, it is astonishing to discover through travels on the island how openly the Chinese of Taiwan today advocate their varied opinions. Even more surprising, these opinions are expressed not by slogans, code words or cliches, but by detailed explications."[16]) The failure on the part of China to grasp the direction and pace of political change in Taiwan is deemed significant by pessimists because it implies that no effort will be made to present Hong Kong as an autonomous entity which pursues a liberal path under PRC rule. (After all, if the political climate in Taiwan is perceived as markedly inferior to that in China, and if the Taiwanese are regarded as people who neither enjoy nor demand elementary freedoms, there is no need to offer inducements other than the prospect of reunification with the politically attractive mainland.)

Another factor to which pessimists attach considerable importance is the likely Taiwanese response to the PRC overtures, which they believe[17] will be decidedly negative—Taiwan will spurn categorically all Chinese advances. Moreover, it will withdraw from Hong Kong in 1997, although some air and sea links between the two places will be maintained through the services of foreign airlines and shipping companies, and perhaps some of Taiwan's offices in the territory will be replaced by new ones in disguise. The sense of frustration which Taiwan's reaction will provoke on the PRC side will further undermine the "one country, two systems" policy. The Chinese, concluding that it apparently serves no useful purpose, will jettison the policy and seek reunification with Taiwan by other means. Nor is this all: Taiwan's hostile response will compel China to adopt an even more uncompromising attitude in Hong Kong than might otherwise be expected. As Pye has suggested:

> China's sensitivity to Taiwan's reaction seems likely to offer better prospects for stability in Hong Kong than either the foreign exchange argument or the advantages of pragmatism in high places. Yet, paradoxically precisely because the Taiwan reunification issue exists it will probably be impossible for Beijing to allow the people of Hong Kong to rule themselves with even the degree of electoral freedom enjoyed on Taiwan. This is because Beijing has already said that it will not tolerate an elected government in Hong Kong because of fear of "interference" from Taiwan. . . . Thus, while the Taiwan factor may have some restraining effects on Beijing, it will also set limits on future administrative arrangements for Hong Kong.[18]

It could be argued, of course, that pessimists overstate the Taiwan problem because of their unwillingness to acknowledge the significant economic changes taking place on the mainland. After all, should the PRC remain committed to a strategy of liberalization, the two Chinas would gravitate towards each other and develop a relationship characterized by fairly close cooperation (although full integration may prove to be an elusive goal) rather than friction. And, should the mainland and Taiwanese economies partially converge, Hong Kong would doubtless benefit greatly because such a convergence would stimulate business activity in the region, enhance the territory's role as a catalyst for reunification, and reduce the threat to it inherent in radical revival in the PRC.

Indeed, pessimists concede that partial convergence of the mainland and Taiwanese economies would be a boon to Hong Kong, but they are convinced this will not occur. Pessimists distinguish between "adjustment" and "reform" and claim that the economic changes witnessed in China since 1978 constitute merely an adjustment, not genuine reform. Furthermore, they assert that a series of adjustments, even if extending over a long period of time, will not result in a transformation of the PRC economy. As Prybyla has observed:

> The word "changes" is used advisedly. It covers two different but related alterations. The first consists of "adjustment" of policy variables within a given institutional structure: intrasystemic changes, rearranging the furniture and opening the windows. The second, "reform" involves the manipulation of institutional-systemic variables: restructuring the system of economic organization. Adjustments are changes designed to make the system work better—whether more efficiently or equitably—without altering it in fundamental ways. They may go quite far and involve redistributions of income, emphasis on self-sufficiency or the division of labour, importation of advanced technologies, exchange of experts to alter the pattern of skills within the system, and so on. But reforms go further and deeper. They change in fundamental ways the institutions of the system. Reforms may be carried out at once, through a revolutionary act, or incrementally by progressive adjustments. Over time, the mass of intrasystemic adjustments can bring about qualitative systemic change. While conceivable, reform through incremental adjustments is not likely to materialize in the "medium" term (20–25 years), as attested to by the post-Stalin experience of the Soviet Union. Resort to adjustments, in fact, may be symptomatic of an unwillingness or (political, ideological) inability to come to grips with deep-seated economic problems through reform.[19]

The unwillingness or inability of the Chinese to reform their economy, pessimists maintain, stems from the fact that economic restructuring would be politically costly. The reason is that reform efforts would need to be predicated on the assumption that the mainland economy cannot take off unless family-based businesses are allowed to assume a pivotal role. This assumption, while difficult to question, is problematic because it necessitates a shift of power from the party to the family unit. The CCP may recognize that the family is the only social institution through which the Chinese can channel their economic energies effectively, but the party is unwilling or unable to share its power (at least in the urban areas where relaxation of controls might have serious consequences).

Pessimists also contend that the idea of reform does not enjoy strong support either within or outside the party, except perhaps among those who live in the countryside. Party cadres and intellectuals are said to be attracted to central planning of the Soviet variety and impressed by the fact that the Soviet Union has been transformed from a feudal society into a world power by relying on a top-down command system. In addition, and at the grass roots, a high degree of dependence on the state appears to have developed, leaving urban dwellers reluctant to subject themselves to the vagaries of market forces. The corollary is that China lacks a constituency for urban economic reform as distinct from urban economic adjustment.

Even if such a constituency did exist, pessimists assert, the leadership would not necessarily be inclined to respond to its demands. Political power in the PRC is concentrated in the hands of a small number of top officials who are insulated from external pressures. These officials can switch at will—and at no cost to themselves—from seemingly reformist policies to ones that have conservative or radical undertones. But their "pragmatism" should not be taken for granted—they would not hesitate to plunge Hong Kong into a crisis if this could serve their tactical objectives. They have created an institutional milieu conducive to the accumulation and maintenance of power, but it cannot sustain reform in China and bring stability to the territory.

Another potential source of instability, according to pessimists, is the fragility of the emerging alliance between the PRC and the Hong Kong business elite. The alliance will inevitably disintegrate because neither side can satisfy the other's expectations: China is incapable of fostering a climate favourable to private enterprise—even one perceived as "friendly"—and the local tycoons, their enormous wealth notwithstanding, are unable to control developments in the territory to the extent believed on the mainland and lack the power needed to guarantee collective prosperity. Pessimists also view the alliance as tactical rather than strategic in nature. That is, it is not based on mutual trust, and the two sides have sought to cooperate for no other reason than short-term expediency.

Local attitudes towards the civil service are regarded by pessimists as an equally serious threat to stability. They do not see in the structure of the Chinese society in Hong Kong any evidence of the availability of a large number of people dedicated to the public good who might form a reservoir from which could emerge an elite civil service. Such people constitute a tiny minority because the very idea of public service runs counter to the survival ethic a hostile environment produces—people are on their own and can trust only their families. Because this ethic prevails in the territory, a strong sense of community has never developed, and thus there is little commitment to community service. What passes in the guise of community service is actually a great deal of self-serving because it is turned to practical use to influence business relationships. Pessimists feel that in the absence of a sense of community service, government efficiency and effectiveness are bound to decline, adversely affecting stability and prosperity.

The problem will doubtless be compounded by a behavioural phenomenon referred to by pessimists as the "last train syndrome." This syndrome does not manifest itself in societies whose members can legitimately expect future rewards—optimistic expectations may induce people to make short-term personal sacrifices in order to contribute to the long-term welfare of the community. Simply stated, people in these circumstances are prepared to wait their turn because it will eventually come. On the other hand, under different circumstances, such as in pre-1997 Hong Kong, it makes little sense to engage in socially responsible conduct. Rather, with the 1997 deadline approaching, there is a strong temptation to accumulate as much capital as possible—as quickly and ruthlessly as possible—and run. This type of behaviour normally results in an erosion of the rules of the game and in corruption and instability. Put another way, as everyone rushes to catch the last train, social discipline breaks down and the economy grinds to a halt.

Leading the rush to catch the last train, according to pessimists, will be the territory's entrepreneurs and professionals, two categories which clearly understand that the concept of "one country, two systems" is unworkable. Local entrepreneurs in particular, haunted by the memories of their experience in postrevolutionary China, are determined not to lose their assets again. These people were shaken by the events of September 1982 when Prime Minister Thatcher went to Beijing and failed to secure an extension of the lease. They expected some kind of a compromise to be struck, with Britain conceding sovereignty but continuing to administer Hong Kong beyond 1997. And because they were caught by surprise, they found themselves holding tangible assets in the territory—assets they could not dispose of when the property and stock markets collapsed. The present upsurge in property and stock values presents the local tycoons with their last opportunity to go liquid and move their capital to places such as Australia, Canada, and the United States. Astute enough to realize this, they are vigorously, albeit often discreetly, seeking new investment outlets.

Pessimists argue that the flight of entrepreneurial and professional talent and capital will deprive Hong Kong of perhaps its most important resource. It is true that the territory is not short of highly motivated and capable young people who could replace the departing entrepreneurs and professionals. It is also true that foreign investors show no signs whatever of contemplating a withdrawal from Hong Kong and that their professional counterparts appear to be more than willing to practice their skills there. Be that as it may, pessimists contend that the transition from British to Chinese rule—more specifically, the institutional changes likely to accompany it—will prevent the emergence of a new generation of successful local entrepreneurs and professionals. Foreigners too, and for similar reasons, will sooner or later scale down their operations in the territory. The inevitable brain drain and flight of capital will leave a gap that will be filled by state enterprises and personnel from the mainland. Hong Kong will thus become a city dominated by a mixture of socialist and state-capitalistic influences. Consequently, pessimists reason, it will lose its dynamism and ability to sustain a high level of prosperity.

Process

Pessimists consider the upsurge in confidence in the territory after the signing of the Sino-British Joint Declaration and the economic boom experienced by it in the late 1980s as temporary phenomena. According to them, the confident mood and the strength of the economy stem from the realization that there is sufficient time to make further financial gains and currency advances in the wake of the steep decline (since September 1985) in the value of the US dollar. Pessimists regard the post-1984 period as the final stage in the territory's golden age—an age during which Hong Kong has been transformed from a fishing village into a thriving metropolis.

This stage will soon come to an end, but pessimists are not in complete agreement as to when exactly the Hong Kong economy will shift into reverse. Some suggest that 1989 may serve as the turning point; others do not foresee any significant changes before 1992. Rather than single out a particular year, many pessimists simply state that the territory will experience a serious crisis of confidence in the early 1990s and that economic conditions thereafter will deteriorate markedly. A measure of stability, although not prosperity, will be restored around 2000, when the second stage in Hong Kong's evolution from a British colony into a Chinese SAR will end and the third one will begin.

It is interesting to note that the crisis of confidence pessimists anticipate in the early 1990s is not linked by them to any specific events, whether in China or the territory. What will precipitate the crisis, they claim, is the recognition that time is running out and that the risks inherent in retaining a stake in Hong Kong exceed the rewards by a critical margin. This recognition will result in a sharp acceleration in disinvestment, outflow of capital (including human capital), and quest for liquid assets. It will also lead to a property market and stock market crash and drastically affect the performance of the banking industry.

Pessimists are divided as to whether Britain will watch these developments with passive resignation or opt for a more decisive course of action. Some believe the UK will remain nominally committed to the territory in order not to incur the wrath of the Chinese. Others think that it will have no choice but to seek a quick retreat from Hong Kong in the mid-1990s (say, 1993–1994) because of the deteriorating economic and political climate. They argue that two factors will tip the balance in favour of an early withdrawal: growing interference by the PRC in the administration of the territory and escalating public protest. (If the local people are unable to express overtly their hostility towards China, they may well turn on the Hong Kong government as the target for their frustration.)

It should be emphasized that pessimists do not envisage a collapse of the public order in the territory during the second stage of the transition from British to Chinese rule. Nor do they doubt the government's ability to respond effectively, should the need arise, to actions which may constitute a challenge to its authority. Nonetheless, some of them are convinced that Britain will be subject to such intense pressure in Hong Kong by 1993–1994 that a retreat from the territory will have to be considered very seriously. After all, operating a "lame duck" government whose authority is undermined both from within and without and which faces a severe economic crisis is not a viable option unless there is reason to assume that the problem is temporary and that the long-term benefits to be derived from resisting the strong urge to depart before 1997 outweigh the short-term costs. Because neither assumption seems valid to highly pessimistic key informants, they believe the British will withdraw from Hong Kong earlier than planned, whether unilaterally or with the consent of the PRC.

Those pessimists who expect an early British withdrawal constitute a relatively small minority. Most are of the opinion that the colonial administration will continue to discharge perfunctorily its responsibilities until 30 June 1997. They also predict that two to three years later the situation in Hong Kong will stabilize almost completely, although an economic turnaround will not be achieved under the new regime. Put another way, as a special economic zone of the PRC, and in the third stage of its transition from British to Chinese rule, the territory will enjoy stability without prosperity—or the type of stability that is detrimental to true prosperity.

Evaluation

If optimists and pessimists reach completely different conclusions and proceed from completely different premises, there are nonetheless some similarities in the way they structure their respective arguments. For instance, both groups tend to rely excessively on monocausal explanations and are vulnerable to criticism on those grounds. As pointed out earlier, optimists engage in a form of analysis referred to as "economism," portraying the PRC leadership as being propelled almost exclusively by economic considerations. On the other hand, pessimists obviously perceive Chinese policymakers as being driven by no other motive than the desire to extend and consolidate party control. They rule out, at least implicitly, the possibility that those who hold political power on the mainland may be pursuing multiple goals (e.g., modernization as well as maximum party control), and they refuse to acknowledge, again at least implicitly, that the pursuit of multiple—and often conflicting—goals is neither an uncommon phenomenon nor an impossible task.[20]

Pessimists go beyond merely depicting top cadres in the PRC as preoccupied above all else with party control. They see them, to paraphrase Downs,[21] as "purely self-interested officials" whose sole aim is to protect their resources and preserve their ability to exert power; maximum party control is just a means to this end. The emphasis on self-interest as a factor motivating players in the Chinese political arena can, of course, be viewed as a useful antidote to the rather naive optimistic assumption that such players are guided largely by the nation's interest. However, it is a moot point to what extent one may legitimately describe the PRC ruling elite as a one-dimensional, self-interested group. Indeed, there is reason to believe that its attitudes and behaviour have complex roots and cannot be attributed to a single cause.[22]

Another related criticism which may be levelled at pessimists is that, like their optimistic counterparts, they generally overlook the fact that Chinese leaders by no means share the same policy preferences. The perception that politics in the PRC is basically a game in which coalitions made up of power-seekers vie for dominance presumably accounts for this tendency to minimize the significance of policy differences on the mainland. Yet as noted previously, a number of leading sinologists[23] deem such differences to be highly significant. Furthermore, these observers contend that there is no dearth of top Chinese cadres strongly committed to genuine reform. Their potential influence on developments in Hong Kong should perhaps not be exaggerated, but neither should it be ignored.

Admittedly, pessimists paint a picture of Chinese politics which is not easy to challenge; their analysis of the dynamics of power in the PRC rests on solid cultural foundations. Nevertheless, they are open to the criticism that their predictions have the hallmarks of cultural determinism. It may well be that the Chinese cultural milieu produces politicians who put a high premium on control and who are motivated primarily by self-interest. However, as social scientists[24] have shown, culture is not immune to change. For instance, it would not be unreasonable to assume that as China opens its door, the encounter with new technologies and other cultures might induce cultural change there. And a more propitious cultural climate could enable a reformist elite to pursue vigorously its agenda and possibly even realize some of its ambitious goals.

Whether or not China undergoes cultural transformation and its leadership steers it in a reformist direction, developments in Hong Kong need not necessarily conform to pessimists' expectations. Like their optimistic counterparts, pessimists tend to overstate the ability of top decisionmakers in the PRC to implement their policy designs. Perhaps because they perceive the Chinese political system as totalitarian[25] in nature, pessimists exaggerate its "conversion effectiveness" (i.e., effectiveness in converting policies into action).[26] There is no denying that a handful of party officials wield enormous power in the PRC. However, as observed earlier and contrary to prevailing opinion, policy implementation is not necessarily an activity the Chinese bureaucracy carries out with a great deal of success. As a corollary, pessimists may be criticized for failing to consider more carefully how countervailing forces, both internal and external, could modify PRC policies in Hong Kong and reshape economic realities there.

Pessimists also appear to be making somewhat questionable assumptions about the behaviour of Chinese politicians. Whereas their rationality draws the optimists' undue emphasis, pessimists portray them as overly irrational. The impression left is that pessimists view the PRC leadership as highly inconsistent, poorly informed, and incapable of learning, but there is evidence indicating these perceptions may not always be valid. For instance, Suttmeier[27] has concluded that the shifts in science policy on the mainland between 1949 and 1974, although reflecting the tension between the forces of revolution and consolidation, proved useful because the experience with opposing models helped science policymakers to develop a national strategy through active learning and systematic accumulation of relevant knowledge. As Suttmeier has summed it up: The Chinese themselves have been unable to decide how science should be integrated with society and social change. As a result they have experimented with competing models and have incorporated what has been learned from those experiments into the design of subsequent models.[28]

A study by Chan[29] is even more instructive in this respect. He has highlighted the stability of the PRC's conflict behaviour from the Korean War (1950) to the Quemoy conflict (1958), the Sino-Indian border disputes (1962), The Vietnam War (1964–1965), and the more recent Sino-Soviet border clashes. Chan has detected no signs of oscillations in this particular domain and has suggested that "the similarities in Peking's actions across different historical contexts imply the presence of a relatively stable and coherent strategy of conflict management.[30] Experience in other policy areas also casts doubt on the pessimists' assertions regarding Chinese decision-making behaviour. For instance, agricultural policy from 1976 to the post-1978 reforms was largely confined to marginal changes in the allocation of private plots and the sanctioning of open markets.[31] It would be misleading, of course, to argue that strategy formulation in the PRC is not characterized by often wide swings, but close examination of specific policies occasionally uncovers patterns of change of varying magnitudes: Some policy swings appear to be circumscribed within narrower limits (agriculture); some are immune from oscillation (defence); and sometimes the oscillations themselves may result in a cumulative learning effect (science).

Another set of somewhat questionable assumptions apparently underlying the pessimistic scenario concerns systemwide change in China. As pointed out earlier, optimists are convinced that politico-economic evolution in the PRC is proceeding in a manner consistent with what students of social change describe as "unilinear theories of social progress." Pessimistic key informants, on the other hand, veer to the other extreme and depict China as a society which is in "stationary equilibrium"[32]—one which almost invariably returns to its initial state once the change-inducing agent has been neutralized. Unlike social systems deemed "open,"[33] such a society does not experience real "growth" (in the sense of moving towards increasing complexity, operational effectiveness, order, and unity).[34]

The initial, or "natural" state to which the PRC system is supposed to return entails the use of coercion as a control mechanism and an emphasis on order goals. (Order goals "involve preventing people from doing the wrong things, more or less without regard to why they refrain from doing them, and without any expectation that they will make a positive contribution."[35] By contrast, ideological goals "involve getting people to understand or believe the right things, or to do the right things voluntarily and for the right reasons."[36] Economic goals "involve inducing people to produce and exchange services."[37]) From time to time, strain within the system produces a change in direction and the leadership's operational code becomes a combination of normative power and ideological goals (e.g., during the Great Leap Forward and the Cultural Revolution) or of remunerative power and economic goals (e.g., at various junctures since 1978). (Power "is normative when it is based on persuasion, promises and the manipulation of symbolic rewards"[38] and remunerative "when it rests on the rationalized exchange of compliance for material rewards."[39]) Pessimists seem to believe, however, that Chinese society is destined to be governed by a mixture of coercive power and order goals.

The pessimists' emphasis on historical determinism is apparently rooted in a perception of the PRC as a country hampered by a rigid political culture and dedicated to a self-perpetuating form of totalitarianism that allows a small elite to enjoy a "triple (i.e., economic, ideological and political) power monopoly."[40] There are scholars who contend that the immobilism thought to characterize the mainland system belies the "underlying reality of a complex daily policy process of development and refinement,"[41] that the frequent and seemingly futile attempts to liberalize or radicalize it constitute a regular "component of Chinese administrative technique geared to achieving an incremental step in national development,"[42] and that the most appropriate model to explain change in the PRC is a "policy experimentation-cum-secular-development model."[43] Some researchers[44] even suggest that China may undertake (or be compelled to undertake) genuine reform, both economic and political, rather than merely a series of superficial adjustments[45]—a possibility perhaps dismissed too lightly by pessimists who foresee a continuing stalemate on the economic and political fronts with unfortunate implications for Hong Kong.

Notes

1. See L.T. Lee, "Chinese Communist Law," *Michigan Law Review* 60 (February 1962): 439–472; V.H. Li, "The Role of Law in Communist China," *China Quarterly* 44 (October-December 1970): 66–111.

2. In the 1950s, the main task of factory managers and party secretaries was to arouse the patriotic sentiments of workers. First they set targets and concocted the relevant political slogans. Then the work hands or teams were encouraged to compete among themselves in "ushering in the new socialist era." Those who broke production records received spiritual rather than material rewards—for instance, personal thanks from national leaders.

3. See A.O. Krueger, "The Political Economy of the Rent-Seeking Society," *American Economic Review* 64 (June 1974): 291–303; J.M. Buchanan, R.D. Tollison and G. Tullock, eds., *Towards a Theory of the Rent-Seeking Society* (College Station: Texas A & M University Press, 1980); K.K. Fung, "Surplus Seeking and Rent Seeking through Back-Door Deals in Mainland China," *American Journal of Economics and Sociology* 46 (July 1987): 299–317.

4. See Harris, "The International Future of Hong Kong;" Wilson, "New Thoughts on the Future of Hong Kong;" Harris, *Hong Kong*; Miners, "Can the Colony of Hong Kong Survive 1997?;" Rabushka, *Hong Kong*; Lawrie, "Hong Kong and the People's Republic of China;" Cheng, "The Future of Hong Kong;" Youngson, *Hong Kong*; Greenfield, "The Hong Kong Solution;" Youngson, ed., *China and Hong Kong*; Au, *Possible Futures of Hong Kong*; Johnson, "The Mouse-Trapping of Hong Kong;" Overholt, "Hong Kong and the Crisis of Sovereignty;" Bonavia, *Hong Kong and 1997*; Ching, *Hong Kong and China*; de Mesquita, Newman and Rabushka, *Forecasting Political Events*; Harding, "The Future of Hong Kong;" Jao, "The Monetary System and the Future of Hong Kong;" Jao, "Hong Kong's Future as a Financial Centre;" Overholt, "Hong Kong and China;" Williams, "The Economies of Hong Kong and Taiwan and their Future Relationships with the PRC;" Domes, "The Impact of the Hong Kong Problem and the Hong-Kong Agreement on PRC Domestic Politics;" Harris, "Hong Kong Confronts 1997;" Jao, "Hong Kong's Future as a Free

Market Economy;" Johnson, "1997 and After;" Kelly, *Hong Kong*; King, "The Hong-Kong Talks and Hong-Kong Politics;" Lau and Kuan, "Hong Kong After the Sino-British Agreement;" Prybyla, "The Hong-Kong Agreement and its Impact on the World Economy;" Chiu, Jao and Wu, eds., *The Future of Hong Kong*; L.W. Pye, "The International Position of Hong Kong," *China Quarterly* 95 (September 1983): 456–468; S.E. Finer, "Hong Kong and 1997," *Political Quarterly* 56 (July-September 1985): 262–270; George Hicks, "The Political Economy of 1997," in *Hong Kong and 1997*, ed. Jao et al., pp. 399–404; J.C. Hsiung, "The Hong Kong Settlement," *Asian Affairs* 12 (Summer 1985): 47–58; A.C. Wu, "One Country, Two Systems," *Issues and Studies* 21 (July 1985): 33–59; J.P. Burns, "The Process of Assimilation of Hong Kong and the Implications for Taiwan," *AEI Foreign Policy and Defense Review* 6 (3/1986): 19–26; Y.M. Shaw, "An ROC View of the Hong Kong Issues," *Issues and Studies* 22 (June 1986): 13–30.

5. L.W. Pye, *The Spirit of Chinese Politics* (Cambridge, Mass.: M.I.T. Press, 1968), pp. 12–13.

6. Ibid., pp. 13–16.

7. See P. Atwell, *British Mandarins and Chinese Reformers* (Hong Kong: Oxford University Press, 1985).

8. See C.D. Howe, ed., *Shanghai* (Cambridge: Cambridge University Press, 1981).

9. See L.W. Pye and N. Leites," Nuances in Chinese Political Culture," *Asian Survey* 22 (December 1982): 1148.

10. See A.Y.C. King, "Administrative Absorption of Politics in Hong Kong," *Asian Survey* 15 (May 1975): 422–439; S.K. Lau, *Society and Politics in Hong Kong* (Hong Kong: Chinese University Press, 1982).

11. See Pye, "The International Position of Hong Kong," p. 459.

12. See ibid.

13. See ibid, p. 462.

14. Ibid., pp. 461–462.

15. L.W. Pye, "Taiwan's Development and its Implications for Beijing and Washington," *Asian Survey* 26 (June 1986): 612.

16. Ibid., p. 612.

17. See J.C. Hsiung, "The Hong Kong Settlement," *Asian Affairs* 12 (Summer 1985): 47–58; Y.M. Shaw, "An ROC View of the Hong Kong Issue," *Issues and Studies* 22 (June 1986): 13–30.

18. Pye, "The International Position of Hong Kong," p. 464.

19. Prybyla, "The Chinese Economy," p. 554.

20. See G.C. Edwards and I. Sharkansky, *The Policy Predicament* (San Francisco: Freeman, 1978).

21. Downs, *Inside Bureaucracy*.

22. See Harding, "Competing Models of the Chinese Communist Policy Process."

23. See Solinger, "The Fifth National People's Congress and the Process of Policy Making;" Hamrin, "Competing Policy Packages in Post-Mao China;" Harding, "Competing Models of the Chinese Communist Policy Process;" Solinger, *Chinese Business under Socialism*.

24. See Ponsioen, *The Analysis of Social Change Reconsidered*; Applebaum,

Theories of Social Change; Boulding, *A Primer on Social Dynamics*; Nisbet, ed., *Social Change*; Moore, *Social Change*; Edari, *Social Change*; Smith, *Social Change*.

25. See L. Shapiro, *Totalitarianism* (London, Pall Mall Press, 1972); S.P. Soper, *Totalitarianism* (Lanham: University Press of America, 1985).

26. See M.E. Olsen, *The Process of Social Organization* (New York: Holt, Rinehart and Winston, 1978).

27. R.P. Suttmeier, "Science Policy Shifts, Organizational Change and China's Development," *China Quarterly* 62 (June 1975): 207–241.

28. Ibid., p. 238.

29. S. Chan, "Chinese Conflict Calculus and Behavior," *World Politics* 30 (April 1978): 391–410.

30. Ibid., p. 40.

31. See Petrick, "Policy Cycles and Policy Learning in the People's Republic of China."

32. See Olsen, *The Process of Social Organization*; W. Buckley, *Sociology and Modern Systems Theory* (Englewood Cliffs, N.J.: Prentice-Hall, 1966); J.J. Monane, *A Sociology of Human Systems* (New York: Appleton-Century-Crofts, 1967).

33. See Buckley, *Sociology and Modern Systems Theory*; Monane, *A Sociology of Human Systems*; Olsen, *The Process of Social Organization*.

34. See Buckley, *Sociology and Modern Systems Theory*; Monane, *A Sociology of Human Systems*; Olsen, *The Process of Social Organization*.

35. See Skinner and Winckler, "Compliance Succession in Rural Communist China," p. 402.

36. See Ibid.

37. See Ibid.

38. See Ibid.

39. See Ibid.

40. See H. Wagner, "Stages of Communist Rule," *Asian Perspective* 11 (Spring-Summer 1987): 152–170.

41. Nathan, "Policy Oscillations in the People's Republic of China," p. 732.

42. Ibid., p. 731.

43. Ibid., p. 733.

44. See, for example, Wagner, "Stages of Communist Rule." See also: Johnson, ed., *Change in Communist Systems*; S.P. Huntington and C.H. Moore, eds., *Authoritarian Politics in Modern Society* (New York: Basic Books, 1970); A. Brown and J. Gray, eds., *Political Culture and Political Change in Communist Systems* (London: Macmillan, 1977); A. Gyorgy and J.A. Kuhlman, eds., *Innovation in Communist Systems* (Boulder, Westview, 1978).

45. As Wagner has observed: There is no doubt, whatsoever, that communist dictatorships are reformable. This is due to the existence and engagement of non-totalitarian, authentic societal forces. They determine the course and the speed of the de-totalization process. The very moment communist regimes abandon their triple power monopoly, voluntarily or compulsorily, they cease to be totalitarian and turn into authoritarian systems." Wagner, "Stages of Communist Rule," p. 170.

SIX

The Trend Scenario for the Hong Kong Economy

Effects

Optimists and pessimists tend to make assumptions and offer predictions which appear to point firmly in one direction. Their stance is unqualified and communicated in a way which leaves little scope for meaningful synthesis. Key informants identified with the trend scenario, on the other hand, seek consciously to integrate the optimistic and pessimistic forecasts. They emphasize the enormous complexity of the task confronting students of the territory's future and maintain that it should be approached with a flexible attitude and an awareness of the pitfalls inherent in oversimplification. For this reason—but without necessarily implying that their scenario is superior to those which lie at the extreme ends of the optimism-pessimism continuum—it may be convenient to refer to them as "realists."

Realists believe that Hong Kong will be neither a fully autonomous SAR nor yet another Chinese special economic zone. Specifically, they think that it will retain its separate status and be given the means to operate in a semi-independent fashion in a number of policy domains, but that the parameters within which its government will be allowed to act in a discretionary manner will be strictly defined and that the PRC will ensure, by exercising both ex ante and ex post facto strategic control, that the "national" interest is never overlooked. (A high degree of ex ante strategic control can be achieved by manipulating public opinion, influencing the recruitment and socialization of bureaucratic and political elites, providing administrative and policy guidance, establishing mechanisms for joint consultation, co-opting local leaders into central and provincial decisionmaking bodies on the mainland, offering positive and negative reinforcement, and so forth.) In fact, realists are of the opinion that strategic decisions having very wide ramifications will be taken in Beijing rather than in the territory, although local views will normally be canvassed, at least on an informal and selective basis.

The "controlled" autonomy envisaged by realists will doubtless fall short of the expectations to which the Sino-British Joint Declaration has given rise both locally and internationally. In most respects, it will also fall short of the substantial de facto autonomy Hong Kong has enjoyed as a Crown Colony/dependent territory. Nonetheless, realists are confident that it will remain sufficiently different from the mainland and sufficiently independent of the central government to be able to function with reasonable effectiveness as a capitalist enclave with its own identity and its own policies (and, of course, the institutional mechanisms needed to sustain that identity and those policies).

Realists anticipate that Hong Kong will differ from the mainland in at least four crucial respects. First, it will continue to rely on private ownership of the means of production and respect for private property rights as key principles of social organization, whereas the mainland will decentralize its industrial structure but not pursue decollectivization beyond the small-enterprise segment of the urban economy. Second, the market will remain the ultimate arbiter of value in Hong Kong; the mainland will not abandon its quest for a balance between central planning and market discipline. Third, the Hong Kong economy will be far more open than its mainland counterpart because those responsible for economic policymaking in the territory will not proceed to erect significant external barriers to the mobility of factors of production and the flow of goods and services—the kind of barriers the Chinese government may contemplate lowering gradually but will certainly not be inclined to remove altogether for a long time to come.

The fourth noteworthy difference between Hong Kong and the mainland will manifest itself, according to realists, in the political domain. The CCP may become a more accountable organization, but it will not abandon its role as the dominant force in Chinese society. By contrast, in the territory the party will be less visible and display a greater degree of self-restraint. That is, it will be content to operate as a "shadow" government and as a rule will exert influence indirectly rather than directly (e.g., through subtle manipulation and manoeuvring, organizational penetration, coaching and guidance of relevant decision-makers, exhortation, policy coordination, and careful "damage control"). As a result, Hong Kong will continue to be administered as an essentially "bureaucratic polity,[1] although its executive branch of government will be subject to more formidable external and internal constraints than at present. (With respect to internal constraints, realists postulate that in addition to a more or less independent judiciary, the local bureaucracy will have to share power with a legislature most of whose members will be either directly or indirectly elected and therefore increasingly reluctant to toe the official line).

The point concerning the high degree of openness of the Hong Kong economy requires an elaboration and a qualification. Specifically, the assertion that the territory will not erect significant external barriers to the mobility of factors of production and the flow of goods and services is coupled by realists with the prediction that the Hong Kong dollar will remain a freely convertible currency. At the same time, they argue that it will be linked to a basket of currencies (a linkage deemed to have greater economic and political advantages than a link to the US dollar) in order to foster a climate of stability. Moreover, realists hasten to emphasize that an open economy should not be equated with a passive monetary stance. On the contrary, they expect the Monetary Affairs Branch of the Hong Kong government to adopt, with the support of the Bank of China, a far more active posture and become as prone to regulatory excesses as is the Monetary Authority of Singapore.

Indeed, realists believe that Hong Kong will evolve into a city similar to Singapore in several other respects. This means that the government's penchant for regulation will not be confined to the monetary sphere, but will manifest itself in many areas of economic activity; particularly affected will be activities which reflect and reinforce modes of political and social behaviour perceived by the CCP leadership as a source of "spiritual pollution." Realists also think that public spending will rise, that the tax burden will be heavier, and that the government will play a more active role in managing the economy (i.e., the policy of "positive nonintervention" will be diluted). Be that as it may, state paternalism will not be carried much beyond the limits witnessed in Singapore, and the territory will remain a fairly attractive business proposition.

In addition to drawing parallels between Hong Kong and Singapore, realists see some similarities between future economic practices in the territory and those in present-day Japan. Thus, they point to the inevitable emergence of a form of protectionism directed at players other than those belonging to the network of mainland-owned enterprises and business entities deemed friendly by China. As is the case in Japan, this protectionism will be of the "invisible" variety, though realists do not expect it to be highly damaging in nature and contend that it will not lead to a significant erosion of market operations. The system will doubtless lose some of its efficiency, but most players will adapt to the marginally different rules of the game and—higher transaction costs notwithstanding—will try to turn them to their advantage by forming strategic alliances and making politically astute investments. Similarly, the system should be able to tolerate a slightly higher level of corruption without experiencing economic paralysis.

The preceding observations suggest that realists anticipate an institutional realignment in Hong Kong. To be more explicit, they posit that economic power will shift from organizations with colonial roots to those with a mainland identity or at least solid mainland connections. This view should not be construed, however, as implying that realists hold the opinion that the territory will undergo a process akin to deinternationalization. Foreign-owned businesses will not encounter blatant discrimination, and even institutions with close links to the colonial establishment, such as the Hong

Kong and Shanghai Bank, will not be denied the opportunity to engage in profitable activities. Furthermore, the English language will be widely used, at least in the commercial domain, and laws governing business operations will continue to reflect international capitalist practices (although the British Commonwealth will not necessarily serve as the sole source of ideas for local law drafters, legislators, and judges).

Although they rule out deinternationalization, realists envisage two significant changes in the international role of the territory. First, they predict that its manufacturing sector will shrink considerably and that it will no longer function as an international manufacturing centre. Second, they are quite optimistic about the prospects of Hong Kong's service industries, but assume that their geographical scope will be largely confined to the PRC, the territory itself, and possibly Taiwan. In other words, Hong Kong will evolve into a key subregional service centre—the economic capital of China (or the various Chinas) rather than of the entire Asia-Pacific region.

Realists do not expect the territory's development to proceed as smoothly as imagined by their optimistic counterparts. Hong Kong will inevitably experience economic and political cycles, and the concept of "one country, two systems" as embodied in the Sino-British Joint Declaration will not be easy to implement. Nonetheless, the territory will adapt and carve out a niche for itself as a metropolis serving the hinterland to its north. As such, it should be able (absent unforeseen international circumstances) to grow at a rate of about 3–6 percent a year in real terms well into the twenty-first century.

Causes

The realistic scenario is supported by arguments which reflect both the optimistic and pessimistic standpoints. Thus, although they do not attach too much importance to the Joint Declaration and other quasi-legal obligations the PRC may undertake, realists postulate that Chinese policymakers are generally aware of the benefits of preserving the economic status quo in Hong Kong and the costs of tampering with it. On the other hand, they harbour no illusions about the CCP's preoccupation with control and its tactics. Unlike their optimistic and pessimistic counterparts, however, realists see no reason why China could not pursue multiple—and often conflicting—objectives in the territory. Indeed, this pursuit might take the form of a policy of "constrained maximization"—endeavouring to maximize the benefits Hong Kong offers subject to the constraint of achieving a fairly high degree of political control.

Realists employ a similar logic in analyzing likely developments in the PRC. They contend that the Chinese leadership is committed quite strongly to revitalizing the mainland economy, but that it is reluctant to undermine the party's monopoly position in most spheres of societal activity. This results in a pattern of behaviour that can be explained in terms of the "germs" theory of modernization.[2] Put another way, the drive to modernize produces unwanted political consequences which the party apparatus proceeds to suppress, with the cycle repeating itself when the costs of suppression escalate beyond a critical threshold. As Myers has elaborated:

> China's modernization plans require innovation, particularly innovation to adjust and maintain the coherence of the explanatory system at the highest levels. Such innovation can only come from the intellectuals who staff the institutions whose semiotic products are the physical and social sciences, economics, philosophy and the arts. To achieve this innovation there must be a relaxation of ideological control. Each time there is a relaxation of ideological control, however, and individuals begin to randomize their behaviour in order to create the necessary conditions for learning a new response, the ideological innovations that result are inevitably threatening to the coherence of the sanctioning ideology. The achievement of modernization requires less ideological control to permit more innovation, but that innovation is precisely the explanation for the increase in cultural and spiritual "pollution," the rise of "liberalism," and the appearance of "unhealthy tendencies" and other "germs."
>
> The leaders of the PRC are thus caught in what appears to be an impossible dilemma. The very sources of innovation that hold out the promise of the sort of future China's leaders profess to want may, in the end, be unavailable to them. By giving the various social institutions and the intellectuals who are part of them the sort of free rein they require to randomize and innovate, the coherence of the sanctioning ideology may be threatened. Conversely, by bringing these intellectuals under the control of that ideology, the main sources of innovation will be shut off.[3]

Unlike their optimistic counterparts, realists do not minimize the seriousness of the dilemma facing policymakers in the PRC. But they do not side with the pessimists either. Realists do not believe the dilemma will necessarily lead to immobilism or force the system into static equilibrium. Rather, while acknowledging that the modernization effort will continue to be marked by cycles of relaxation and repression in the years ahead, realists assert that the dilemma inherent in reconciling the objectives of economic efficiency and political control will not prevent gradual progress which may prove significant in the long run. In other words, they posit that the Chinese system is in dynamic equilibrium:[4] As it oscillates between the extremes of relaxation and repression, it does not return to its natural state, but instead settles at new points which over time show a tendency to move somewhat closer to the relaxation end of the spectrum.

Of course, progress is bound to be more limited in the face of policy swings than in their absence. Clearly, therefore, the realistic scenario is less reassuring than that offered by optimists. Nonetheless, those who subscribe to the realistic position anticipate sufficient strides to be made on the mainland towards the goals which inspire relaxation efforts to enable capitalist Hong Kong to avoid the kind of a painful readjustment foreseen by pessimists. The assumption is that the PRC will pursue economic efficiency somewhat more vigorously than it will party control and that the forces of relaxation will prove somewhat stronger than the forces of repression. Doubtless, the territory will have to adapt to the slightly harsher environment—but by merely modifying some of the prevailing rules of the game rather than discarding them altogether.

Realists are also of the opinion that the implementation of the "one country, two systems" policy, although a daunting task, should not pose insurmountable difficulties. They concede that Chinese officials are not well informed about Hong Kong and that the mainland bureaucracy is capable of thwarting the intentions, good or otherwise, of top decision-makers in Beijing. Implementation failures, perhaps even serious ones, are thus inevitable. Notwithstanding, realists dispute the pessimistic contention that policy learning is absent in the PRC and argue that in time Chinese party and state organs will become more effective in addressing the problems of the territory. The modus operandi of post-1997 Hong Kong may not correspond fully to that envisaged by the drafters of the Sino-British Joint Declaration, at least those representing the British side, but Chinese implementation failures will not set off a process of irreversible economic decline.

Obviously, other parties with a stake in the territory cannot be expected to wait patiently until the PRC achieves a better balance between economic efficiency and party control and learns how to manage Hong Kong without causing excessive disruption. Indeed, realists believe that uncertainty about China's intentions and ability to deliver will persist and that its occasionally heavy-handed and counterproductive tactics will continue to alienate both the local people and foreigners. Brain drain and capital flight will thus remain a cause for concern, and attracting skilled personnel and investment to the territory may prove difficult. Yet Hong Kong—in itself as well as in its status as gateway to the PRC—will present considerable business opportunities for what will be no dearth of economic actors willing to take the risks involved in trying to capitalize on them.

Realists are aware that inappropriate policies, implementation failures, departure of entrepreneurs and professionals, and disinvestment—even on a limited scale—are bound to have harmful consequences. However, China's generally accommodating policy towards the territory and the gradual improvement in the economic and political climate on the mainland should have a mitigating effect. Therefore, realists deduce, the Hong Kong economy might escape a severe downturn and be able to grow at a respectable annual rate of 3–6 percent in the long run. Such a performance, though scarcely impressive by historical standards, will be perceived as more than satisfactory given the circumstances and will in turn contribute to a growing sense of prosperity and stability.

Realists rule out the possibility of faster growth on the grounds that the business environment will be slightly less favourable than at present and that the service sector, which normally enjoys lower gains in productivity, will assume the role of an economic locomotive. The shift from manufacturing to services, which according to realists is already apparent, will accelerate for five principal reasons. First, investment in manufacturing entails greater political risk because of its capital-intensive nature; it will be deemed safer to channel resources into service operations. Second, labour-intensive and land-intensive manufacturing activities will be undertaken in the SEZs and the Pearl Delta region (and in other countries in Asia where production costs are well below the level prevailing in Hong Kong). Third, greater reliance on automation, particularly industrial robots, in developed countries will bring about a decline in investment in offshore manufacturing facilities. Fourth, local exporters will find it increasingly difficult to penetrate overseas markets in the face of escalating protectionist pressures.

The fifth factor realists consider a serious hindrance to further manufacturing expansion in the territory is perhaps the most interesting. They argue that in view of the challenge from low-cost producers, local industrialists must provide more sophisticated output but that their management style would be a liability in a high-tech environment. The Chinese, or rather overseas Chinese, excel in running small, family-owned, and highly flexible businesses, but seem to lack the ability attributed to the Japanese and Koreans of guiding in a disciplined fashion a large-scale organization, in the forefront of the technological battlefield, towards its long-term objectives. On the other hand, they make skilful business intermediaries and professionals and will thus help spur growth in the service sector.

As indicated, however, realists expect the territory to evolve into a subregional (rather than a regional or an international) service centre. They are convinced that Tokyo will eclipse all the other major Asian cities in this regard and that the relationship between the Japanese capital and Hong Kong will be similar to that between London and Zurich. The territory will enjoy a comparative advantage in the areas of entrepôt trade and the provision of financial and business services to the PRC, but in the regional/international sphere it will be unable to mount an effective challenge to Tokyo and will be reduced to playing a supplementary role to Asia's leading financial centre. (Realists claim that Hong Kong is the world's third largest financial centre only insofar as the number of financial institutions is concerned; otherwise Tokyo has already overtaken the territory.)

Japan's coming of age financially at this juncture reflects, of course, the nation's underlying strength and remarkable accumulation of surplus wealth. Noting Japan's prominence as a capital exporter, realists say they see a new era coming in which it will exercise much of the influence on the world economy that Britain and the United States wielded over the past century. Historically, a creditor nation has led growth in each period of global economic expansion, and Japan, as the largest supplier of capital to the world, will inevitably emerge as the dominant financial power. Tokyo, therefore, will enjoy considerable advantages over cities such as Hong Kong and Singapore.

It is true that relative to the size of its economy, Japan's financial markets have been midgets, stunted by protective regulations (and overcautious regulators) dating back to the period when the country was regaining its strength in the 1950s and 1960s. However, these markets are growing at a very rapid pace—perhaps too rapid for Japan's conservative financial planners who, because of external pressures, find themselves in the rather unusual position of having to react to events rather than dictating developments. Furthermore, realists believe that despite bureaucratic footdragging and the proliferation of cultural barriers, Japan will be compelled to embark on a radical deregulation programme and that by the end of this century it will enjoy a lower level of government intervention than any other industrialized country.

By implication, it would be erroneous to dismiss the Tokyo offshore banking market as a token gesture. Realists argue that it has got off to a better start than its New York counterpart, after which it was modelled and formally named, and that its performance thus far has exceeded expectations. Although tight regulation—somewhat tighter than in New York or Singapore—is preventing more robust growth of the Tokyo offshore market, there can be little doubt that the authorities recognize that the opening-up process will have to be carried further when it is fully established and trading has settled down. The Tokyo operation in its present form is just a first step, and more ambitious liberalization measures will eventually allow it to rank alongside London and New York as a key financial centre.

Realists contend that no major bank could afford not to be in the Tokyo offshore market, at which point a separate and probably competing presence in Hong Kong might be difficult to rationalize. Tokyo, not the territory, would be the natural funding centre for the yen lending that is gaining ground in the Asia-Pacific region at the expense of the US dollar. It is even possible, though improbable in the medium term, that Tokyo might be a more liberal place than an increasingly regulated Hong Kong. The territory would doubtless always offer some tax advantages over Japan, making it attractive as a place to book loans, but it could not vie with Tokyo for supremacy as an international/regional financial centre.

Japan will also benefit from the growing trend towards "securitization," realists assert. Tokyo, of course, already dwarfs other Asian stock markets—their combined capitalization is only a fraction that of the Tokyo Stock Exchange (TSE)—and Japan's dominance is in fact likely to become more pronounced in coming years. This will come about, inter alia, through increased listings by non-Japanese Asian companies on the TSE and the Osaka stock exchange. At present, only one of the foreign stocks listed in Tokyo (National Australia Bank) is from the West Pacific region. However, more are expected to be added soon—initially from Hong Kong, Singapore, and South Korea.

The reason Japan will dominate regional securities markets is simple. As sovereign lending by banks declines, borrowing in their own names by state-run and private-sector enterprises will accelerate in several Asian countries. Domestic capital markets are unlikely to be able to satisfy all of these needs, so at least part of the fund raising will take the form of tapping foreign equity markets, primarily Japan's. Undoubtedly, Hong Kong has similar ambitions of listing regional stocks, but its liquidity compared with Tokyo's is puny. Singapore is equally, perhaps even more, constrained in this respect.

State and private enterprises in several Asian countries have also joined their governments quite recently in tapping the bond markets as an alternative to bank borrowing or being funded through the national budget, action which highlights an interesting and little-recognized aspect of Tokyo's potential dominance. The so-called Asiadollar bond market (centred nominally in Hong Kong and Singapore) competes with the Euroyen bond and samurai bond markets. It is dollar-dominated (though yen issues are growing) and attracts Japanese as well as many Asian issuers. Increasingly, however, Japanese securities companies are underwriting Asiadollar bond issues and marketing them among Tokyo institutions. As a consequence, the Asiadollar bond market is becoming practically an offshore dollar market within the sphere of influence of the Tokyo market.

Furthermore, the Euroyen bond and samurai bond markets are also expected to grow very rapidly as eligibility criteria are progressively relaxed. The fact that more foreign companies will be listed on Japanese stock exchanges will allow them to issue convertible bonds and bonds with warrants attached on both Euroyen and samurai markets. In addition, the advent of swaps means that both markets will become closely integrated with the Asiadollar bond market. As a result of these developments, the yen will probably account for about a quarter of transactions on international bond markets within ten years, and a similar proportion of all issues will be floated in Tokyo.

Realists to not dispute either the validity of the "bigger-pie" theory or the optimist's assumption that Tokyo's growth will not necessarily be achieved at the expense of Asia's other regional financial centres, Hong Kong and

Singapore. They acknowledge that these smaller rivals may possibly benefit because Tokyo's internationalization will in all likelihood serve to increase the volume of financial transactions taking place in the Far East at the expense of London and New York. Perhaps Hong Kong and Singapore will have a smaller slice of the pie, but the pie itself will be bigger. Nonetheless, realists caution that the bigger-pie theory, although reassuring, may be only partly true. After all, as pointed out earlier, the more Tokyo grows as an international financial centre, the less logical it becomes for commercial and merchant banks to maintain parallel offices within the same region. The structural changes discussed previously may have a similar effect because as more of the world's debts are packaged into negotiable securities, financiers will want to conduct their main business alongside the customers to and from whom those securities are being bought and sold. In Asia, that means Japan, which has a dozen of the world's largest commercial banks, four of its largest merchant banks, the world's largest industrial corporations outside the US, and a stock market several times the size of all those of the rest of Asia put together. To state it differently, if regulatory liberalization makes Tokyo an available option, any other Asian market may be reduced to a mere sideshow.

On balance, therefore, realists conclude that the outlook for Hong Kong as a financial centre is one of provincialization rather than internationalization. The territory's standing as the largest Asian financial centre after Tokyo, they add, is also facing a serious challenge as a result of recently introduced disincentives to foreign banks. Of these, by far the most damaging is likely to be a decision by Japan's tax authorities to bring Hong Kong–registered subsidiaries of Japanese banks into the Tokyo tax net for the first time.[5] Another problem confronting Japanese deposit-taking companies (DTCs) in the territory, whose paradoxical emphasis is lending rather than taking deposits, is enforced compliance with Hong Kong's revised capital adequacy provisions. In this case, although the Japanese argued that letters of comfort from their city and trust bank head offices should suffice, the local Banking Commission was resolute in its demands that all banks and DTCs comply by September 1988 with a 5–8 percent capital-to-asset ratios laid down in the Banking Ordinance.[6]

A third negative factor—one whose impact will take some time to gauge—is the elevation to statute of a long-discussed proposal in Macau to establish an offshore banking unit (OBU) there. Although the Macau OBU may be little more than a booking centre for business actually conducted in nearby Hong Kong, realists assert that its liberal parameters could well attract substantial interest from the territory. Indeed, Macau's sudden decision to go ahead with an OBU, five years after it was first contemplated, is viewed by them as an opportunistic move to capitalize on the reluctance of many foreign banks to adhere to Hong Kong's existing and expected balance-sheet structures.

Realists emphasize that the problems and challenges confronting the territory in the financial domain should not be overstated. Hong Kong has played a preeminent role in the non-yen syndication business for Japanese banks and of late has attracted a growing share of Australian loan-syndication activity. Denied the tax advantage once enjoyed by their local subsidiaries, Japanese banks nonetheless appear unlikely to depart en bloc, partly because their branches will continue as before, consolidated by the parent, and also because they are allowed to deal in securities, an option not yet available to them in Japan. This fact, in conjunction with the proximity to China and the convenient location for financing trade with countries such as South Korea and Taiwan, will ensure the continued presence of the major Japanese banks, around twenty-five of which have full licenses.[7]

Furthermore, realists are confident that Hong Kong will remain a buoyant subregional service centre even in the face of the kind of problems and challenges previously highlighted. Booming entrepôt trade (which would benefit industries such as communications, construction, and transport), a rapid expansion in PRC-related financial and business services, and a thriving tourist industry will propel the economy along a growth path. Because its economic system will be characterized by a fairly high degree of flexibility and openness, realists also see no reason why the territory should not continue to show signs of vitality in areas in which it has traditionally performed well—such as bullion dealing, local corporate finance, and retail financial services to high-net-worth Southeast Asian overseas Chinese. In conclusion, Hong Kong may be about to shift from a pattern of spectacular growth to one of solid growth, from internationalization to provincialization, but it will emerge as the economic capital of a modernizing (although by no means modern) China—a status conducive to the steady development of all segments of the service sector other than those in direct competition with Tokyo.

Process

Realists are less inclined than their optimistic and pessimistic counterparts to divide the period up to and beyond 1997 into distinct subperiods. Rather, they expect a gradual evolution towards slower growth, deindustrialization, and provincialization. The process may extend over more than a decade and be completed only after 2000. Hence, to the extent that realists refer to specific developmental phases, they tend to confine themselves to the distinction between the transition period, which is likely to end around the turn of the century, and the period characterized by less marked change that will follow it.

Their emphasis on gradual evolution notwithstanding, realists acknowledge the probability of shocks to the system. Events such as swings to the left in the PRC, death of Deng Xiaoping, actions and statements by

Chinese officials perceived as unfavourable to Hong Kong, escalation of protectionist pressure, global recession, brain drain, capital flight, acceleration in the flow of business to Tokyo, British departure, and arrival of the PLA will have a detrimental effect on the territory's economic climate. However, such events will cause short-term rather than long-term dislocation and will influence the pace of economic change rather than its direction. Put another way, the assumption is that the Hong Kong system is capable of withstanding the type of shocks that realists envisage and adapting successfully in the face of the kind of environmental turbulence they anticipate.

Evaluation

One problematic feature of the realistic scenario is the reluctance or inability of those who espouse it to provide more detailed and less vague observations. To achieve a high degree of detail and avoid vagueness is, of course, an objective which often eludes futures researchers; the optimistic and realistic scenarios are also not entirely satisfactory in this respect. Realists argue, with some justification, that the lack of detail and the tendency to be vague which others may attribute to their forecasts stem from caution and a desire not to oversimplify and that the gaps in their scenario and the imprecise statements to which they are occasionally compelled to resort can legitimately be viewed as a virtue rather than a weakness. Nonetheless, one is left with the impression that realists might not be facing certain issues and that they are excessively flexible in their employment of some of the variables.

Another possible shortcoming of the realistic scenario lies in the somewhat naive belief that the conflicting forces likely to shape Hong Kong's destiny will inevitably be reconciled in a dialectical fashion: When the capitalist thesis is exposed to the socialist antithesis, the interpenetration between the two systems will result in a synthesis consistent with the goal of maintaining the territory's prosperity and stability. Such reasoning is often relied upon by social scientists who study processes of conflict and accommodation.[8] Be that as it may, the one-dimensional scenarios offered by optimists and pessimists appear in some respects more plausible than the halfway house constructed by realists. Interestingly enough, it is easier to accept positions indicating success or failure than those settling for the complex middle ground.

Realists also tend to overestimate Hong Kong's ability to withstand shocks to the system and adapt in the face of environmental turbulence. The confidence they display in this regard apparently stems from the fact that they look at each shock to the system and each episode of environmental turbulence in isolation—the cumulative effects are not considered. To ignore cumulative effects is conceptually problematic because there is evidence to suggest that response functions which are reasonably smooth over wide ranges can, without warning, exhibit very dramatic discontinuities once a critical threshold is reached.[9] (For instance, rivers cleanse themselves naturally of certain quantities of sewage, but above some threshold they can remove no more. Social systems show analogous properties as in, for example, the neighbourhood "tipping" phenomenon: When the proportion of black families or overcrowded dwellings passes some crucial threshold, the present residents flee en masse, leaving the neighbourhood to become all black or all slum.)[10] One should not rule out the possibility that a series of mutually reinforcing shocks to the system and episodes of environmental turbulence might cause a major breakdown and undermine prosperity and stability.

In addition to overestimating the territory's adaptive capacity, realists seem to underestimate the difficulties inherent in reforming the Chinese economy. The assumption that the PRC, without necessarily embracing capitalism or even market socialism, will progress sufficiently towards the goal of economic restructuring to allow Hong Kong to pursue policies conducive to prosperity and stability may not be valid. Neither the experience of Hungary nor that of Yugoslavia is encouraging in this respect. Both countries have been engaged for about two decades in efforts to liberalize their economies, but these efforts appear to have reached their limits and have not prevented an economic decline in recent years.[11] It is conceivable that the implementation of China's reform programme would prove equally difficult.

The realistic scenario is vulnerable to criticism on methodological as well as substantive grounds. Although they attribute to themselves a high degree of realism, those who espouse this scenario offer, like their optimistic and pessimistic counterparts, "categorical" rather than "hypothetical" predictions. (According to Popper,[12] categorical predictions specify what as a matter of fact is going to happen in the future; hypothetical predictions, on the other hand, indicate what will happen *if* certain conditions come about.) However, because realists are at least willing to contemplate the possibility of revising their scenario or parts thereof in the light of changing circumstances, it is reasonable to assume that their forecasts will take on an increasingly hypothetical character. In any event, notwithstanding their shortcomings, the three scenarios presented in this book provide a useful framework for exploring Hong Kong's future development.

Notes

1. See S.K. Lau, *Society and Politics in Hong Kong* (Hong Kong: Chinese University Press, 1982).

2. See J.T. Myers, "China—the 'Germs' of Modernization," *Asian Survey* 25 (October 1985): 981–996.

3. Ibid., p. 996.

4. See Buckley, *Sociology and Modern Systems Theory*; Monane, *A Sociology of Human Systems*; Olsen, *The Process of Social Organization*; A.O. Hirschman, *Journeys Toward Progress* (New York: Twentieth Century Fund, 1963).

5. With a corporate tax rate of 18 percent, Hong Kong has been highly attractive as a booking centre for Japanese institutions, burdened with a domestic corporate tax rate of almost 50 percent. By the end of 1986, assets held by Japanese-owned institutions in the territory amounted to a staggering HK$980 billion (US$125.6 billion), a consequence largely of Hong Kong's beneficial tax rate. This represented more than the total assets held by American, European and mainland Chinese banks and DTCs operating in the territory.

6. The tax and capital-adequacy problems are interrelated for the former will have a direct bearing on the ability of Japanese DTCs to meet capital adequacy requirements. Specifically, they will not be able to accumulate reserves because profits from Hong Kong will be needed by their head office to pay the extra tax. As a consequence, some may switch loans to other financial centres, such as Singapore.

7. Resigned to the tax liability, Japanese institutions will however be looking to the Hong Kong authorities to provide other sweeteners to encourage them not to reduce their level of activity in the territory.

8. See, for example, G.R. Leslie, R.F. Larson, and B.L. Gorman, *Order and Change* (London: Oxford University Press, 1980).

9. See A.E. Kahn, "The Tyranny of Small Decisions," *Kyklos* 19 (1, 1966): 23–47; R. Rose, "Coping with Urban Change," in *The Management of Urban Change in Britain and Germany*, ed. R. Rose (London: Sage, 1974), pp. 5–25; E.C. Zeeman, "Catastrophe Theory," *Scientific American* 234 (April 1976): 65–83; G.B. Kolta, "Catastrophe Theory," *Science* 196 (April 1977): 287, 350-351.

10. See R.E. Goodin, *Political Theory and Public Policy* (Chicago: University of Chicago Press, 1982).

11. See P.G. Hare, H.K. Rudice and N. Swain, eds., *Hungary* (London: Allen and Unwin, 1981); F. Singleton and B. Carter, *The Economy of Yugoslavia* (London: Croom Helm, 1982); I.T. Berend and G. Rank, *The Hungarian Economy in the Twentieth Century* (London: Croom Helm, 1985).

12. K.R. Popper, *The Poverty of Historicism* (London: Routledge and Kegan, 1960).

SEVEN
Policy Implications

The economic future of Hong Kong is a subject which can be approached both from a descriptive and a normative perspective. In fact, the two approaches should ideally complement one another: Description should serve as a basis for prescription; prescription should alert researchers engaged in description to environmental changes which may result from actions taken by influential decision-makers with a view to shaping future developments. Therefore, although this book has a clear descriptive bias, an attempt is made in this chapter to offer some policy ideas which might facilitate progress in the direction envisaged by optimists and realists–or at least help moderate the impact of the negative forces identified by pessimists.

The descriptive constructs outlined in preceding chapters have their source in the key informants I interviewed. The same key informants are also the source of the policy ideas sketched in this chapter. Those ideas were obtained by asking them the following question: "If you believe that the present status quo in Hong Kong should be maintained as far as possible, what practical steps could be taken to ensure this?" The most pessimistic among the key informants expressed reluctance to consider any practical measures to promote prosperity and stability, either because they perceive the future of the territory as an "uncontrollable" variable[1] or because they sense nothing can realistically be done to avert a significant economic decline. The majority of those interviewed, however, were willing to address themselves to this issue.

The practical steps suggested by the key informants can be grouped into a number of broad areas. Their proposals fall in the following categories: (1) political reform, (2) general policies, (3) specific economic policies, (4) the government's role during the transition period, (5) the civil service, (6) the relationship between Hong Kong and China, and (7) the territory's relationships with other external parties. While many of the proposals put forward pertained to noneconomic policy domains, they were offered with a view to rendering Hong Kong's economy less vulnerable to adverse pressures.

In the political realm, more than half of those interviewed were of the opinion that the territory should embrace some form of direct elections. The supporting arguments were expressed in "instrumental"—as distinct from "terminal"—terms. (Instrumental values are attached to means, whereas terminal values are attached to ends).[2] Specifically, the key informants contended that democratization was a prerequisite for capitalist institutions, particularly in the face of an erosion of the British link, and that it could act as a barrier against potentially harmful influences from the mainland where a more arbitrary form of government prevails. They also stressed that growing political participation might enhance the sense of social involvement, especially among members of the middle class, and therefore contribute to stability. Some even suggested that the opportunity to exercise the "voice" option would make local residents less inclined to resort to the "exit" option[3] and leave the territory.

It should be noted, however, that in many cases the support for direct elections was qualified. Several of those interviewed expressed anxieties about the possibility that democratization might result in a shift in emphasis from the creation of wealth to its redistribution. (As Olson[4] has observed, the ascendancy of groups concerned with redistributional objectives and economic decline are linked phenomena.) Another consequence of direct elections singled out as a cause for concern was the emergence of "political business cycles"[5]—the tendency of politicians to manage the economy with a view to gaining electoral advantages rather than optimizing performance in the strict sense of the term. A preoccupation with the redistribution of wealth and the existence of political business cycles could, of course, prove to be economically costly.

The perception that democratization may entail costs as well as benefits led some of the key informants to propose that in redesigning its political institutions, Hong Kong should use Japan as a model. According to those who took this position, Kaidanren (i.e., the Federation of Economic Organizations) is the pivotal force in Japanese politics. Kaidanren leaders normally do not seek political office—very few businesspersons in Japan do. The task is left to full-time politicians who are often succeeded by sons or other close male relatives. Kaidanren's vehicle is the Liberal Democratic Party (LDP), a broadly based organizational entity with no strong ideals whose members range from ultraconservatives to those slightly left of centre.

The key informants who proposed emulating Japan saw no reason why Hong Kong's leading businesses and their professional allies could not form a Kaidanren-style organization by superimposing it on the associations and chambers of commerce now in existence. In fact, they maintained that the "Group of 76"—Basic Law drafters who are in business and the professions—could probably be regarded as the nucleus of the territory's own Kaidanren. Furthermore, they argued that because of the apparent convergence of interests between capitalists and communists, an all-embracing party such as the LDP might be established in Hong Kong and comfortably accommodate the local business and professional establishment as well as leftists and other pro-China groups (i.e., virtually all the main political actors except for diehard liberals and fringe Marxists).

To establish such a party would doubtless pose a serious challenge in view of the strong feelings in the territory and in Beijing about party politics. Nonetheless, those interviewed were of the opinion that a convincing case could possibly be made for setting it up. (It would mean, of course, allowing others to form rival parties as well.) Failing this, the capitalist elite could field a "pressure group" of either like-minded people or "professional" politicians who would be funded by it and would espouse the politics advocated by the business and professional establishment.

The key informants favouring such a system emphasized that it would not be inconsistent with an executive-led type of government supported by the PRC. According to them, Japan also qualifies as an executive-led system because the bureaucracy is the other crucial component in the power structure. The Japanese civil service enjoys considerable autonomy; politicians in fact exercise only limited control over the bureaucrats, who often work more closely with the business community than with the politicos. From China's standpoint, a style of governance like the one that has evolved in Japan would presumably prove attractive because it might ensure prosperity and stability in the face of largely symbolic attempts by some politicians to promote seemingly abstract ideals.

The LDP is not a mass party. The Japanese system leaves the great mass of the people depoliticized, a feature the PRC leadership may find reassuring because it dovetails with Hong Kong people's putative apathy towards politics. Two additional characteristics of the local political scene were portrayed by those interviewed as being congruent with such a system: the avoidance of "adversarial politics" and the emphasis on "consensus." Many people in Japan apparently take considerable pride in having achieved these. Genuine democrats and liberals there enjoy, of course, the freedom to make their beliefs public and seek support for them. However, their actual influence remains limited, and they do not play a significant role in policy-making. Rather, the electorate is constantly exhorted to vote for prosperity, stability, and international prestige. And it is often reminded at election time of the danger posed by nonmainstream groups, particularly the communists, to the high living standards attained by Japanese society. The mild scepticism I expressed regarding the appropriateness of such practices in the territory's present circumstances elicited the following response from one key informant:

> It works. And there is no reason to believe that similar exhortations will not work here. Even the communist bogey can be used. Just imagine Sir Y.K.

Pao standing up and warning the people: "If the liberals get in and the whole place falls apart, Beijing's bureaucrats will come barrelling down to set things right." Who would want to vote for Martin Lee and Szeto Wah?

No doubt such a system will not make an earthly paradise of Hong Kong. With the exception of North Korea, however, where that has been officially proclaimed, there is no paradise on earth anywhere else.

It is interesting to note, however, that even this interviewee was careful to point out that political change was both inevitable and desirable. He and those holding similar views were clearly convinced that the future governmental system should rest on the two pillars of the business and professional establishment and the bureaucracy. Yet they expressed preference for a system rooted in the community-at-large and one in which political power flows through institutional channels. Consistent with this preference, most thought that at least 40 percent of the members of the legislature should be directly elected, that those not directly elected should be either elected by functional constituencies of the corporatist[6] type or appointed following a recommendation by a semi-independent body (i.e., one not controlled by the chief executive), and that mechanisms should be constructed to ensure executive accountability to the legislature. Whatever the outcome of the efforts to redesign the political system, virtually all the key informants who were willing to consider the policy implications of the transition from British to Chinese rule were of the opinion that these efforts should be guided by a spirit of compromise between the values of efficiency and liberty. As one interviewee summed it up:

> There are two politically significant groups in Hong Kong: the capitalists and the middle class professionals. Apparently, these two groups have somewhat divergent ideas. But if the territory is to have a future, they have to cooperate. The capitalists must understand that in the long run liberty is indivisible. Authoritarianism and capitalism can, of course, go together for a while, as in South Korea and Taiwan, but never for long, because capitalism fosters independence and ultimately the demand for liberty, while authoritarianism breeds a ruling class that will wittingly or unintentionally work against the interests of capitalism.
>
> For their part, the middle classes in Hong Kong must realize that unrestricted majoritarianism erodes the bases of individual freedom as well as economic growth. The territory definitely does not need high taxes, extensive regulation, and the protection of special interests. Together, these two groups should therefore try to design a constitutionally constrained political "democracy" where the government enjoys something akin to a popular mandate but where its powers (particularly economic powers such as those to tax, borrow, print money, and regulate the economy) are limited.

Indeed, several of the general policy proposals and the specific economic policy proposals put forward by the key informants were inspired by the perception that government powers ought to be constrained through a combination of effective constitutional and institutional measures. The general policy steps favoured included the introduction of a bill of rights as part of the Basic Law, the distancing of the judiciary from the civil service, the establishment of an independent office to perform functions similar to those of an ombudsman (ideally, to be supplemented by a freedom of information law giving individuals, among other things, the right of access to any files the government holds on them), and the strengthening of the role of the director of audits. (The director would be made completely independent of the executive branch and provided with more resources; the scope of the reviews undertaken would be extended beyond financial and compliance audit and economy and efficiency audit into policy/programme audit.)

The specific economic policy proposals made by the interviewees with a view to ensuring governmental restraint centred largely on the need to adopt constitutional rules which would reduce the room for manoeuvre available to the authorities in managing the economy. In particular, they were inclined to emphasize the advantages of a mandatory balanced-budget mechanism, arguing that the budgets formulated (both proposed and adopted) and implemented by the government in each fiscal year ought to be either balanced or in surplus. (Departures from this rule should be allowed only if supported by, say, at least three-quarters of the members of the legislature). They also tended to suggest that a substantial majority of the members of the legislature (again, three-quarters was a figure mentioned often) ought to be required for increasing tax rates or introducing new taxes.

Similar proposals were put forward in relation to the management of the territory's currency and its money supply. Thus, several key informants maintained that the free convertibility of the Hong Kong dollar should be constitutionally guaranteed. A considerable number also expressed strong opposition to the establishment of a central bank and asserted that a linked exchange rate system—provided the peg was to a basket of currencies rather than to the ailing US dollar—would serve a useful purpose in restraining automatically the money supply and relieving the government of the pressure from interest groups to manipulate it.

Another specific economic policy proposal made with the aim of curbing potential excesses on the part of the authorities and preventing mismanagement of the economy was to privatize as many public services as possible. As one interviewee stated: "The objective should be to fill up the economic space with property rights, as it were, to constrain government." In the case of services which cannot be financed by the private sector or which involve considerations of the public interest, it was suggested that the government could withdraw from the production process and confine itself to providing finance through a voucher scheme. (Under the voucher system, individuals receive authorizations to spend public funds—vouchers—which they use to purchase goods and services in the open market. Suppliers return those vouchers to the issuing agency for payment.)

Not all the general policy proposals and specific economic policy proposals put forward by the key informants were directed at restricting government powers. Some interviewees, for instance, placed considerable emphasis on the need not only to avoid succumbing to the urge to discourage local residents from emigrating but also to condone unofficial efforts to facilitate the quest for second passports. The point stressed by those who adopted this position was that the option of exit paradoxically reinforces the incentive to stay. Similar views were expressed with respect to the strategy of precautionary diversification which local entrepreneurs have been pursuing in managing their investments. Such a strategy, it was contended, is both sensible and conducive to stability and should therefore under no circumstances be subject to official disapproval.

The general policy proposal to foster a climate of tolerance with regard to emigration, if implemented, could of course further weaken the supply side of the economy by aggravating the problem of labour shortage. However, the key informants were confident that market forces would help to rectify imbalances in the demand for and supply of blue-collar workers (though they urged the adoption of creative solutions such as the provision of day-care centres, which could enable working mothers to join the labour force). The dearth of white-collar workers was seen as a greater cause for concern, but even this apparent constraint was viewed by the interviewees as amenable to policy manipulation, which could include the following specific (economic) policy proposals: (1) to allow key staff time off to obtain foreign residency papers (ideally, by orchestrating "emigration shifts" to avoid a flood of vacancies in the 1990s); (2) to better integrate international operations, which could be used as leverage positions to obtain residency papers for key personnel; and (3) to start recruiting overseas in countries such as Australia, Canada, and the US, which have absorbed a large number of former Hong Kong residents who have already fulfilled their residency requirements.

Several additional specific economic policy proposals were made by the interviewees. One area which received considerable attention was assistance to industry. Although no key informant suggested that Hong Kong should move into the more exotic high-tech spheres of activity, such as biotechnology and superconductivity, many advocated substantial upgrading of manufacturing processes and products with some help from the government. Thus, they called for a more active government role in the dissemination of technological information, provision of technological services to industry, promotion of vocational training, development of a "Silicon Valley" type of science park, and a lobbying effort to ensure that the territory is not placed on the list of countries embargoed by the Coordinating

Committee for Multilateral Export Controls (COCOM) upon the transfer of sovereignty from (capitalist) Britain to (communist) China. (For the lobbying of COCOM to succeed, the interviewees cautioned, Hong Kong may have to introduce legal measures to prevent the post-1997 diversion of high-tech products from the territory to the PRC.) A number of key informants were even favourably disposed towards the idea of offering tax incentives to manufacturers who upgrade their facilities—a surprising view in light of their Hong Kong orientation.

A closely related subject which elicited comments was the financing of industry. The interviewees were quite keen to have an over-the-counter (OTC) market established in order to increase the supply of capital to fledgling companies which cannot meet the more stringent criteria of the established stock market; their view was that London's Unlisted Securities Market (USM) could serve as a model for the territory's "second market." They were also of the opinion that the government should nurture the growth of venture capital financing both in its classical form (provision of capital to new ventures) and in the form of "mezzanine financing" (investment in companies which have progressed beyond the stage of starting their operations). However, the key informants expressed doubts, given the sophistication of the local banking sector and proliferation of light industries not requiring long-term financing, about the need for an industrial development bank in Hong Kong.

It should be emphasized that the support for the establishment of an OTC market was not unconditional. The interviewees counselled that any moves in this direction should be preceded by an overhaul of the management structure of the securities industry and the regulations governing its operations. Above all, they maintained that the running of the stock and futures exchanges ought to be placed in the hands of disinterested professionals rather than parties with direct interests in the markets and should be subject to closer monitoring by a securities commission better-equipped to perform its functions. They also perceived an urgent need for concrete measures to curb insider trading, improve disclosure rules, and tighten listing requirements (i.e., upgrade regulation to a level more in line with practices in other major financial centres).

In addition to targeting the securities industry as an area in need of policy attention, some of the key informants thought that steps should be taken to stabilize the banking sector. One policy measure which enjoyed a fair degree of support was the introduction of a deposit insurance scheme, which, it was argued, could contribute significantly to stability if the premiums charged reflected the riskiness of each bank's portfolio, thus penalizing stockholders for risky loan extensions. Two of the interviewees, a banker and a financial economist, also emphasized the potential benefits that might accrue from the use of a discount window to loan funds to troubled financial institutions. At least one interviewee, however, contended that the existence of such a facility could give rise to the problem of "moral hazard" (i.e., result in more careless management of financial institutions than without a safeguard in the form of a discount window mechanism).

The last specific economic policy proposal—the setting up of a central provident fund (CPF)—produced no agreement among the key informants. Several of those who addressed themselves to this issue expressed reservations about the scheme: It would prove unmanageable, create turbulence in the financial markets, strain the economy, erode the competitive advantage of the local business sector, exert a downward pressure on wages and increase unemployment (because employers would reduce the size of subsequent wage increases and/or reduce the number of employees), induce workers to seek leisure at the expense of productive effort (by shifting the emphasis from voluntary to compulsory savings), and encourage public borrowing. They favoured measures to promote awareness of the CPF concept among private employers, better regulation of existing schemes to safeguard workers' entitlements, improving the terms of the old-age allowance, and expanding the scope of the Long Service Payment (LSP) scheme to provide pension benefits to employees. (At present, the LSP is a compensation fund for workers unfairly dismissed from their jobs. The government has already decided to extend benefits to employees who retired because of old age or ill health and to the dependents of those who died on the job. An amendment under consideration is based on a scheme in Australia, in which the LSP gratuity is transferable when a worker acquires a new job after dismissal.)

However, a number of interviewees dismissed suggestions that a CPF might present insurmountable management problems and undermine macro- and microeconomic performance. One of them went further and argued that a modest central pension scheme could be established to provide an adequate social net for no more than 6 percent of earnings, with the contributions from employees, employers, and the government set at 2 percent each. A central pension scheme, he maintained, would contribute to stability more than a CPF because the latter may fail to guarantee an adequate income support to those living long after retirement even if the payout is conservatively managed; it also entails risks for those who invest their payout unwisely. Yet he stressed that introducing a CPF would be preferable to adhering to the status quo: He reasoned that although filial piety remains a potent force in the territory, the strong communal bond of the agrarian world is weakening; furthermore, by the turn of the century, 19 percent of the then 8 million Hong Kong residents will be over 65, and the burden on the young for caring for the old will be excessive in an overcrowded, highly urbanized society.

Policy proposals relating to government's role during the transition period were less wide-ranging and more general in nature. One point most key informants tended to emphasize was the obvious need to preserve and further develop the institutional and physical infrastructure to manage possible environmental turbulence—without, however, departing significantly from the traditional noninterventionist stance. Another aspect of government's performance often referred to was the almost deliberately low-key leadership style of top public officials. Many key informants stated that the enormous challenges which lie ahead demand a more forceful leadership style to inspire greater confidence and that this should be reflected in selection and promotion decisions within government. The government's "reactive"[7] decisionmaking mode was also perceived as a cause for concern, and a number of interviewees suggested that "environmental scanning groups"[8] be established in major policy areas in order to enable the government to anticipate environmental threats and opportunities rather than merely react to them. Such suggestions were frequently coupled with the observation that because the government is now operating in a transitional (as opposed to a stable) environment, it ought to transform its organizational structure from a "directive" one into a "delegative" one.[9] (See Figure 7.1 and Table 7.1.)

Two of the policy proposals relating to government's role during the transition period proved somewhat problematic in that they either were expressed in rather vague terms or provoked strong disagreement. Thus, one key informant was in favour of fostering a climate supportive of individuals who occupy "vanguard" roles (i.e., brokers of ideas who "move ideas to public awareness, supplying the energy necessary to raise them over the threshold of public consciousness"),[10] but he conceded that creating such an atmosphere was a formidable task and could offer no concrete steps towards this end. (He raised the possibility of setting up broadly-based think tanks, only to conclude that such groups tend to become "institutionalized.") The policy proposal which provoked strong disagreement focused on whether the government should prepare the population for "alternative futures." Some interviewees insisted that the authorities should face this problem openly because evasive tactics would be unethical and might even backfire; others voiced fears that any attempt to conjure up scenarios other than the optimistic one could develop into a "self-fulfilling prophecy."[11]

Proposals concerning the civil service revolved largely around the issue of "localization." Several key informants warned against the dangers of pursuing this objective too aggressively and turning the civil service into an inhospitable territory for expatriates. They saw no reason why an open city like Hong Kong should go beyond the provision in the Sino-British Joint Declaration which stipulates that the most senior positions in the civil service will be reserved for Chinese nationals. On the other hand, they emphasized the need for careful succession planning to ensure that the inevitable outflow

Figure 7.1 Environmental States

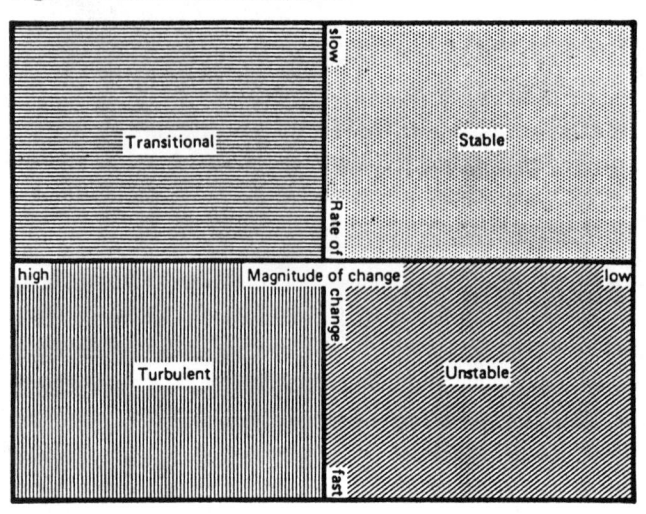

A 2x2 matrix with axes "Rate of change" (slow/fast, vertical) and "Magnitude of change" (high/low, horizontal):
- Top-left: Transitional (high magnitude, slow rate)
- Top-right: Stable (low magnitude, slow rate)
- Bottom-left: Turbulent (high magnitude, fast rate)
- Bottom-right: Unstable (low magnitude, fast rate)

Table 7.1 Matching Organization and Environment

(1)	(2)	(3)	(4)
\multicolumn{4}{c}{Environmental States}			
Stable	Transitional	Unstable	Turbulence
\multicolumn{4}{c}{Organizational States}			
Directive	Delegative	Matrix	Modular
\multicolumn{4}{c}{Orgaizational Characteristics}			
Functional standardization	Rational task segmentation, decentralization	Tasks combined in project or product group	Management by temporary teams
Authority-based leadership	Delegated decision authority	Dual technical-administrative supervision	Problem-solving orientation
Formalized communication hierarchy	Profit centres for control, incentives	Emphasis on task coordination	Mission-directed technical and administration coordination
Control via budgets and standards	Results-based leadership	Slight upward job mobility	Self-destruct criteria
Rewards for upward mobility	Infrequent downward communication, management by exception	Professional rewards sought, functional identity	Interteam competition allowed
			Multiple channels of mobility

of expatriates does not leave critical gaps which might undermine government performance during the transition period and beyond. It is interesting to note that the continued presence of expatriates in the civil service was viewed as being of considerable symbolic as well as practical importance. As one interviewee asserted:

> It is one thing to put locals in charge, but quite another to dismiss expatriates altogether. Their continued presence in the civil service is important if only to act as a safeguard for those who believe in Western ideals and concepts that currently do not exist in China, such as freedom of choice and expression. But their presence is vital for a more important reason.
>
> It will be seen as a reassuring gesture to those who are the most jittery about the future—the territory's affluent and flight-prone business and middle-class people.
>
> Many of these people have been exposed to Western values and democratic ideals. While they may not embrace them, they are aware that the flip side is less appealing. Living under a benevolent dictatorship is more desirable than living under an autocratic and authoritarian regime.
>
> A government without expatriates would be an alarming prospect. Unfortunately, such a prospect cannot be ruled out. Although they make up only a small percentage of the 170,000-strong civil service, expatriates are already leaving at a rate of about 300 a year. If this trend accelerates, it can bode only ill for Hong Kong.
>
> This is where it is vital for the government and China to take measures now to halt the crisis of confidence among expatriates. If they do not, it will not be the expatriates alone who will be affected. After all, they always have another country to call home.
>
> But without expatriates to act as a buffer and an act of faith, there can be little scope for manoeuvre if the territory is to achieve its cherished ideal of a high degree of autonomy.

In addition to drawing attention to the dangers inherent in an overzealous localization drive, the key informants advocated measures to preserve the integrity of the civil service and to maximize the satisfaction civil servants derive from their jobs. Constitutional safeguards designed to insulate the civil service from potentially damaging external influences were seen as the most effective means of achieving the first of these two objectives, although the need to "professionalize" the bureaucracy, particularly the administrative grade which dominates it,[12] was also strongly emphasized. The task of boasting job satisfaction, with a view to preventing high turnover and providing incentives to optimize performance, was perceived as more manageable and was largely equated with offering an attractive package of material benefits (such as the new pension scheme which gives civil servants who leave government employment after ten years the right to a government pension when they reach retirement age).

The relationship between Hong Kong and China was another policy area which elicited diverging opinions. No interviewee took exception to the proposal that the objective of influencing mainland opinion, particularly at the elite level, should be accorded priority and pursued vigorously (albeit, selectively, given resource constraints) by sponsoring visits from the PRC, sending delegations there, granting scholarships, embarking on joint ventures, and so forth. On the other hand, there was lack of agreement regarding the role of confrontational tactics in addressing issues on which the territory (or at least some groups there) and the Chinese side do not see eye to eye. Some key informants objected strongly to such tactics on the grounds that backdoor politics, manoeuvres designed to avoid loss of face, patience, strict adherence to diplomatic protocol, and subtlety would be more effective in securing a satisfactory compromise. However, a number of interviewees argued with equal conviction that mainland officials are by no means averse to tough bargaining and that an open confrontation may be both unavoidable and desirable in certain situations.

Proposals concerning Hong Kong's relationships with other external parties did not emerge as an area of major interest—presumably because of the perception that the territory's future depends largely on the actions and inactions of the PRC. Nonetheless, some key informants thought that a worthwhile strategy vis-à-vis the external environment should include a determined effort to elicit the active support of potentially influential overseas Chinese communities. These, in turn, being sympathetic towards the territory and its aspirations, may bring direct or indirect pressure on the PRC, which is anxious in its own right to cultivate those nationals presently living abroad in places such as Australia, Canada, Southeast Asia, and above all, the US. Informants felt the attempt to mobilize the overseas Chinese could be undertaken with or without the overt encouragement of the government, but its blessing would be most welcome. The realization that Hong Kong is more than a parochial annex to the mainland and has extensive informal links is an asset that ought to be exploited more fully to the territory's long-term benefit. A prevalent feeling among the optimistic and realistic interviewees was that policy proposals as outlined here could go some way towards ensuring a degree of prosperity and stability in the period leading up to 1997 and beyond.

Notes

1. See R.L. Ackoff, *A Concept of Corporate Planning* (New York: Wiley, 1970); R.L. Ackoff, *Redesigning the Future* (New York: Wiley, 1974); R.L. Ackoff, *The Art of Problem Solving* (New York: Wiley, 1978); R.L. Ackoff, *Creating the Corporate*

Future (New York: Wiley, 1981).

2. See D.M. McAllister, *Evaluation in Environmental Planning* (Cambridge, Mass.: M.I.T. Press, 1980).

3. Exit and voice are explored in A.O. Hirschman, *Exit, Voice and Loyalty* (Cambridge, Mass.: Harvard University Press, 1970); A.O. Hirschman, *Shifting Involvements* (Princeton, N.J.: Princeton University Press, 1982).

4. M.L. Olson, *The Rise and Decline of Nations* (New Haven, Conn.: Yale University Press, 1982).

5. See E.R. Tufte, *The Political Control of the Economy* (Princeton, N.J.: Princeton University Press, 1978); B.L. Frey, *Modern Political Economy* (Oxford: Robertson, 1978); B.L. Frey, *Democratic Economic Policy* (Oxford: Robertson, 1983); J.E. Alt and K.A. Chrystal, *Political Economics* (Brighton: Wheatsheaf Books, 1983).

6. The term "corporatist" is employed to refer to a process of interest intermediation which involves the negotiation of policy between state agencies and interest organizations arising from the division of labour in society, where the policy agreements are implemented through the collaboration of the interest organizations and their ability and willingness to secure the compliance of their members. See R. Marris, ed., *The Corporate Society* (London: Methuen, 1976); A.S. Miller, *The Modern Corporate State* (Westport, Conn.: Greenwood Press, 1976); H. Wilensky, *The New Corporatism, Centralization and the Welfare State* (Beverly Hills, Calif.: Sage, 1976); J. Zysman, *Political Strategies for Industrial Order* (Berkeley: University of California Press, 1977); P.C. Schmitter and G. Lembruch, eds., *Trends Towards Corporatist Intermediation* (Beverly Hills, Calif.: Sage, 1979); S. Berger, ed., *Organizing Interests in Western Europe* (Cambridge: Cambridge University Press, 1981); M. Buxbaum, *The Corporate Politea* (Washington, D.C.: University Press, 1981); O. Newman, *The Challenge of Corporatism* (London: Macmillan, 1981); A. Cawson, *Corporatism and Welfare* (London: Heinemann, 1982); G. Lembruch and P.C. Schmitter, eds., *Patterns of Corporatist Policy-Making* (Beverly Hills, Calif.: Sage, 1982); C. Landauer, *Corporate State Ideologies* (Berkeley: Institute of International Studies, University of California, 1983); M.L. Harrison, ed., *Corporatism and the Welfare State* (Aldershot, England: Gower, 1984); P.J. Katzenstein, *Corporatism and Change* (Ithaca, N.Y.: Cornell University Press, 1984); J. Zysman, *Governments, Markets and Growth* (Ithaca, N.Y.: Cornell University Press, 1984); A. Cawson, ed., *Organized Interests and the State* (Beverly Hills, Calif.: Sage, 1985); W.P. Grant, ed., *The Political Economy of Corporatism* (London: Macmillan, 1985); W. Streeck and P.C. Schmitter, eds., *Public Interest Government* (Beverly Hills, Calif.: Sage, 1985); P.J. Williamson, *Varieties of Corporatism* (Cambridge: Cambridge University Press, 1985); I. Scholten, ed., *Political Stability and Neo-Corporatism* (Beverly Hills, Calif.: Sage, 1987).

7. Reactive decisionmaking modes are contrasted with "preactive" and "interactive" ones. (Emphasis added.)

> Preactivists are not willing to settle for things as they are or once were. They believe that the future will be better than the present or the past, how much better depends on how well they get ready for it. Thus they attempt to *predict* and *prepare*. They want more than survival; they want to grow—to

become better, larger, more affluent, more powerful, more many things. They want to do better than well enough; they want to do as well as possible, to *optimize*. . . . Interactivists are not willing to settle for the current state of affairs or the way they are going, and they are not willing to return to the past. They want to design a desirable future and invent ways of bringing it about. They believe we are capable of controlling a significant part of the future as well as its effects on us. They try to *prevent*, not merely prepare for, threats, and to create, not merely exploit, opportunities. . . . They are neither satisficers nor optimizers; they are *idealizers*.

See Ackoff, *Redesigning the Future*, p. 25.

8. For a further discussion, see D.C. Basil and C.W. Cook, *The Management of Change* (New York: McGraw-Hill, 1974).

9. See ibid. for a further discussion.

10. See D.A. Schon, *Beyond the Stable State* (London: Temple Smith, 1971), p. 131.

11. See R.K. Merton, "The Unanticipated Consequences of Purposive Social Action," *American Sociological Review* 1 (December 1936): 894–904; R.K. Merton, "The Self-Fulfilling Prophecy," *Antioch Review* 8 (1948): 193–210; R.L. Henshel and L.W. Kennedy, "Self-Altering Prophecies," *General Systems* 18 (1973): 119–126; R.L. Henschel, "Self-Altering Predictions," in *Handbook of Futures Research*, ed., J. Fowles (Westport, Conn.: Greenwood Press, 1978), pp. 99–123.

12. See M. Mushkat, *The Making of the Hong Kong Administrative Class* (Hong Kong, Centre of Asian Studies, University of Hong Kong, 1982).

Index

Asiadollar bond market, 145
Australia; as new economic frontier, 88-89
Aviation communications technologies; scenarios, 29 (table)

Bank of China, 73, 111, 139
Banking industry; future of in New York, 23

Capitalism; in Asia, 74
Chiang Kai-Shek; supporters of in Hong Kong, 83-84
China. *See* People's Republic of China, Taiwan. *See also* Hong Kong
Chinese business style; and Japanese business style compared, 143; and Korean business style compared, 143
Chinese leaders; adjusters, 100 (table), 101; as self-interested players, 101; behaviour of, 98-101, 100 (table); conservers, 100 (table), 101; developmentalists, 101; different generations of, 101; discontinuity of policymaking, 102; eclectic modernizers, 99; factional conflicts among, 101; liberals, 101; militant fundamentalists, 99; and policymaking, 102; radical conservatives, 99; reformers, 99, 100 (table), 101; restorationists, 99; utopians, 101; Westernized Chinese, 99; "zealots," 101. *See also* Deng Xiaoping, Mao Zedong, People's Republic of China
Chinese people; nature of, 5-6, 14 (note); and shortcomings in large-scale business organization, 143; and small, family-owned businesses, 143; overseas Chinese and Hong Kong, 162
Communist dictatorships; reformability of, 136 (note)
Coordinating Committee for Multilateral Export Controls, 156-157
Corporatist; defined, 163 (note)

Decision-making modes; contrasted, 163-164 (note)
Deng Xiaoping, 104 (note)

Environmental states; and organizational characteristics, 160 (table)
Environmental turbulence, 148-149, 160 (figure), 160 (table); defined, 1
Euroyen bond market, 145

Fei Yiming, 122
Free trade; and automatic corrective mechanism, 7-8, 10-11, 14-15 (note)

Future; attitudes towards, 25; trends, 27 (table)
Futurism; examples of approach, 22-23; and scenarios, 19, 20, 24. *See also* Scenarios

Hong Kong; access to foreign markets, 95; adaptability, 3-5, 11, 12-13, 148-149; asset diversification in, 87; and Australia, 147; balance of factor endowments with China, 89; Banking Commission, 146; banks, 73; Basic Law, 76, 96, 152; British and Chinese positions, 1, 12(*See also* Sino-British Joint Declaration); British people in, 6-7; British presence in, 84, 130; capitalists, 154; as centre for foreign presence in China, 80-81; as credit source for People's Republic of China, 79, 93-94; and Chinese dissidents, 81; and Chinese labour, 87-88; and computerization, 95-96; Chinese people in, 5-6; Chinese refugees in, 84-85; Chinese-British relations in, 119-120; Chinese-Japanese relations in, 119-120; Chinese-U.S. relations in, 120; chronology of significant events, 64-65 (table); civil service, 127-128; direct elections, 152, 154; as doorway to new economic frontiers, 88-89; economic future and scenario types, 35; economic policy suggestions, 155-158; economic status, 2; economic threat from South Korea, 89-90; economic threat from Taiwan, 89-90; as export centre for People's Republic of China, 77-78; and foreign passports, 87; and free enterprise, 7-10; as foreign exchange centre for People's Republic of China, 77, 123-124; foreign presence in, 114; general policy suggestions, 154-156; geographic description, 4-5; human resources, 5-7; investment in China, 79, 93-94; and Japan, 93, 139, 147; and Japanese corporations, 150 (note); and key informant method, 61-67; key informants interviewed, 62 (table); "localization" of civil service, 159-161; and London, 3; Long Service Payment scheme, 158; as market for Chinese products, 77; middle class professionals, 154; Monetary Affairs Branch of government, 139; and New York, 3; and other Asian financial centers, 73; and People's Republic of China, 3-4, 11-12, 76-83, 120, 127; policy suggestions, 151-162; political apathy in, 153; political reform, 151-154; and "positive non-interventionism," 8, 10, 15-16 (note); post-war challenges, 2; preserving integrity of civil service, 161-162; redistribution of wealth, 152; reduction of uncertainty over future of, 96-97; refugee mentality in, 87; as regional centre, 94; resources, 4-5; and scenario approaches, 58 -59, 61-67; and Shanghai, 90; and Singapore, 94, 139; social climate, 121-122; socioeconomic development, 2-3; and South Korea, 147; and Southeast Asian Chinese, 147; suggested central provident fund, 158; suggested changes in government role, 159-162; suggested emigration policy, 156; suggested emulation of Japanese political system, 152-154; suggested improvement of technology, 156-157; suggested over-the-counter market, 157; suggested role of government during transition period, 159; suggested stabilization of banking sector, 157-158; suggestions regarding civil service, 159-162; suggestions regarding relationship with People's Republic

of China, 162; suggestions regarding relationships with overseas Chinese, 162; and Sydney, 90; and Taiwan, 82, 83-84, 147; taxation, 150 (note); third-ranked financial centre, 3; "three-legged stool" notion, 12; and Tokyo, 3, 4, 90-91, 143, 144, 145, 146; and tourism in China, 79-80; turbulent environment in, 1, 10; U.S.-Chinese relationship in, 83-84. *See also* Optimistic scenario, Pessimistic scenario, Trend scenario
Hong Kong and Shanghai Bank, 139-140
Hong Kong Bank, 73

India; as new economic frontier, 88; and People's Republic of China, 86

Japan; and Hong Kong, 93, 139, 147; and internationalization of yen, 93; Kaidanren, 152; Liberal Democratic Party, 152, 153; relations with Soviet Union, 89; role in international economics, 144

Key informants in this study, 62 (table)
Korea; and People's Republic of China, 86
Korean War, 83

London; relation to other European financial centers, 90

Macau; offshore banking unit, 146
Mao Zedong, 82
Mushkat study; key informants, 62 (table); methodology, 61-67; optimistic scenario, 66-67; pessimistic scenario, 66-67; questions asked, 63-66, 63 (table); trend scenario, 66-67

New China News Agency, 111
New York; offshore banking market, 90-91, 144
New Zealand; as new economic frontier, 88-89

Optimistic scenario; and actions of Chinese policymakers, 98-99; causes, 75-96; and Chinese leaders' rationality, 98; and Chinese policymaking, 102; and economism, 97, 131; effects, 71-75; evaluation, 97-103; fiscal conservatism, 71; free enterprise, 71, 73-74; and "free political market," 74; government regulation, 72; growth rate, 74-75; Hong Kong and People's Republic of China, 72-73; Hong Kong and U.S. dollars, 72; and Hong Kong's economic advantages to People's Republic of China, 97; macroeconomic adjustment, 72; manufacturing, 73-74; and overestimation of economic variables, 97; People's Republic of China, 73, 75-83; and People's Republic of China's "national mission," 98; and perceptions of change in People's Republic of China, 133; and perceptions of Chinese policymakers, 132; and pessimistic scenario, 130-134, 137; process, 96-97; public finance, 71; public sector, 72; service sector, 74; Sino-British Joint Declaration, 75-76; and underestimation of political variables, 97-98; and "unilinear theories of social progress," 103. *See also* Pessimistic scenario, Scenarios, Trend scenario

People's Republic of China; attitude toward family as economic unit, 126-127; balance of factor endowments with Hong Kong, 89; and British presence in Hong Kong, 84; discontinuity of policymaking, 102; early role of factory managers and party secretaries, 134 (note); economic conditions, 77-78; and foreign presence in Hong Kong, 80-81; and Hong Kong, 76-83, 116, 120, 127; Hong Kong as outlet for dissidents, 81; and Hong Kong prosperity, 116; and India, 86; international affairs, 104 (note), 104-105 (note); investment in Hong Kong, 78-79; and Korea, 86; as market for Hong Kong products, 88; misperception of Hong Kong's capitalist lifestyle, 121-122; misunderstanding of Hong Kong system, 120-121; as new economic frontier, 88; noninterference with Hong Kong, 87; policy changes, 75-76; policy in Weihaiwei, 118-119; policymaking, 102-103; political factors regarding Hong Kong, 81-82; relations between North and South, 116-117; and Sino-British Joint Declaration, 75-76; and Southeast Asia, 80; and Taiwan, 116, 124-126; and Tibet, 86, 124; tourism in, 79-80; uses of force in Asia, 86; and Vietnam, 83, 86; withholding of force against Hong Kong, 85. *See also* Chinese business style, Chinese leaders, Chinese people, Macau, Taiwan, Shanghai, Weihaiwei

Pessimistic scenario; British retreat from Hong Kong, 130; causes, 116-129; and change in Hong Kong's values, 114; and changes in bureaucracy, 112; and changes in judiciary, 112-113; and changes in legislature, 112; and Chinese attitude towards family as economic unit, 126-127; and Chinese authoritarianism, 117-118; and Chinese Communist Party's role in Hong Kong, 112, 113-114; and Chinese economic development, 122-123; and Chinese misperception of Hong Kong social climate, 121-122; and Chinese misunderstanding of Hong Kong system, 120-121; and Chinese officials' arrogance, 122-123; and Chinese reversion to central planning, 113; decline of service industry, 115; economic growth, 115-116; economic reversals in Hong Kong, 129; effects, 111-116; evaluation, 130-134; flight of talent (brain drain), 128-129; flight of upper and middle classes, 115; and foreign presence in Hong Kong, 114; and Four Cardinal Principles of communism, 112; and Hong Kong as Special Economic Zone, 111-112; Hong Kong civil service, 127-128; Hong Kong's role as foreign exchange centre, 123-124; Hong Kong relations with People's Republic of China, 127; industrialization of Hong Kong, 115; "last train syndrome," 128; and less autonomy for Hong Kong, 111-112; and market economy, 113; and optimistic scenario, 130-134, 137; People's Republic of China and Taiwan, 124-126; and perceptions of change in People's Republic of China, 133-134; and perceptions of Chinese policymakers, 131-133; process, 129-130; reform in People's Republic of China, 127; and retention of some free enterprise in Hong Kong, 113; Sino-British Joint Declaration, 119; standard of living, 116; and taxation in Hong Kong, 114-115. *See also* Optimistic scenario, Scenarios, Trend scenarios

Postindustrial society; characteristics, 22 (table), 22-23. *See also* Futurism

Protectionism, 95

Public officials; typology of, 107-108 (note)

Samurai bond market, 145

Scenarios; anticipatory, 25-26, 34-35; barometric techniques, 44-46; beginning state-driven, 31, 33; "bootstrapping," 57; causal techniques, 53-55, 54 (figure); classical decomposition analysis, 43-44; construction of, 21 (figure); continuity models, 42-43; cross-impact analysis, 51-52, 51 (table); cyclical variation factors, 44; defined, 20-22; Delphi method, 50-51, 58-59; descriptive, 24-25; descriptive-anticipatory, 25, 35; descriptive-exploratory, 25, 35; development of term, 19; developmental, 33-34; econometric, 58; econometric modeling, 47; economic forecasting, 46; end state-driven, 31, 32-33, 35; exploratory, 25-26, 34-35; factor-listing technique, 42, 43 (table); historical analogies, 49; holistic approach, 24; idealization method, 32-33, 34; indirect methods, 52; input-output analysis, 48, 48 (table); irregular factors, 44; key-informant method, 60; leading series, 44-45, 45 (table); learned-behaviour models, 52; linear approaches, 55; market research, 50; methods of construction, 32-35; morphology, 31 (figure), 32; multiple, 28-30; naive methods, 42-44, 53-54, 54 (figure); need for typology, 21; normative, 24-25; normative-exploratory, 34; objective techniques, 53; opinion polling, 46-47; opportunistic forecasting, 48-49, 58; panel consensus, 50; peripheral, 26, 28; for planning and decisionmaking, 31-32, 32-33, 34; for prediction, 31-32, 33, 34-35; pressure indexes, 45-46; process type, 30-31, 32-33; prophecy type, 33, 35; regression/correlation analysis, 52; sales forecasting, 46-47; seasonal variation factors, 44; selectivity, 24; simulation type, 33, 35, 53; state type, 30-31, 35-36; subjective techniques, 53; survey, 58; technological or social system Delphi type, 34, 35; time-series analysis, 42-44, 52; trend factors, 44; trend type, 26; typologies, 26 (table), 27 (figure), 31 (figure), 32, 41-42, 47, 49, 52, 53, 55-58, 56 (figure); and U.S. think tanks, 19-20; value Delphi type, 34; visionary forecasts, 49. *See also* Mushkat study, Optimistic scenario, Pessimistic scenario, Trend scenario

Shanghai, 119, 122

Shenzen, 122

Siberia; as new economic frontier, 89

Singapore, 94-95; and Hong Kong, 94; and Indonesia, 94; and Malaysia, 94; and Tokyo, 144, 145-146

Sino-British Joint Declaration, 71, 75, 76, 82, 97, 103, 104-105 (note), 119, 129, 138, 140, 159. *See also* Hong Kong; British and Chinese positions

South Korea; and Hong Kong, 89-90

Soviet Union; relations with Japan, 89

Standard Chartered Bank, 73

"Standard worlds," 27, 28

"Surprise-free projections," 27-28, 30

Taiwan; and Hong Kong, 82, 83-84, 89-90; and People's Republic of China, 124-126. *See also* Chinese business style, Chinese people, People's Republic of China

Thatcher, Margaret, 128; visit to Beijing, 1-2

Tibet; and People's Republic of China, 86, 124

Tokyo; as financial centre, 90-93; offshore banking market, 90-92, 144

Tokyo Stock Exchange, 145

Trend scenario; and adaptability of Hong Kong, 148-149; anticipated differences between Hong Kong and mainland, 138; and "categorical" predictions, 149; causes, 140-147; changes in internationalism, 140; dialectical reconciliation of conflicts over Hong Kong's future, 148; and economic development of People's Republic of China, 140-142; economic growth of Hong Kong, 140, 142-143; effects, 137-140; English language, 140; and environmental turbulence, 148-149; evaluation, 148-149; flight of capital, 142; flight of talent (brain drain), 142; growth of service industry, 143; Hong Kong as subregional service centre, 140, 143, 146, 147; Hong Kong dollar, 139; integration of optimistic and pessimistic scenarios, 137; manufacturing sector, 140; market economy, 138; Monetary Affairs Branch of Hong Kong government, 139; open economy, 138-139; parallels between Hong Kong and Japan, 139; parallels between Hong Kong and Singapore, 139; perceptions of Chinese policymakers, 140; power shift to mainland-oriented organizations, 139-140; private ownership, 138; process, 147-148; and reform of Chinese economy, 149; role of Chinese Communist Party in Hong Kong, 138; semi-independent status of Hong Kong, 137-138; shocks to Hong Kong system, 147-148; shrinking of manufacturing industry, 143; Sino-British Joint Declaration, 140; transition period, 147; vagueness of, 148. *See also* Optimistic scenario, Pessimistic scenario, Scenarios

United States; and People's Republic of China, 83-84; protectionism, 95
Unlisted Securities Market (London), 157

Victoria Harbour, 5
Vietnam; and People's Republic of China, 86
Vitenam War, 83

Weihaiwei, 118-119

About the Book and the Author

Contrary to widely expressed hopes, the leadership of the People's Republic of China has opted not to treat the 1997 landmark change of sovereignty in Hong Kong as essentially irrelevant, but to take concrete steps toward incorporating Hong Kong into the Chinese body politic before the end of the twentieth century. Miron Mushkat explores the likely ramifications of the "one country, two systems" formula that the PRC has devised for Hong Kong as a starting point, identifying the possible paths along which the local economy may be propelled in the next decade or so.

The emphasis throughout the book is on economic futures, because—the spate of political reforms in the territory notwithstanding—Mushkat continues to perceive Hong Kong largely as a business conglomerate headed by a board of directors, rather than as a full-fledged polity, and because there is a tendency among people residing there to define welfare primarily in economic terms. (Political and social issues, however, are addressed as well.) He is quick to point out that, given the volatility of the Hong Kong environment, a substantial divergence between extrapolations based on the status quo and future events is highly probable. That does not, however, detract from the value of the "optimistic," "pessimistic," and "trend" scenarios that he provides.

Dr. Miron Mushkat has been affiliated since 1987 with Baring Securities, the securities arm of the British investment bank Baring Brothers, as director with special responsibility for regional economic research. Prior to joining his present employers, Dr. Mushkat taught at the University of Hong Kong (where he currently holds honorary lecturing and research positions), Victoria University of Wellington (New Zealand), University of Manchester (UK), Carleton University (Canada), served as a special assistant for corporate planning and finance to the chairman of the Broadcasting Corporation of New Zealand, and worked as an economist for the Canadian government. Dr. Mushkat's principal research interests lie in the areas of political economy, public finance, applied policy analysis, and quantitative analysis. He is the author of over 50 monographs, book chapters, and articles that deal with theoretical and methodological developments in this area.